"For over a decade, my family has planned vacations around visits to Eventide in Portland, Maine, which is a full six-hour drive from our house. The menu feels like it was designed expressly for us, from their insane oyster selection and simple pickled vegetable salads all the way to their indulgent brown butter lobster and crab rolls. You can only imagine the collective joyous shriek in our house when we found out we could have a little Eventide-inspired Maine magic in our own kitchen all year-round. Thank you, Arlin, Andrew, and Mike, this book is destined to be well-used and well-loved."

JENNY ROSENSTRACH
New York Times bestselling author of *Dinner: A Love Story*

"From the moment Eventide opened in 2012, it clarified a dream we'd all nurtured without quite realizing it: a longing for a place where the crowd was salty, the smack of the sea was ever-present, and every morsel of food reminded you why you'd been making a beeline for the ocean since childhood. It was the seafood shack that showed you why seafood shacks mattered. What a gift to have that Eventide magic poured into a book. Now the world is your shack."

ROWAN JACOBSEN
author of *A Geography of Oysters*

"EVENTIDE (the restaurant and the cookbook!) is what happens when three Maine-loving friends with the just the right combination of talent, heart, and moxie put passionate vision in front of practical know-how and commit to figuring out any kinks along the way. Arlin, Andrew, and Mike's delicious risky business created a framework for contemporary New England seafood shack fare. The recipes in their gorgeous cookbook offer the perfect blueprint for bringing their Maine seacoast magic home."

MINDY FOX
food writer and bestselling cookbook co-author of *Antoni in the Kitchen*

RECIPES FOR CLAMBAKES, OYSTERS, LOBSTER ROLLS,
AND MORE FROM A MODERN MAINE SEAFOOD SHACK

EVENTIDE

ARLIN SMITH, ANDREW TAYLOR, AND MIKE WILEY
WITH SAM HIERSTEINER

Photographs by Zach Bowen
Illustrations by Aaron Staples

TEN SPEED PRESS
California | New York

FOREWORD

My views on food, cooking, and hospitality are clear and simple. First and foremost, I love an oyster bar that offers ice cold beverages and fresh seafood. It means everything to me and Eventide is all that: a bustling, small oyster bar with crackling fresh seafood that fully represents its time, place, and community.

Portland and the state of Maine feature prominently in my cooking. You could say the food represents my holy grail, something I search for, something I long for. As a young cook I read a feature on a Maine-based chef in *Saveur* magazine, and it brought me to Portland several times. Portland was my secret place, my secret getaway where I could relax and enjoy great food.

On one such getaway, a bartender many years my senior, a man by the name of Tom, told me that the gentlemanly group who owned Hugo's, itself a venerable Portland institution, had opened a neat oyster bar called Eventide, and it was worth checking out.

I meandered in the next day for lunch. The place was decorated simply—all white and blue—and it was packed. And everyone was smiling, working with a sense of urgency, but you got the feeling that they were just trying to be great hosts, working not for the sake of profits, but for the sake of hospitality.

"We're trying to get everyone fed and hydrated," the bartender said with a big grin. I felt instantly at home, savoring multiple types of local oysters and ice cold drinks. A regular overheard me ordering—it was that kind of friendly, casual place—and said, "Get any of the buns, man. Trust me!" I ordered the clam bun *and* lobster bun *and* the Jonah crab, a bit of tuna, more oysters, a tostada.

With food this beautifully sourced and prepared, Eventide isn't your run-of-the-mill oyster bar. This is an oyster bar executed by a team of highly skilled career cooks and restauranteurs with impeccable taste, esthetics, and vision. Interesting right? Eventide is the type of restaurant we all wish we had on our street corner, so we could drop in regularly because every neighborhood deserves a little democratic seafood restaurant just like this.

Eventide is a place I pine for, offering up food I crave. When I do get there and sit, joy fills my heart just as the seafood fills my belly.

-David McMillan, co-owner and chef of Joe Beef, Liverpool House,
Le Vin Papillon, Mon Lapin, and McKiernan

INTRODUCTION: BREEZE BLOWIN' IN

Sometimes inspiration strikes like a lightning bolt, and other times it's a slow burn. The groundwork for our little restaurant was laid decades ago, during happy summers spent with family traversing New England's coast, including the rocky shores in Maine. Our childhood experiences scavenging crabs, clams, in-shore fish, and seaweed deeply influenced the Eventide concept and menu, as did the clam shacks and lobster pounds that are given altar-like reverence in New England. These singular, superlative experiences became so ingrained in our minds that when we set out to put modern touches on them, we had an incredible sense of nostalgia to build on.

But as we look back on the journey, we also have to be transparent about something: we didn't know what the hell we were doing, really. By most of the laws and conventions of the restaurant industry and common business sense, Eventide should have been the entrepreneurial equivalent of a spectacular dumpster fire.

We opened in the summer of 2012 in quaint Portland, Maine—population 67,000. Although we put in some years together at Hugo's, a trailblazing restaurant in terms of Portland fine dining, we had no hands-on experience in getting an establishment up and running. Our budget was a frayed shoestring, and we didn't base many (any?) of our key decisions on sound restaurant business practices.

The seemingly bold decisions were actually naivety at work. We designed the restaurant ourselves on drafting paper and hired a local residential carpenter to build it out. We put in only two tables because, well, we didn't like tables. We decided not to build a kitchen and had no hood fan. Our stovetop firepower included one induction burner and a tabletop fryer to match. We failed to foresee that our monumental stone oyster basin, dubbed "The Rock," was going to destroy multiple floors with plumbing issues and condensation in the years to come. We opened with absolutely no art on the walls because we couldn't afford any.

Discoveries of setbacks and our own mistakes grew more frequent, as did the daily, anxiety-driven vomiting in the shower. A peek behind the scenes at the chaos suggested that it was exactly the rookie disaster that it deserved to be.

And yet—and we say this with the same mix of shock and bemusement we've had all along—Eventide has been busy since day one. People even found it charming.

The bighearted little city of Portland took the leap with us from the moment the doors opened. Man, do we love this town.

THE BACKSTORY

The first thing our first customer said to us, after he wandered in, not knowing we were open yet, and looked incredulously around the space, was, "Where are all the seats?" For a bunch of greenhorns who could have used some positive reinforcement at the time, that hurt. The proverbial pain was amplified because that first customer happened to be Dana Street.

Dana and his James Beard Award–winning partner, chef Sam Hayward, are the proprietors of Fore Street, which opened in 1996 as the first real, excellent, farm- and fishery-to-table restaurant in Portland. To this day, it remains the quintessential Maine restaurant (the team also owns Street and Co., Standard Baking Co., and Scales). Dana and Sam, along with James Beard Award–winners chef Rob Evans of Duckfat and Rob Tod of Allagash Brewing, were the first to bring any kind of national food and beverage media attention to Maine.

In fact, it was at Hugo's, Rob Evans and his wife Nancy Pugh's restaurant, that the three of us (Arlin, Andrew, and Mike) met. Arlin arrived first as general manager in 2009, after graduating from the Culinary Institute of America in Hyde Park, New York, and working a mix of front-of-house positions in restaurants in the Hudson Valley. Andrew came through a short time later as sous chef, after stints at Thierry Rautureau's Rover's in Seattle and Ken Oringer's Clio in Boston. The last piece of the puzzle was Mike, who started in 2010 as a line cook, after working restaurants, getting a graduate degree, and skiing sick lines in Colorado.

At the time, Hugo's was considered a pioneering restaurant, bringing modern elements into the tradition-bound fare of New England and, more specifically, the cuisine of Maine. And it punched above its weight, because Rob had come to Portland in 2000 from chef Thomas Keller's The French Laundry in the Napa Valley, one of the world's best restaurants and an incredible wellspring of culinary talent. Hugo's was a modern restaurant that followed high gastronomic trends from Napa, New York, and western European capitals. Despite the accolades that it garnered, it had never really been embraced with open arms by the community the way Eventide was later (things have changed now, but that's for another book). We learned that Mainers like things that are simple and low-key, rather than superconceptual.

Nevertheless, the heritage, heretical element, and ethos overall at Hugo's spoke to us at a deep level, and given that Rob and Nancy had largely stepped away from

the day-to-day at the restaurant by the time Mike arrived, the three of us had the chance to develop our own collective point of view. That's pretty rare, to be thrust into that kind of creative opportunity together, and we intended to push in our own direction.

Fast-forward two years, and some pretty powerful forces (hubris, opportunity, and pregnancy among them) coalesced to vault us into the terrifying world of restaurant owner-operators. And while we were in way over our heads in so many ways, we were lucky to have a few things going for us: a wave of change in the restaurant world and in Portland, an incredibly supportive local community, and the best ingredients on earth at our fingertips, to name a few.

A RABELAISIAN DETOUR

Don Lindgren and his wife, Samantha Hoyt Lindgren, owners of one of the two or three greatest culinary bookstores in the world, Rabelais: Fine Books on Food & Drink, are the spirit guides and keepers of the culinary flame in Maine. We are in their debt in more ways than one. The original Rabelais location next to Hugo's was a place where chefs, cooks, barkeeps, and all manner of others would go to escape the grind for just a minute. We'd duck over there during prep for Hugo's service, aprons and all, just to double-check this or that from the 1999 El Bulli cookbook. We basically had this world-renowned culinary research institution, run by two scholars of gastronomy, at our disposal. We learned more there than we could have in just about any other way (none of us had the time or resources to travel widely and immerse ourselves in global cuisine).

Don's memories of that moment in time ahead of Eventide's opening set the scene. "The question we got asked the most was, 'Where should I go to get a good drink and eat some oysters and clams?' and I didn't have much of an answer," he often says with an incredulous laugh. The three of us were in the same predicament, and we grew more and more focused on the idea that there was a gap in Portland that needed filling.

THE IMPORTANCE OF SEAFOOD SHACKS

It's hard to overstate how important the shack experience—sitting down to slurp shellfish and eat fried seafood with loved ones and friends—is in this part of the world. Like soul food joints in the South, barbecue houses down the Mississippi and in Texas, and roadside diners in the Midwest, these informal seafood houses are the hallowed ground of our food culture in New England. Fancy restaurants come and

go, leaving their mark and helping push American food forward, but good seafood shacks, serving tried-and-true New England staples, endure.

It'd be tempting to call places like J. T. Farnhams in Essex, Massachusetts, and Beal's in Southwest Harbor, Maine, relics that survive because they've been around forever and they have a view, but that's missing the point. They are as relevant as ever because they serve unpretentious food that people nearly universally love. Moreover, there is nothing that feels more honest than a place that simply prepares the bounty that is close at hand.

And because the best of these restaurants seem to spring out of the fisheries of the area, it's fascinating to see how they change as one moves up and down the New England coast. New York and Connecticut are famous for their oyster bars; the smell of fried scallops and clam chowder drifts from every seafood house in southern Massachusetts and Cape Cod. Northern Massachusetts, the land of the soft-shell clam, is famous for its fried clam shacks. Moving north to southern and Midcoast Maine, you'll begin to see more and more lobster rolls. Once you reach "Down East," the term used for the northern third of Maine's coast, it's full-on lobster pound territory, where you'll find the best lobsters in the world, live or steamed, in abundance.

Our Top Seafood Shacks in Northern New England (North to South)

Whenever we can, we like to shout out the amazing families and proprietors that keep these gems alive and kicking.

1 ABEL'S LOBSTER POUND

13 Abels Lane, Mt Desert, ME 04660

YEAR OPENED: 1939
OWNERS: THE SQUIRES FAMILY

Go for the steamed lobsters, lobster rolls, lobster bisque, steamed clams, and clam chowder

2 BEAL'S LOBSTER PIER

182 Clark Point Road, Southwest Harbor, ME 04679

bealslobster.com

YEAR OPENED: 1969 (WHOLESALE OPERATION OPENED IN 1932)
CO-OWNER: STUART SNYDER

Go for the steamed lobsters and clams

3 YOUNG'S LOBSTER POUND

2 Fairview Street, Belfast, ME 04915

youngslobsterpound.webs.com

YEAR OPENED: 1930S
OWNERS: FOURTH-GENERATION FAMILY OWNED

Go for the steamed lobsters and clams

4 MCLOONS LOBSTER SHACK

315 Island Rd, South Thomaston, ME 04858

mcloonslobster.com

YEAR OPENED: 2012
OWNERS: THE DOUTY FAMILY

Go for the lobster roll and clam dip

5 FIVE ISLANDS LOBSTER CO.

1447 5 Islands Road, Georgetown, ME 04548

fiveislandslobster.com

YEAR OPENED: 2007
OWNERS: KEITH AND GINA LONGBOTTOM

Go for the steamed lobsters, lobster rolls, steamed clams, fried shrimp, and fish chowder

6 HOLBROOKS WHARF

984 Cundy's Harbor Road, Harpswell, ME 04079

holbrookwharf.com

YEAR OPENED: 2005
OWNER: THE HOLBROOK COMMUNITY FOUNDATION

Go for the fried seafood of all kinds, steamed lobsters, and steamed clams

7 DAY'S CRABMEAT & LOBSTER

1269 US-1, Yarmouth, ME 04096

daysmaine.com

YEAR OPENED: 1920
OWNERS: RANDALL CURIT AND JENNIFER RIEF

Go for fried seafood of all kinds, and the lobster and crab rolls

8 THE CLAM SHACK

2 Western Ave, Kennebunk, ME 04043

www.theclamshack.net

YEAR OPENED: 1968
OWNER: STEVE KINGSTON

Go for fried seafood especially fried whole belly clams; boiled lobster; lobster rolls; and clam chowder

9 BOB'S CLAM HUT

315 US-1, Kittery, ME 03904

bobsclamhut.com

YEAR OPENED: 1956
OWNER: MICHAEL LANDGARTEN

Go for clam chowder, lobster stew, fried whole belly clams, and the Lillian fried clams

10 CHAUNCEY CREEK LOBSTER PIER

16 Chauncey Creek Road, Kittery Point, ME 03905

chaunceycreek.com

YEAR OPENED: 1948
OWNER: RON SPINNEY

Go for raw oysters and clams, chowders, lobster and crab rolls, and steamed clams

11 J. T. FARNHAMS

88 Eastern Avenue, Essex, MA 01929

jtfarnhams.com

YEAR OPENED: 1941
OWNERS: TERRY AND JOSEPH CELLUCCI

Go for fried whole-belly clams, seafood chowder, lobster and crab rolls, crab cakes, and lobster bisque

12 WOODMAN'S OF ESSEX

119 Main Street, Essex, MA 01929

woodmans.com

YEAR OPENED: 1914
OWNERS: THE WOODMAN FAMILY

Go for fried seafood of all kinds, especially fried whole-belly clams; boiled lobsters; and clam chowder

MAINE'S MIDCOAST: CENTER OF THE UNIVERSE

We recognize how lucky we are, trust us. Not only do we have a rich regional tradition of simple, honest food, but we also have the natural bounty of Maine. Lobster may be what the state is best known for, but overall, there's no place on earth with better fish and shellfish. Portland sits on the southern edge of Casco Bay, a fertile kingdom for fish like mackerel, cod, haddock, striped bass, bluefish, and Western North Atlantic bluefin tuna. The innumerable marshes and finger estuaries that marry the Casco Bay and the surrounding Gulf of Maine to the coastal mainland are perhaps the most brilliant oyster beds in the world.

Although Dana Street, Sam Hayward, Rob Evans, and Rob Tod were the first to bring national food media attention to Portland, the general public and even some bold-faced food names have been hip to Maine for a while. Of course, the oyster bars and seafood shacks of New England have drawn people for decades, but it's still kind of an open secret that some of the most legendary chefs in America of the last fifty years have built their reputations in part on, and in partnership with, Maine's watermen and waterwomen.

Giants like Thomas Keller of The French Laundry, Eric Ripert of Le Bernardin, Jean-Georges Vongerichten of Jean-Georges, and the late Jean-Louis Palladin of Jean-Louis at the Watergate all built deep relationships with local entrepreneurs, such as Rod Mitchell of Browne Trading Company, the late Ingrid Bengis-Palei of Ingrid Bengis Seafood, and George Parr of Upstream Trucking. This is the pipeline that helped introduce America to a wider variety of high-end seafood in the 1980s and 1990s, including such delicacies as razor clams and sea urchins, and lesser-known types of fish, oysters, and other shellfish. Concurrently, Japanese processors were quietly setting up buying stations along the coast of Maine for bluefin tuna, sea urchin, glass eels, and surf clams to buy cheaply and ship directly to the Tsukiji fish market in Tokyo.

In addition to the bounty from our waters, we're also lucky to have access to great vegetable and livestock farms up and down the state, many of which are banded together in the Maine Organic Farmers and Gardeners Association (MOFGA), the oldest and largest such state network and certifying body in the country. Our close partners at Stonecipher Farm in Bowdoinham, North Star Sheep Farm in Windham, Southpaw Farm in Freedom, and Green Spark Farm in Cape Elizabeth all navigate a short season to raise, grow, and preserve products like pork, lamb, and an amazing panoply of vegetables. It is really hard to mess up products this good if you care even a little bit.

What truly sets the whole ecosystem apart is how incomparably cold, clean, and resilient it is. There's still a lot of work to do to protect local waters and lands, and we will continue to play our part contributing to the effort. It's an existential issue for us (and humanity, of course), because any success we've had has a lot to do with Maine's ecosystem and status as a vacation and tourism destination.

The buildup to Eventide was decades in the making, thanks to our childhood experiences with seafood shacks. When we did decide to take the leap and open, we caught lighting in a bottle. As we noted, we opened Eventide in part because you couldn't experience the amazing variety of Maine oysters in Portland restaurants as recently as 2012.

That seemed crazy, but it also represented a huge opportunity. Portland was the perfect place to seize it. Don Lindgren explained why it made some economic sense to give Eventide a go:

> Portland has a couple of things going for it. First, the city's commercial storefronts and spaces are predominantly small and inexpensive, relative to big cities. That sets up the ability for chefs to own their own restaurants, even without partners or venture capital backing, which in turn means that Portland eateries are more likely to exhibit the vision of the chef, rather than investors. It leads to more chance taking and more creativity.

In the aftermath of the Great Recession of 2008, Portland took off from the starting line to become what Lindgren described as one of the best food cities in America. Almost by necessity, there's a thriving restaurant culture here. Without the kind of widely diversified economy that bigger cities have, a larger relative percentage of Portlanders work in full-service restaurants than in any other city in the Northeast. A pipeline of great talent from other cities finds its way here because rents are relatively cheap (for now), the restaurants are great, and the quality of life is outstanding. And the national food media, in its infinite wisdom, has chosen Portland as one of its poster children for what a great small city dining and drinking scene looks like.

ONE GOOD REASON TO TRY

This was the ideal backdrop against which we stumbled forward into Eventide. Rewind to 2012: Rob and Nancy had made no secret of their interest in selling Hugo's to focus on their more casual and higher-volume restaurant, Duckfat, down the street. Nancy even had Mike, an English major, help write the real estate listing. Around the same time, Don and Sam Lindgren announced their plans to move the Rabelais bookstore out of Portland and relocate it about twenty miles south to Biddeford.

The idea of buying Hugo's had been something of a running joke among the three of us, because we were the ones using literal and proverbial zip ties to hold the restaurant together. If buying one seemed like a bad idea, then throwing a second restaurant into the mix should've seemed preposterous.

But there we were, with unfounded confidence and an opportunity to be owner-operators of two restaurants for basically the price of one. With very little planning or lead time, we cobbled together barely enough money from family and friends to purchase Hugo's and the Rabelais space, which would later become Eventide (we shared one kitchen for both restaurants at the beginning, and still do, to some extent). What we lacked in business sense, experience, and resources we resolved to make up for with really hard work, deep respect for the food we were serving, and the desire to make people really happy.

After signing the final Hugo's purchase papers with our mentors over a pint at an Irish pub, we were new owners of a turnkey, high-end, low-volume restaurant and a tiny raw space. As a result of our inexperience, we laid out endless little stumbling blocks in our own way, but we had to get moving quickly, because every minute lost was a dollar lost that we couldn't afford to burn. Instead of trying to tiptoe our way through the thicket, we just decided to barrel ahead. We wanted to do the unexpected, often and unselfconsciously, with our food and the level of generosity we showed our customers.

PUSHING OUT THE WALLS

Over more wings and beer than we care to admit, we dragged our fantasy of a modern New England oyster bar and seafood shack into reality.

Arlin, the one among us with solid front-of-house experience, got things started by drawing space plans for Eventide on draft paper. As we looked at the weird, stubby little L-shaped footprint over and over and over again, all we knew was that we wanted to create a space where people were going to have fun and let their guard down. We planned as big a traditional bar as was feasible and lined the huge glass windows with countertop seating facing the street. Why? Because bars are more fun, in the minds of three young dudes.

With most of the space allocated to barstool seating, we had enough room remaining for just two picnic tables, like the ones you might find out back of a seafood shack. Andrew's brother-in-law built them. The grand total seating number was thirty-two.

The raw bar, which we explain in detail in chapter 1, was where we really wanted to break boundaries—both in New England and beyond. Variety was priority one. It felt critical to showcase a wide range of Maine oysters, which was still pretty much unheard of, even in Portland. We wanted the bar to be full of at least a dozen types every day, piled high and shucked to order in front of the guest. It was all about keeping things honest.

Beyond the oysters themselves, we also wanted to provide creative accoutrements like shaved ices made from kimchi, horseradish, and hot sauce. That felt almost radical when you consider what traditional oyster bars and seafood shacks usually serve. Even all these years later, we challenge you to think of the last time you ordered a dozen raw oysters and were even given the option of embellishments beyond cocktail sauce, mignonette, lemon slices, and maybe hot sauce (not that there's anything wrong with any of that). We just saw so many opportunities to elevate rich, salty oysters with bright, spicy, creative touches.

We also dreamed of building out the raw bar concept with our idea of "New England Sushi"—giving raw shellfish and fish a bunch of new preparations as crudos. We weren't going to balance tiny tranches of fish atop vinegared rice, but we definitely wanted to take cues from great sushi chefs. We know that doesn't sound novel, but at the time, crudos were not on every high-end restaurant menu, regardless of cuisine, as they are today.

FINISHING SPEED

Then came the sacred sea cows: classic seafood shack fare and traditional Maine cuisine. The former, as we mentioned, is a singular dining experience that draws loyalty from generations of families and waves of attention from summer weekenders and global food adventurers. The latter is less well known, or perhaps less well defined, because it's not that different from any other homespun regional cuisine. Maine is all about simple, hearty, honest food with lots of soups, stews, potatoes, local seafood, and preserves, but not a lot of frills. Make that no frills. But we were trained in the cuisine of ambitious, high-end restaurants that forever ask, "Can't there be more frills, tweaks, or embellishments?"

We found our footing between those competing forces with Eventide's Brown Butter Lobster Roll (page 112), the foundation of any success we've achieved. After playing around a lot with classic setups of hot buttered lobster chunks and cold, creamy lobster salad on a variety of buns, we eventually figured out that we didn't want to go the classic, split-top, griddled hot dog bun route. We didn't have a griddle, for one, but more importantly, we knew that we wanted to do something different and (respectfully) plant our own flag in the sand.

Being part of the generation of chefs who swam in Chef David Chang of Momofuku's wake means we're *not* satisfied with conventional wisdom, and we're big fans of steamed bao buns. The bao is a perfect, tender little pillow to wrap around your delicious filling of choice. It is a little miracle of Chinese gastronomy, because it unfailingly elevates (and never detracts from) whatever you cram in there.

We already had a steamed bun recipe wired for a bar snack at Hugo's, and we just rolled it differently to create the split-top look. With the lobster, we found our way pretty quickly to brown butter, which has a jammier and richer flavor than uncooked butter; it provides the roll with caramelized flavor that was lost without the griddled bun. Creating the lobster roll was the most calculated culinary project we took on ahead of opening the restaurant. Everything else was wild improvisation and survival-based cooking.

People came in droves more or less from the beginning. A week or so after his initial visit, Dana Street came back with his entire management staff, and we put them in front of "The Rock" to drink in the general liveliness and all the interaction between customers. People were coming in and having drinks and eating a whole meal standing at a stone ledge. Everyone in the restaurant seemed like as if they were at a shindig together. As it turns out, thirty-two seats were enough to party.

TAKE A LEAP

Now that you've heard the backstory, here's our pitch on the food and recipes that follow in this book. We hope you will come back to this book every summer, just as tourists and locals flock to the classic New England oyster bars and seafood shacks that are the inspiration for Eventide Oyster Co. It's a book made to pack for a week at the beach or to stumble upon while perusing the bookshelf at the summer rental. For any time of year and wherever you may be, it offers the best insight we have, acquired in almost a decade of hard labor and lessons, about buying and preparing fresh, seasonal seafood and other coastal favorites.

We want you, dear reader, to feel comfortable putting together a raw seafood spread for appetizers at your next brunch get-together; a brown butter lobster roll (page 112) with a green salad and a glass of pale wine, solo on a Tuesday night; some lobster stew (page 126) for a meal on the deck or the balcony; or a halibut tail bo ssam (page 148), our version of the ultimate Korean BBQ party spread, at your next dinner gathering. You can make them all possible with help from this book. Our only request is that you share with others what we're sharing with you, whenever you can. It's about spreading the familial magic that comes with picking up your loaded trays at the oyster bar or seafood shack counter, after a wait across seasons and long lines, and getting them to the table for friends and loved ones.

Go ahead and confidently serve fish in your home! Take a leap! Do something unexpected and fun, because it's worth it. When we opened Eventide, we didn't really know what we were doing either, but we just took the leap and trusted that fresh, high-quality seafood would do most of the work on its own. Done right and responsibly, it's about the cleanest and most beautiful eating there is.

Final note: These recipes were developed and refined by all of us, with help from a huge supporting cast, including our opening bar manager (and wartime consigliere) John Myers, and our pastry chef Kim Rodgers. Sometimes we have a personal story to share about the recipe or a really important tip for making the dish, which is why you'll see our names after some headnotes. No names means the recipe comes from all of Team Eventide.

CHAPTER 1

THE ROCK: EVENTIDE'S RAW BAR PROGRAM

Most people seem to think that serving shellfish on the half shell at home is some kind of Herculean feat. It's fine on the one hand, because they keep coming back to Eventide for their fix (we thank you!). But it's a shame on the other, because both oysters and littleneck clams are approachable luxuries, and there's just no better way to kick off a memorable dinner party, summer lunch, or cook-at-home date than with a raw bar spread. It's a way to beat people's expectations and set the stage for a warm, sparkly kind of night. In that sense, it's bringing the spirit of Eventide into your home.

THE ROCK

The raw bar program at Eventide is one of the things we are proudest of, because it brought an ultralocal, top-quality, widely varied oyster list to the fore in a casual, upscale restaurant setting in a way that hadn't been done much before. We opened Eventide partly because nobody else was capitalizing on the staggering breadth of Maine oysters. We figured if we chose wisely and served everything simply and as fresh as possible, we might do well for ourselves.

One of the most fateful decisions we made during the run-up to opening Eventide was to have a custom stone oyster basin created as the centerpiece of the restaurant and our boundary-pushing raw bar program. No ubiquitous, stainless steel oyster displays would do. That's how we found ourselves at Cosmic Stone, Lance Linkel's stone yard in Topsham, Maine.

Being surrounded by giant earth-moving machines, massive slabs of granite, and the childlike energy of a man-monument like Lance all have a way of influencing a person. We arrived looking for a quaint little piece of stone to sit atop our new bar, which wasn't even poured yet, and we soon found ourselves standing on top of a trapezoidal boulder the size and weight of a Ford Festiva. Lance had a wild look in his eyes and seemed as if he were having none of the reticence in ours. It didn't take him long to close the deal. He "hogged out" a shallow tray across the top of the boulder and a drainage hole down through it before trucking it to Portland. We muscled it into the restaurant with the help of a Bobcat, an engine hoist, and fifteen line cooks.

The granite beast became known as "The Rock," and we poured our concrete bar around it, on a whim adding a little lip on the outside at bar height that is now known as "the rail." Through some stroke of dumb luck, the rail ended up being exactly the size of the used fish-poaching vessel lids that we stumbled upon and planned to repurpose as oyster-serving trays. Today, standing at "The Rock" and enjoying a dozen from the rail is the best spot in the house. So many things fell together that way, and we are skeptical that Eventide would be breezy like it is if we had followed some strict blueprint.

THE OYSTERS WE'RE FORTUNATE TO SERVE

It just felt intuitive for us to have a huge selection of oysters and shuck each one to order in front of guests. As we kept improving and building on the program, we realized it was pretty unique. However, what most sets Eventide apart is not our shucking protocol, but the fact that we live on the doorstep of elysian shellfish beds. We believe that the shellfish grown here are the best in the world, thanks to the cold, clean, unparalleled quality of Maine's coastal water, particularly the Damariscotta River.

More than three-quarters of the state's farmed oysters and a lot of other products come out of the Damariscotta, which is actually a twelve-mile-long estuary northeast of Portland that drains into the Gulf of Maine. The next time you're eating an oyster that transports you with its balanced salinity and freshness, let your mind wander to the Damariscotta. These are the forested, rocky-shored wilds of Maine, where freshwater runoff meets saltwater in a vibrant natural intersection. Thirty billion gallons of water surge through to cleanse the Damariscotta during every tidal cycle, making it an ideal setting to grow filtering bivalves like oysters, millions of pounds of which are harvested from these waters every year. The dynamic ecosystem is also home to seals, osprey, eagles, lobsters, horseshoe crabs, and numerous species of fish, including striped bass, bluefish, herring, flounder, and many more. It is close to the perfect biological interface, a place infinitely greater than the sum of its parts.

We came to appreciate the beauty and power of Damariscotta and similar rivers, like the New Meadows, through our friendship with John Hennessey, who along with his dad, Jim, owns and operates Winter Point Oyster Farm. During the stressful times running up to the opening of Eventide, John would show up in our doorway with bags of his oysters and clams. We'd sit and shuck them and drink beer and listen to him talk about oyster ecosystems and oyster farming. He helped us fully understand and appreciate one of the two local products, alongside lobster, that are the cornerstones of what we do.

There is such a deep love for the Damariscotta's and Maine's products here, and that signaled an opening as much as a barrier. From the beginning, our aim with our oyster program and broader menu has been to give people a new way to experience what they love, without completely unmooring them from their nostalgia. It's our nostalgia, too.

EXPANDING THE REPERTOIRE

We knew we wanted to offer a more expansive oyster menu than just about anyone had ever done, and we started by taking a closer look at Maine oysters, which had yet to find much distribution outside of the Northeast. At the time, there wasn't really enough variety of Maine specimens alone to carry a broad program like ours, so we contented ourselves with whatever high-quality ones we could find, including from beyond Maine, which we dubbed as "From Away" on the menu.

As demand for oysters shot up in the restaurant world and a bunch of places opened to celebrate the slurp—for example, The Ordinary (Charleston, South Carolina), The Walrus and The Carpenter (Seattle, Washington), Peche (New Orleans, Louisiana), Island Creek Oyster Bar (Boston, Massachusetts), Neptune Oyster (Boston, Massachusetts), and the John Dory (New York, New York)—entrepreneurial Mainers saw oyster farming as a more attractive way to make a living in a sustainable fishery. The results for us and for Maine's economy were huge. From 2011 to 2017, the Maine oyster business nearly quintupled, with more than ten million shells harvested every year.

That is still a fraction of what is harvested in the Chesapeake Bay and the Gulf of Mexico, but with oysters, more than almost any other product, quality is everything, and the only thing. We have it here. All of a sudden, there were more varieties available in Maine, and the numbers we were moving meant that people wanted to develop relationships with us. Those bonds are written on our menu today: Winter Point, Norumbega, Johns River, Basket Island, Pemaquid, Flying Point, North Haven, Glidden Point, Otter Cove, Long Reach, Dodge Cove, Nonesuch, Wet Smacks, and Eros. We've all but abandoned the "From Away" portion of the oyster list at this point.

ELEMENTS OF SURPRISE

We had big plans to innovate on accoutrements, too, because the word *hidebound* doesn't even do justice to the dressing situation for shellfish. We saw endless opportunities for playful, delicious accompaniments.

At Hugo's, we experimented a lot with granités (shaved ices) to embellish oysters, and we took things a step further when we opened Eventide. First, we tested all kinds of ices and used a fork to scrape them into snowflakes for serving with raw shellfish. This is the approach that the home cook can use very effectively, which we map out in a few pages, but as demand started to go up, we eventually pulled the trigger and bought a shaved ice machine. That allowed us to mass-produce a good variety of concoctions, including many recipes in this chapter.

A BEAUTIFUL RAW BAR CAN BE YOURS

There is no scientific formula for putting out an amazing raw bar spread. The two most important factors are getting the highest-quality shellfish possible and handling it properly. Fortunately, it's not just restaurateurs who have it easier today: sourcing products for a great raw bar experience has gotten dramatically easier for at-home shuckers, too. And handling your oysters properly takes some practice, but not to worry—we have tips for you.

Your local specialty fish market, high-quality grocery store, or the internet are great places to start the search for high-quality specimens. If you end up in a shop, you should ask the fishmongers working the counter what is freshest and most recommended. While it is technically true that oysters can live up to a month properly stored in the refrigerator, we certainly don't recommend it. Five to seven days after they are harvested, they will not taste nearly as fresh and run the risk of drying out. Ask to see harvest tags (the tracking information that the Department of Marine Resources requires all handlers to have) or ask them to tell you the harvest date. If they're reluctant to comply, you should be reluctant to buy.

Another option is going online to grab overnight delivery of Maine oysters harvested that day from the Pemaquid Oyster Company (pemaquidoysters.com), Glidden Point Oyster Farms (gliddenpoint.com), Johns River Oysters (johnsriveroyster.com), and many other producers. Take your time with the search and learn about the great farmers working all over the country.

Before you get your oysters, you'll need a good oyster knife, which you can buy online, and a towel to protect your oyster-holding hand from injury. Once you get your oysters, you just need practice shucking. It could get a little messy. There will be some failures. But trust us, you can get the hang of it, just like we did (actually, Mike is still pretty lousy at it).

Here are our step-by-step guides to shucking oysters (page 26) and clams (page 29).

Once you've gotten reasonably confident about your shucking skills, the rest is lickety-split, if you follow our instructions.

Oyster Breakdown

1 Lay oyster on top of a towel, with the hinge facing you. Be sure that the cup of the oyster is on the bottom and the flatter shell is on top.

2 Fold the towel over the top of the oyster, leaving the hinge peeking out at the bottom. This will help protect your hands from the shell and oyster knife.

3 With one hand on top of the towel, holding the oyster down, work the tip of the knife into the hinge, using it like a crowbar to delicately pop open the shell.

4 Wipe away any grit or silt that might've collected on the knife with a paper towel or the towel under the oyster.

5 Work the knife back into the oyster and slide the knife tightly along the underside of the flat top shell.

6 To sever the adductor muscle, which holds the meat to the shell, work the knife away from you and all the way through the top of the oyster.

7 Remove the top shell and inspect the oyster.

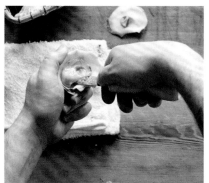

8 Slide the knife between the underside of the oyster meat and the shell to sever the bottom of the adductor muscle.

9 Remove any bits of shell that may have splintered off, and slurp.

GET AHEAD OF IT. Before you plan to serve your spread, think about getting the easy, non-perishable stuff out of the way. Pick your accoutrements, make a list, and do a grocery store run for ingredients. Then whip up the goods—like Classic Cocktail Sauce (page 31), Red Wine Mignonette (page 31), Kimchi Ice (page 33), and Tabasco Ice (page 33)—and store them in jars in the fridge (or freezer for ice).

GET CRISP, COLD DRINKS. Do not flout this rule. Stock up on lean, mineral-driven white wines like Muscadet and Sancerre. Up the ante with pale pink, high-acid rosés from Provence, France, or from some of the up-and-coming vineyards on Long Island, New York, like any of the fine white wines from Channing Daughters Winery. When it comes to bubbles, you can't go wrong with dry, non-vintage blanc de blanc Champagne. If you're a beer-drinking oyster eater, we suggest light-bodied Pilsners, citrusy American pale ales, and refreshing wheat beers. For an unexpected and surprising beer and oyster pairing, we enthusiastically recommend the bigger, bolder Allagash Tripel. This beer has been our go-to oyster pairing for years because its perceived sweetness nicely offsets an oyster's complex brine, and its carbonation acts to wipe the palate clean between slurps. If spirits are your thing, stick with light, refreshing options like vodka, gin, and tequila. Cocktails or mocktails with vegetal or citrus notes (did somebody say Celery Gimlet, page 239?) definitely fit the bill. Buy three times as much alcohol as you think you'll need, and put it all in a large ice bucket somewhere very near the raw bar setup.

CALIBRATE YOUR FRESH SEAFOOD BUYING. The best approach, bar none, is to buy your oysters, clams, and fish the day you're serving, provided you've internalized our dictates about freshness above. If you're having anything shipped, make sure it arrives absolutely no more than a day or two in advance of putting out your spread.

CHOOSE STURDY, SEAFARING VESSELS. A wide, shallow, good-looking ceramic tray or platter is great for heaping with crushed ice and shellfish (or in a pinch, a foil tray—we won't judge you). Small jars, ramekins, and cups with small serving spoons are good for your accoutrements. A couple of large slate or wooden boards are also worth having on hand, for things like our smoked shellfish (see page 206) or a dramatic crudo board. Anything boosted from your eccentric Grandma's collection will shine here. If you want to give it a real seafood shack touch, buy a batch of red-and-white checkered paper boats for people to use as hors d'oeuvres plates.

DON'T OVER-SHUCK YOURSELF. We all know that your Uncle Duke once ate one hundred oysters in one sitting at the Acme Oyster House in New Orleans, but think smaller scale for a dinner party. Assuming oysters aren't the only food at your party, people need only a few slurps to be happy, so plan on three oysters per person alongside the other dishes you're serving. If you're hosting a happy hour where the focus is on oysters, plan for a half dozen per guest. Give yourself a good chunk of time (around 30 minutes) before serving to get the shellfish shucked and arrayed on a large platter covered with a 1-inch layer of crushed ice. Position the oysters so they sit sturdily facing up, to keep the liqueur from spilling out, and leave a little space between each one, arraying your sauces around the platter. Around the same time, you should be slicing and plating your crudo if you're adding it to the spread (see chapter 2 for more detail). Do not be tempted to shuck the oysters or clams more than an hour ahead of time and store them in the refrigerator. You're basically sacrificing the beautiful freshness of the product, because they will dry out and develop a kind of skin across the oyster that is not pleasing.

KEEP A SHARP EYE ON THE DETAILS. There are three things to avoid when presenting a raw bar setup:

1. Dead shellfish: Before you start shucking, sort through the shellfish and check that all the shells are tightly closed. Shells that are open even a fraction or sound hollow when tapped, oyster meat that looks dried out when you open the oyster, or oysters that are off-smelling are no-nos and should definitely be tossed.
2. Shells in your oysters or clams: You should make every effort to remove any remnant shell pieces with your oyster knife or finger (while being careful to preserve all the liqueur in the shell).
3. Scrambled oysters: Oysters shucked so poorly the meats are totally mangled. This is pretty much unavoidable for the novice shucker, and the good news is they still taste great, so don't worry about it too much. But always keep it in mind that there is platonic ideal to strive for!

There's an unavoidable learning curve when it comes to the raw bar, but take heart! Every time you screw up and pierce the belly of an oyster or make some other faux pas, you get to eat a free oyster. Good for you!

Clam Breakdown

1 Make sure to have a clam knife and work over a towel.

2 Hold the clam with the hinge in the palm of your hand and the round side—called the 'lips'—facing your fingertips.

3 Place the clam knife blade carefully between the lips, and wrap your fingers around the dull edge of the clam knife.

4 Using a squeezing motion, pull the clam knife towards the hinge, and when done properly, the knife will slide in easily. Pull knife all the way to the hinge.

5 Open the clam and using the tip of the clam knife, work the knife around the top shell and slide the clam meat onto the bottom shell.

6 With a twisting motion, remove the upper shell from the bottom shell and discard.

7 Using the tip of the knife, work under the clam meat to sever the adductors and free the meat from the shell.

8 Double-check that the clam meat is completely free of the shell.

9 Slurp.

CLASSIC COCKTAIL SAUCE AND SOPHISTICATED MIGNONETTES

Cocktail sauce and red wine mignonette sauce are two trusty old oyster warhorses we had to have as a part of our raw bar program. Why? Because (most) people love them. They are great with shellfish. We offer relatively straightforward versions, but look no further than our recipe for Black Trumpet and Rosemary Mignonette for a more adventurous take.

CLASSIC COCKTAIL SAUCE

MAKES ABOUT 2 CUPS

½ cup prepared horseradish

2 tablespoons fresh lemon juice

2 teaspoons Worcestershire sauce

1½ cups ketchup

In a small bowl, mix together the horseradish, lemon juice, Worcestershire, and ketchup. Serve immediately or store in an airtight container in the fridge for up to 1 month.

RED WINE MIGNONETTE

MAKES ABOUT 1 CUP

1½ teaspoons whole black peppercorns

2 shallots, minced

1 cup red wine vinegar

1 tablespoon balsamic vinegar

In a dry pan over medium heat, toast the peppercorns for 30 to 60 seconds, until they become fragrant, then remove them from the pan to cool slightly. In a spice grinder, grind the peppercorns to a coarse powder. In a small bowl, stir together the peppercorn powder, shallots, and both vinegars, and let sit for at least an hour, or up to overnight, so the flavors can meld. Store in an airtight container in the fridge for up to 1 month.

BLACK TRUMPET AND ROSEMARY MIGNONETTE

MAKES ABOUT 1¼ CUPS

1 sprig rosemary

1 pound fresh black trumpet mushrooms, finely chopped (fresh shiitakes and reconstituted dried black trumpets are suitable substitutes)

1 small shallot, minced

1 tablespoon water

½ cup balsamic vinegar

½ cup rice wine vinegar

2 tablespoons honey

Finishing salt

Turn on your gas range or light a torch or lighter and lightly wave the rosemary sprig over the flame until the leaves pick up a little char here and there. Kill the flame and set the sprig aside to cool. Pull the rosemary leaves from the stems and very finely chop the leaves.

Add the chopped rosemary, mushrooms, shallot, and water to a pan over medium-low heat and sweat until the mushrooms release their liquid and the liquid evaporates, about 3 minutes. Add both vinegars and bring the mixture to a bare simmer, then remove the pot from the heat. When the mixture cools to room temperature, stir in the honey and salt to taste. Serve immediately or store in an airtight container in the refrigerator for 1 month.

FLAVORED ICES

If shucking a smorgasbord of local oysters à la minute in front of our guests was the single most important concept behind Eventide's raw bar program, then serving unique accompaniments was a close second. For R&D before opening the restaurant, we ate a lot of oysters and shellfish all over Portland, the rest of New England, New York, Charleston, northern California, and beyond. We were collectively stunned by the lack of creativity put toward such an essential aspect of the raw bar.

Flavored ices (also known as granités) were something we had started to play with as an accompaniment to shellfish at Hugo's, and we ramped up our exploration when we were developing the Eventide raw bar program. Savory plays on ices aren't found that often outside of fine dining restaurants, but we saw them as a great way to twist the classic oyster accoutrements, like our Tabasco or horseradish varieties. They are also a tool for cutting down on waste in the kitchen, which we do by using leftover pickling liquid in our beet and red onion ices. Flavored ices can capture and preserve the beautiful, height-of-season flavor of veggies like summer tomatoes and green chiles. Or, they can just give you a chance to try something new and different, like the kimchi or yuzu kosho ices that find their way into the rotation on our menu.

There are no hard-and-fast rules when making flavored ices. Generally speaking, you will see that most of our ices balance sweet and acidic ingredients because that's what people typically associate with oyster accompaniments. Sugar is essential to making the ice easy to work with and giving it the right texture in the end. Don't worry about precision here; our recipes will yield a delicious ice. If you want to be a nerd about it (like us), get a refractometer (see Glossary), which can measure the brix level (sugar content) of a solution. Generally speaking, for our purposes here, you want the brix level to be about 14°Bx.

As we mentioned, because of the sheer volume of ices that we go through, we use a shaved ice machine at Eventide, but all of these ices can be made by scraping with a fork, so they're easy to do at home by hand. You'll need only ½ teaspoon of ice for each oyster, so portion out a batch depending on how many oysters you're serving and keep the rest frozen for use in slurping later.

PICKLED RED ONION ICE

MAKES ABOUT 1 CUP

1 cup brine from Pickled Red Onion (page 192)

Freeze the red onion liquid completely by placing it in a bowl in the freezer for 3 hours. Once frozen, use the tines of a fork to scrape the mixture into a light, fluffy ice. Serve immediately or return to the freezer in a covered storage container. The ice will last for 2 months in the freezer; when you want to deploy it, just use a fork to scrape it again.

GREEN CHILE ICE

MAKES 3 CUPS

1½ cups freshly roasted green chiles (alternatively you could use any manner of store-bought roasted red peppers or frozen chiles from New Mexico), stemmed and seeded

¼ cup Simple Syrup (page 244)

1 cup water

½ cup rice wine vinegar

In a blender, combine the chiles, simple syrup, water, and vinegar. Puree the mixture on high speed until completely smooth.

Freeze the mixture completely by placing it in a bowl in the freezer for 3 hours. Once frozen, use the tines of a fork to scrape the mixture into a light, fluffy ice. Serve immediately or return to the freezer in a covered container.

The ice will last for 2 months in the freezer; when you want to deploy it, just use a fork to scrape it again.

TABASCO ICE

MAKES 1½ CUPS

½ cup Tabasco hot sauce

3 tablespoons Simple Syrup (page 244)

1 cup water

Thoroughly mix the simple syrup, Tabasco, and water in a small bowl. Freeze the mixture completely by placing it in the freezer for 1 hour. Once frozen, use the tines of a fork to scrape the mixture into a light, fluffy ice. Serve immediately or return to the freezer in a covered storage container. The ice will last for 2 months in the freezer; when you want to deploy it, just use a fork to scrape it again.

KIMCHI ICE

MAKES ABOUT 2 CUPS

2 cups brine from Kimchi (page 194, or drained from a good-quality store-bought kimchi)

Freeze the kimchi liquid completely by placing it in a bowl in the freezer for 3 hours. Once frozen, use the tines of a fork to scrape the mixture into a light, fluffy ice. Serve immediately or return to the freezer in a covered storage container. The ice will last for 2 months in the freezer; when you want to deploy it, just use a fork to scrape it again.

HORSERADISH ICE

MAKES ABOUT 3⅓ CUPS

1¼ cups prepared horseradish

½ cup champagne vinegar

⅓ cup Simple Syrup (page 244)

1¼ cups water

Whisk all ingredients together in a bowl and freeze the mixture completely by placing the bowl in the freezer for 3 hours. Once frozen, use the tines of a fork to scrape the mixture into a light, fluffy ice. Serve immediately or return to the freezer in a storage covered container. The ice will last for 2 months in the freezer; when you want to deploy it, just use a fork to scrape it again.

PICKLED BEET ICE

MAKES ABOUT 1½ CUPS

1½ cups brine from Pickled Beets (page 193)

Pour the liquid into a bowl and freeze completely by placing it in the freezer for 3 hours. Once frozen, use the tines of a fork to scrape the mixture into a light, fluffy ice. Serve immediately or return to the freezer in a covered container. The ice will last for 2 months in the freezer; when you want to deploy it, just use a fork to scrape it again.

CONTINUED

FLAVORED ICES

CONTINUED

TOMATO WATER ICE

MAKES ABOUT 3 CUPS

2¼ pounds super-ripe tomatoes, cored and cut into medium pieces

1½ teaspoons kosher salt

2½ tablespoons sugar

In a nonreactive bowl, toss the tomatoes with the salt and allow the mixture to sit for a couple of hours at room temperature. Pour the mixture into a blender and puree until totally smooth. Pour the mixture through a fine-mesh strainer lined with a double layer of cheesecloth into a nonreactive bowl. Place the strainer and bowl in the fridge and allow the tomato water to drain for at least 24, and up to 48, hours. Your yield will vary a bit depending on the juiciness of your tomatoes, but you should end up with just shy of 3 cups of tomato water.

In a blender, combine the tomato water and the sugar, and puree until the sugar dissolves.

Freeze the mixture completely by placing it in a bowl in the freezer for 3 hours. Once frozen, use the tines of a fork to scrape the mixture into a light, fluffy ice. Serve immediately or return to the freezer in a covered storage container. The ice will last for 2 months in the freezer; when you want to deploy it, just use a fork to scrape it again.

YUZU KOSHO ICE

MAKES ABOUT 5⅓ CUPS

3 to 4 tablespoons yuzu kosho (see Glossary)

4 cups water

⅔ cup rice wine vinegar

1 cup sugar

⅓ cup yuzu juice (or substitute 3 tablespoons fresh lemon juice and 2 tablespoons fresh lime juice)

1 teaspoon kosher salt

In a saucepan, combine 3 tablespoons of the yuzu kosho, the water, vinegar, sugar, yuzu juice, and salt. Taste and add another tablespoon of the yuzu kosho if you want it spicy. Bring to a simmer over medium-high heat, stirring frequently to dissolve everything, then transfer to a bowl and let cool to room temperature.

Freeze the mixture completely by placing the bowl in the freezer for 1 hour. Once frozen, use the tines of a fork to scrape the mixture into a light, fluffy ice. Serve immediately or return to the freezer in a covered storage container. The ice will last for 2 months in the freezer; when you want to deploy it, just use a fork to scrape it again.

BLACK PEPPER AND LEMON ICE

MAKES 1½ CUPS

2 tablespoons plus 1 teaspoon peppercorns, preferably Tellicherry (see Glossary)

1 cup water

¼ cup sugar

¼ cup fresh lemon juice

⅛ teaspoon kosher salt

In a dry pan over medium heat, toast the peppercorns for 1 minute or until they become fragrant, then remove the peppercorns from the pan and set aside.

In a small pot with a lid, combine the water and sugar and bring to a boil, stirring to dissolve the sugar. Add the peppercorns, cover the pot, turn the heat down, and simmer for 30 minutes. Turn off the heat, let the mixture cool for a few minutes, and then puree it in a high-powered blender. Strain through a fine-mesh strainer into a bowl and let cool.

Add the lemon juice and salt and freeze the mixture completely by placing the bowl in the freezer for 1 hour. Once frozen, use the tines of a fork to scrape the mixture into a light, fluffy ice. Serve immediately or return to the freezer in a covered storage container. The ice will last for 2 months in the freezer; when you want to deploy it, just use a fork to scrape it again.

CHAPTER 2

NEW ENGLAND SUSHI: EVENTIDE'S CRUDO PROGRAM

Lightly Cured Char	47	**Black Bass Ceviche**	66

Lightly Cured Char 47

BAGEL, PICKLED BEET,
CRÈME FRAÎCHE

Lightly Pickled Mackerel 48

CARAMELIZED ONION, DASHI,
PUFFED SUSHI RICE, NORI

American Unagi 53

KABAYAKI, CELERIAC, BOK CHOY,
CANDIED SESAME, GARLIC CHIVE

Chawanmushi 57

BLACK TRUMPETS,
GRILLED SCALLION, UNI

Razor Clam 59

PARSLEY, LARDO,
GRILLED BREAD CRUMBS

Grilled Squid Salad 62

CITRUS, CASTELVETRANO OLIVE,
KALAMATA OLIVE, CONFIT POTATO

Cured Salmon 64

SCALLION TOFU,
FURIKAKE, YUZU KOSHO

Black Bass Ceviche 66

PIQUE DE PIÑA, CILANTRO,
LIME, MASA

Mussels en Escabeche 67

GRILLED BREAD, CHORIZO, CHIVE

Bonito Tataki 69

CHICHARRONES, CHILE,
TOMATILLOS

Fluke Crudo 71

CARAMELIZED CRAB, SEA BEANS,
CHILE, PICKLED KOMBU

Tuna Crudo 77

GINGER SCALLION, TARE, RADISH

Toro Carpaccio 78

CELERY, SESAME, YUZU

Chu-Toro 81

RAMP LEAF–ALMOND PISTOU,
PICKLED RAMP, GARLIC CHIPS

Tuna Tartare 84

RAMEN CRACKER, UMEBOSHI,
PICKLED SEA VEGETABLES

Eventide was founded with the conviction that raw fish preparations are among the most sublime culinary pleasures, but despite Mike's masters in rhetoric (or maybe because of it), we have a hang-up with words when it comes to trying to categorize or define them.

Japanese sashimi and nigiri are obviously the most recognizable ways to serve raw fish, but many other cultures take advantage of this perfect culinary arrangement. In Central and South America, heavy doses of citrus and spice are often included. Italians, who use the word *crudo* to mean "raw," dress their fish with little more than good olive oil, salt, and lemon.

At Eventide, *crudo* is used more broadly to mean a dish served cold. It doesn't need to be fish nor does it need to be raw, but it does need to strike a balance between savoriness and acidity, demonstrate textural complexity, and embellish the finest attributes of the main ingredient. Our cooks at Eventide are well versed in this loose formula, which keeps them in constant competition to bring new variations to the table. Our daily board of specials is a place their talents can be rewarded as we showcase their ideas for our customers.

Once you begin to understand the relationship between salt and acid and the importance of crunchiness and crispiness and have gained enough familiarity with your base ingredients, it's easy to have a lot of fun. The recipes in this chapter run the gamut from raw preparations to cooked ones, with a huge range of flavors and garnishes. Because the raw versions take some understanding and finesse, we spend a little extra time explaining them here.

HOW TO MAKE CRUDO AT HOME

Did you train under a Japanese master sushi chef for ten years before you were allowed to handle raw fish? No? Neither did we. Glad we got that out of the way. It is okay if you are not a master at scoring gizzard shad skin at perfect intervals and depth. Again, neither are we. These deficiencies haven't slowed us down much, and they won't get in your way either. What you pull together may not end up looking quite as refined as what you see at a five-star restaurant, but if you focus on the right details, it will be just as delicious.

SOURCING

Good purchasing is the most important aspect of preparing a crudo. There is no amount of skill that can salvage old and poorly handled fish. Conversely, it takes almost no chops to make something awesome if you're starting with a pristine product. You can literally scrape a beautiful piece of tuna with a spoon, put some salt on it, and put it on a cracker. Voilà!

Buying fish is way more intuitive than people think. The first misconception to get over is thinking you have to buy a specific fish when you walk into a market. Focus on procuring the freshest fish that will work for your purpose. Once you're at the market, be practical. You've seen a fish that is still alive, right? It has clear eyes, bright and vibrant colors, firm flesh, red gills, and no overly fishy smell. Try to find the closest thing to that as possible. Talk to your fishmonger about what is fresh, seasonal, and local.

Fish varieties that are ideal for crudo include striped bass, black bass, rockfish, arctic char, porgy/scup, fluke, hamachi, tautog, tilefish, halibut, flounder, mackerel, gizzard shad, tuna, and salmon. You can also use many shellfish and crustaceans such as scallops and shrimp. But don't limit yourself! There are tens of thousands of species to choose from; just do your research and be sure to avoid fish that are notoriously parasitic.

WHOLE FISH VERSUS FILLETS

Whole fish are way easier to gauge for freshness than fillets, which is why we almost exclusively buy whole fish. If you're going the fillet route, remember that firmness is a virtue in raw fish. Look for fillets that bounce back when they are poked and hold a sharp edge wherever they've been sliced. The colors should be sharp: redder reds, whiter whites, and vibrant oranges. Again, trust your reptilian brain and make sure the fillet doesn't smell. If you get a strong whiff of anything, avoid it. Also, ask your fishmonger for a center-cut fillet, rather than a tail piece, which has more connective tissue and is poorly suited to crudos. It's also worth asking your fishmonger to remove the skins from the fillets if your recipe calls for skinless.

TIMING

Preferably, buy your fish on the day of serving and slice and plate as close as possible to meal time. To store the fish, take it out of the paper wrapping you brought it home in and pat it dry with paper towels. Then wrap the fish in dry paper towels and seal it in a ziplock bag before putting it in the fridge, preferably nestled in a bowl of ice or on a perforated pan buried in ice. Drain the bowl and/or replenish the ice as needed.

SLICING FRESH FISH FOR CRUDOS

If you've got a razor-sharp knife, good for you! Your cuts will be gorgeous, more uniform, and liable to garner more "likes." Even if you're not well versed in bevel angles and elk horn bolsters, you can still prepare serviceable and delicious crudos with a sharpish knife. What's most important is that your cuts are confident, uniform, and bite-size, which should lead to a melt-in-your-mouth experience. Once you've dialed in your ability to balance salt, acid, sweetness, and heat, we give you permission to start spending ungodly amounts of money on knives, whetstones, honing tools, and hand-wrought sayas.

The colder the fish, the cleaner the cut. As the fish warms toward room temperature, it gets harder to handle. When you are working with smaller fillets, trim the sides of the fish so you have an even, rectangular shape, almost like a block. If you are working with a larger fillet or loin of tuna, trim the fish similarly and then slice the larger blocks into smaller ones that are easier to handle.

That said, you have some flexibility. If your block of fish is a little small, cut on an angle to make the slice bigger. You can also experiment with the thickness of the slice. Fattier fish (like tuna) with less connective tissue shine when served in generous slices, whereas leaner fish with more structure (like fluke) benefit from thin slices.

All that said, the end game you're looking for is a manageable bite. If you're unsure, eat a piece with a sprinkle of salt, making sure it is texturally pleasant, because you don't want to feel like you're working too hard to chew a slice of fish. You can use trimmings for tartares or reserve and freeze them to make any number of other recipes, including stews and fish cakes. The trimmings will last in the freezer for a month, for cooked preparations only!

Roundfish Breakdown

1. Set up your work area with a knife, scissors, fish tweezers, and some paper towels.

2. With a smooth and confident stroke, slice the fish along its length starting at the head and culminating at the tail. You should hear your blade "clicking" as it moves along the spine.

3. Gently lift the fillet away from the bones while running your knife along the spine to facilitate a clean separation of fillet from bone. Leave only the rib bones.

4. Using a pair of culinary scissors, snip through the smaller ribcage bones, following the spine all the way up to the head.

5. Cut behind the gill plate behind the pectoral fin from the top of the fish to the belly. You should be able to remove the entire filet at this point.

6. Repeat with the other side.

7. With a single, confident stroke, remove the ribcage and any pin bones. Trim the edges of the fillet.

8. Separate the top loin from the bottom loin by cutting from the top of the filet to the bottom where the bloodline is.

9. With a sharp knife, cut the top loin into thin slices. If your fish is soft and fatty, cut fatter slices; if it's leaner, cut thinner.

Flatfish Breakdown

① Set up your work area with a knife, scissors, and some paper towels.

② Using your scissors, cut away all fins.

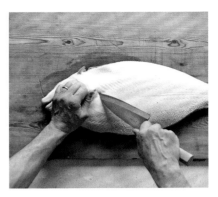

③ Make a cut just behind the gill plate from top to bottom doing your best not to let the knife plunge deep and cut into the internal organs. Repeat on both sides.

④ With scissors, snip through the exposed spine and pull away the head and viscera and discard. Make a confident chopping cut to remove the tail.

⑤ Run your blade down the fish's medial line. Your knife should ride along the spine, between the two loins.

⑥ Starting at the tail and working up, make smooth cuts from the spine outward, lifting the fillet away from the bones to facilitate a clean separation. Remove the fillet.

⑦ Repeat the process to remove the other loin. Start by running the tip of your knife at an angle along the spine.

⑧ Remove the second loin, flip the fish over, and repeat steps 5 through 7 on the other side of the fish.

⑨ Remove the skin by running the knife underneath the fillet. Thinly slice the fish, testing for quality. If chewy, slice thinner.

THE ARRANGING

There are no laws that govern how to place the fish on a crudo plate, beyond the principle of balance we talked about before, which means you can play around with the possibilities.

Dominoes or tiling: Think of the way dominoes look when they fall and you'll have a good vision of how we plate our tuna crudo. Lay your slices in a line, or chain them in a circle or other shape with slight overlaps on each piece.

Scatterplot: It's also fine to lay pieces out so they don't touch each other, or twirl the pieces into little rosettes and place them on a plate randomly. Just make sure there is enough room between the pieces for your garnishes to evenly cover them. This setup will also make it easier for your guests to grab a single piece at a time, rather than massacring the plate.

Carpaccio: You can very thinly slice or pound fish and lay it flat like a canvas. This provides an excellent vehicle to absorb sauces and dressings, while making for a great visual backdrop for various garnishes.

Tartare: Another option is to finely chop your fish, à la the ubiquitous tuna tartare, and toss it with your sauce and garnish for serving. If you go this route, you can just pile the tartare on your plate, in a bowl, or, if you're a true child of the 1990s, you can use a ramekin, cookie cutter, or ring mold to shape your tartare into a uniform cylinder.

Overall, remember the rule of thirds (high school art class, anyone?): if you were to overlay a large hashtag over your plating surface, the most compositionally interesting zones fall along the lines and at their intersections.

Some are inspired by the Japanese insistence on plating only odd numbers of ingredients (not a rule we always follow, however).

THE REAL KEY: FLAVORINGS

Shoot for complementarity as well as contrast. Savoriness is probably the most important factor when thinking about seasoning your crudos, because salt and its many delivery vehicles—like Tare (page 168), Maitake XO sauce (page 170), fish sauce, and miso—draw out the natural flavor of everything they touch. On top of that, acid is an important counterbalance, and it can be delivered with citrus, pickles, or flavored vinegars. Textural components that pop or crunch, like raw, pickled, or fermented vegetables, are excellent additions. So are Puffed Snacks (page 188) and fried grains like Puffed Sushi Rice (page 51), quinoa, and buckwheat. Finally, don't shy away from adding a little piquancy with hot sauce, slivers of hot pepper, or spice blends. Unfortunately, there's no ratios or shortcuts to balancing a crudo, but the point is to let the main ingredient shine. Use a light touch with sauces and garnishes to start.

PUTTING IT ALL TOGETHER

Don't just stir together your chosen garnishes and dump them on your fish, because you're not tossing a salad. It's worth layering the components one at a time, making sure not to drown the pieces of fish, so that the experience of eating the crudo is layered and nuanced. Crudos are a great way to kick off a meal, and we often serve them before heavier cooked food. They can be presented individually in a formal dinner setting or as larger presentations meant to serve a group. At the restaurant, we frequently use a large platter or wooden board for a six-person tuna crudo by simply scaling the portion sizes accordingly. As we noted before, making the dish as close as possible to the time you're serving it will keep the flavors from muddling and textures from softening. Tempering fish a little bit is a good thing. Letting it sit out for hours is not.

In the granddaddy of crudos at Eventide—the Tuna Crudo (page 77)—you can see how all the pieces fit together. The dish includes five tender, toothsome slices of ruby-red bluefin tuna tiled on a plate, then topped with bright and bracing aromatics: crunchy, peppery slices of radish and a salty-sweet tamari-based glaze. When you take a bite, the immediate impression is of the tuna's richness, followed by the salty pungency of the glaze, the bright punch of the ginger and scallion, and the crunch of the radish.

Our final piece of crudo advice: Don't be cowed. People love rules and laws and guidelines for achieving the "perfect" result, but try to avoid getting bogged down in such thinking. We know you've gotta run before you can fly, so don't worry too much.

LIGHTLY CURED CHAR

Bagel, Pickled Beet, Crème Fraîche

Every so often, I get it in my head that I'm going to make really great flatbread, but I've failed over and over again. During one such fit of inspiration and dejection, I tossed a scrap of flatbread dough into a nearby fryer. And, wouldn't you know it? That little throwaway scrap turned into a savory donut with a pleasant, alkaline flavor that was very bagel-like. I rolled another portion of the dough in some everything bagel spice and tried again. It worked like a charm and helped develop this dish—but I still can't make good flatbread. —*Mike*

To cure the char, lay out a large piece of plastic wrap and mix the sugar and salt in a bowl. Sprinkle one-third of the cure on the center of the plastic wrap. Place the char on top. Scatter the remainder of the cure atop the fillet and wrap tightly in the plastic wrap. Store in the refrigerator for 3 hours.

Rinse the fish thoroughly under cold water, pat dry, wrap in a clean paper towel, and store in a ziplock bag in the refrigerator.

To make the bagel, stir the water and yeast together in a large bowl an allow to bloom for 3 minutes. Add the flours and salt to the yeast and water mixture. Stir until just incorporated, cover the bowl with plastic wrap, and place in a warm spot. Allow the dough to rise until doubled in volume, about 2 hours, depending on temperature (the warmer the temperature, the less time needed to rise).

Portion the dough into three uniform balls and roll them into long snakes. Spread the seeds on a plate and roll the dough through the seeds. Cut the dough into 2-inch lengths.

Fill a large pot with 3 inches of canola oil and heat on high to 350°F (or bring a deep-fryer to 350°F). Line a plate with paper towels. Making sure not to overcrowd the pot, fry the dough pieces in batches until evenly browned, about 5 minutes. With a slotted spoon, transfer the pieces to the prepared plate. Once cooled, slice into bite-size pieces and set aside.

To assemble the dish, cut the lightly cured char against the grain into ¼- to ⅛-inch uniform slices. Swipe the crème fraîche artfully across a large platter or four plates. Place the pieces of char and bagels in a pleasing array over the crème fraîche, then spoon and scatter the pickles and sorrel evenly over the top. Serve within 30 minutes.

SERVES 4

½ cup kosher salt

½ cup sugar

10 ounces char fillet, skin and pinbones removed

BAGEL

1¼ cups warm water

2¼ teaspoons active dry yeast (1 packet or ¼ ounce)

2 cups all-purpose flour

1 cup rye flour

1 teaspoon kosher salt

¼ cup poppy seeds or white and black sesame seeds, for coating

Canola oil for frying

4 tablespoons crème fraîche

7 to 10 pieces Pickled Beets (page 193)

A couple of pinches Pickled Red Onion (page 192)

Micro sorrel (see Glossary) for garnish

LIGHTLY PICKLED MACKEREL

Caramelized Onion, Dashi, Puffed Sushi Rice, Nori

SERVES 4

MACKEREL

1-inch knob peeled ginger

1¼ cups water

⅓ cup rice wine vinegar

4 teaspoons mirin

4 teaspoons tamari

4 whole fresh mackerel
(about ½ pound each)
or 8 skin-on fillets
(2 ounces each)

½ cup Caramelized Onion
Puree (recipe follows)

½ cup Dashi Gelée
(recipe follows)

½ cup Puffed Sushi Rice
(recipe follows)

Thinly sliced scallion greens
for garnish

2 tablespoons Nori Vinaigrette
(page 199)

Finishing salt

Mackerel can be a tough sell in the States due to its reputation as a bait fish, but when it's fresh and handled well, it is delicious. If you're near a coast—any coast—some type of mackerel is probably local to you, and virtually all species of mackerel are affordable and rated as highly sustainable. It's also an easy and satisfying fish to butcher, making it particularly good for practicing your fish-cutting skills.

This dish actually predates Eventide. We concocted a version of it for the Hugo's menu after being inspired by tasting things like pickled *saba* (mackerel) and *kohada* (gizzard shad) on trips to Japanese restaurants. Mackerel is a full-flavored, full-bodied fish, and the light vinegar pickle really complements the assertive flavor of the fish. Additionally, mackerel have a tough, unappetizing membrane on the outside of their skin that looks like translucent wrapping, which has to go and, thankfully, pickling the fish makes removal possible. —*Andrew*

To make the mackerel pickling liquid, grate the ginger finely. In a nonreactive container with a lid, combine the ginger, water, vinegar, mirin, and tamari and stir thoroughly. Refrigerate the mixture for 1 to 2 hours, until thoroughly chilled.

Fillet the mackerel, if whole, and rinse the fillets with cold water. Using a sharp knife, trim the fillets to be uniform in size, but maintain the natural shape of the fillet. Don't remove the pinbones just yet—they'll be much easier to take out once the fish is pickled.

Place the fillets skin-side down in a nonreactive container. Pour the cold pickling liquid over the mackerel and drape plastic wrap over the surface of the brine to ensure that mackerel floating near the top are fully submerged. Refrigerate for 20 minutes.

Remove the mackerel from the brine. Use fish pliers or tweezers to carefully remove the pinbones, running your hand over the fish to make sure you've gotten them all. Do your best to avoid tearing the fish.

CONTINUED

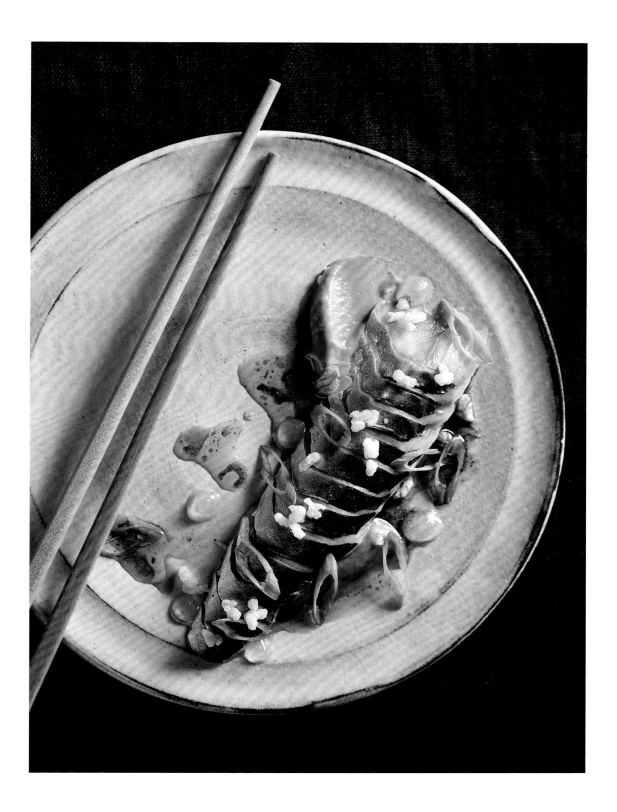

LIGHTLY PICKLED MACKEREL

CONTINUED

Now for some trickery. With either your fingers, the corners of your fish pliers, or even a paper towel, try to lift a corner of the membrane and peel it back from the skin, removing as much as you can. When pickled properly, the thin membrane should come off in one piece but leave behind the colorful markings of the fish skin. Pat the fish dry with paper towels and return to the refrigerator in an airtight container for up to 48 hours before serving.

To assemble the dish, swipe a few streaks of caramelized onion puree across a large platter or four plates. With a sharp knife, slice the mackerel on the diagonal into ½-inch pieces and arrange them on top of the onion puree. Season the fish with salt. Dip the tip of a clean spoon into the dashi gelée and drop pieces of it around the mackerel. Scatter some puffed rice over everything and finish with a shower of scallions and a liberal splash of the vinaigrette. Serve within 30 minutes.

CARAMELIZED ONION PUREE

MAKES ½ CUP

¼ cup canola oil

3 yellow onions, thinly sliced

Water (optional)

Pinch of kosher salt

Pinch of sugar

In a sauté pan, warm the oil over medium heat and add the onions. Cook slowly and methodically until the onions are deeply browned and soft, 30 to 60 minutes. Should the onions catch the bottom and start to brown too quickly, add a splash of water to deglaze and scrape the fond at the bottom of the pan. When the onions are fully browned, season with the salt and sugar. Transfer the caramelized onions to a blender. Starting on low speed and gradually cranking up the power, puree the onions, adding water in small increments to reach a smooth consistency. Strain the mixture through a fine-mesh strainer into an airtight container and chill. Any unused purée can be refrigerated for up to 3 days and used to add a sweet, umami-heightening, oniony essence to dressings, marinades, stews, and other dishes.

DASHI GELÉE

MAKES 2 CUPS

5 sheets gelatin

2 cups Dashi (page 177)

Kosher salt

In a small bowl, cover the gelatin sheets with ice water and soak for 5 minutes, until pliable (bloomed). Remove the gelatin sheets from the water and squeeze them lightly to remove excess water. In a small pot, combine the dashi and the bloomed gelatin and warm slowly over low heat until the gelatin melts completely. (The slower and lower you warm the mixture, the more holding power the gelatin will have.) Add salt to taste. Pour the mixture into a nonreactive container with a lid and cool to room temperature. Transfer to the refrigerator to set completely, at least 2 hours. It will be stiff enough to slice, like Jell-O. Extra dashi gelée will keep in the fridge for 1 week and can be added to soups, stews, and rice bowls for an extra umami kick.

PUFFED SUSHI RICE

MAKES 1 TO 2 CUPS

½ cup sushi rice

6 cups water

Kosher salt

Canola oil for frying

Rinse the sushi rice until the water that drains from it is clear.

In a saucepan, bring the water and a generous pinch of salt to a boil. Line a baking sheet with parchment paper and lightly grease the paper with canola oil.

Add the rice to the boiling water and cook like you would pasta, stirring frequently for approximately 15 minutes. Your goal is to overcook the rice, with each grain ending up a little soft and well past al dente. Drain the rice in a colander. Scatter the cooked rice grains on the prepared baking sheet, taking care to avoid clumping (clumps can result in uneven drying and worse, spoilage). Allow to dry overnight at room temperature or in the refrigerator, uncovered, until each grain is almost completely dry.

Fill a large pot with 3 inches of canola oil and heat on high to 400°F or bring a deep-fryer to 400°F. Line a plate with paper towels.

Test a few grains of rice at a time by dropping them in the oil. If they float to the surface and puff up, you're good, and you can fry the whole batch, transferring the puffed grains to the paper towel–lined plate and seasoning with salt. If the test rice isn't puffing, it may be too dry. In the event it won't puff, mist the dried-out rice with water from a spray bottle and transfer it to a container with a lid. Allow a couple of hours for the rice to absorb the water, then try frying again.

Let the puffed rice cool and store in an airtight container until you are ready to serve. The puffed rice will keep for up to a month if stored in an airtight container at room temperature. Extra puffed rice can be used as garnish for other crudos or added to salads to give a bit of extra crunch.

AMERICAN UNAGI

Kabayaki, Celeriac, Bok Choy, Candied Sesame, Garlic Chive

The eels we use at the restaurant are a really special product. Sara Rademaker raises them to full size at her American Unagi aquaculture facility in Thomaston, Maine. We know that may not sound revolutionary, unless you consider that nearly every other eel landed in Maine is shipped to Asia, raised to harvest weight, cooked, Cryovaced, and shipped frozen back to the United States. It goes almost without saying, but eel is more delicious when it hasn't made a couple of intercontinental flights. Sara's eels always arrive alive and kicking, and we're thrilled to have access to such a wonderful Maine-made product to present to our guests. Good fishmongers will have eel in stock from time to time, or you can ask them to help you source them. Alternatively, you can do what most sushi joints do and simply purchase cooked and vacuum-sealed barbecued eel. If you're using store-bought eel, you can skip all cooking steps apart from the final broiling step. —*Mike*

In a large nonreactive container with a lid, stir together the water and salt. Place the fillets in the container, cover it, and put it in the refrigerator for 4 hours, or overnight.

Remove the fillets from the brine and blot dry with paper towels. Place a wire rack inside a baking sheet, and place the eel fillets on the rack, skin-side up. Preheat the broiler to high with an oven rack in the uppermost position. Broil the eel until the skin is completely dried and lightly browned, 2 to 3 minutes. This step helps to remove some of the sliminess that is inherent in eel skin.

Preheat the oven to 250°F.

Place the eel fillets in a Dutch oven or braising pan with a lid on the stove and pour the dashi over them. Bring the mixture to a simmer over medium heat, then cover the pan, and move it to the oven for 1 hour. Check the eel fillets for doneness by piercing one with a cake tester or skewer, which should pierce the eel with no resistance. If it's not done, return the eels to the oven, checking in 15-minute intervals, until the eel is fully cooked.

CONTINUED

SERVES 4

EEL

4 cups water

3 ½ teaspoons kosher salt

4 cleaned, skin-on eel fillets

2 quarts Dashi (page 177)

1 cup Kabayaki Sauce (page 167)

1 small head baby bok choy

1 cup Celeriac Puree (recipe follows)

¼ cup Candied Sesame (recipe follows)

Finely chopped garlic chives or regular chives for garnish

Finishing salt

AMERICAN UNAGI

CONTINUED

Remove the pan from the oven and allow to cool to room temperature. Carefully transfer the eel fillets to a container with a lid.

In a pot with a steamer insert or a bamboo steamer set over a wok, steam the bok choy for 5 minutes, or until tender. Transfer it to a bowl and season with kosher salt.

Put the eel fillets skin-side up on a lightly greased sheet pan. Preheat the broiler to high with an oven rack in the uppermost position, then broil the eel until it is caramelized, 1 to 2 minutes. Brush it with the kabayaki sauce and broil again until glazed, 1 to 2 minutes.

To assemble the dish, drop a large dollop of the celeriac puree onto a large platter or four plates and use the back of a spoon to streak it across the plates in a thin layer. Place one eel fillet on top of the puree and season with finishing salt. Arrange the baby bok choy or cut pieces around the eel, and sprinkle the candied sesame and garlic chives over the plates. Serve within 30 minutes.

CELERIAC PUREE

MAKES 4 CUPS

1 celeriac (celery root), peeled and cut into 1-inch cubes

3 cups whole milk

¼ cup (½ stick) unsalted butter, cubed

Kosher salt

Combine the celeriac and milk in a small pan. Bring to a simmer over medium heat and cook until the celeriac is fork-tender, about 35 minutes.

Use a slotted spoon to transfer the celeriac to a blender. Start the blender and slowly increase the speed, adding enough milk from the pan to get the mixture to catch the blade and create a vortex (it will take a decent amount of milk). Process the celeriac and milk on high until it is completely smooth, then add the butter and process again until smooth. Season with salt to taste.

Strain the puree through a fine-mesh strainer into a bowl. Store any extra in an airtight container in the fridge for up to 1 week. It can be used as a side dish (replacing mashed potatoes, for example) or as a flavor bed on which cooked protein can recline.

CANDIED SESAME

MAKES 2 CUPS

½ cup sugar

¼ cup water

1¼ cups white sesame seeds

In a stainless steel, small saucepan with a flat bottom, mix the sugar and water to achieve the consistency of wet sand. Over medium heat, bring the sugar and water to 270°F, stirring often.

While you're cooking the sugar, toast the sesame seeds in a separate, small, dry pan over medium heat until they are fragrant and darkened, 30 to 60 seconds, then remove them from the pan.

Once the water and sugar reach 270°F, remove the pan from the heat and carefully add the toasted seeds. Stir with a rubber spatula, breaking up any clumps that may form. Pour the contents into a heatproof bowl and cool.

Any extra mixture can be stored in a covered jar in the fridge for a week, or frozen in a covered container for up to a month. It can be used to garnish noodle or rice dishes or grilled fish, chicken, or beef.

CHAWANMUSHI

Black Trumpets, Grilled Scallion, Uni

I used to eat at this little hole-in-the-wall Japanese spot in Seattle called Shiki, where the owner, a portly Japanese man usually sporting a Harley-Davidson T-shirt and leather chaps, also happened to be an incredible cook of lesser-known Japanese regional comfort food. In addition, he was one of the only chefs in Seattle who was licensed to serve blowfish. Shiki was my introduction to a wide variety of strange and delicious foods like poached cod milt (look it up), fried river crabs, vegetable and loach pancakes, raw blowfish and, of course, a version of the sublime dish you see here.

Chawanmushi is a dashi-based Japanese custard that is so delicate and velvety that it barely holds together. It is served as simple home or peasant food in Japan, especially on the north island of Hokkaido, which is a shellfish-rich, ski-crazy winter paradise that can get as much as five hundred inches of snow in a season. At Shiki, the chawanmushi was served hot with udon noodles, seafood, and a gingko nut set inside the custard. Since it's pretty hard to regulate the cooking of the seafood inside the custard, we like to cook the custard first and then garnish it extravagantly. —*Andrew*

To clean the sea urchins, with one hand in a work glove or in a thick kitchen towel and working over a small baking sheet, hold the sea urchin with its circular mouth (known as Aristotle's lantern) facing up. In your other hand, use a pair of kitchen scissors (preferably Joyce Chen's) to make a cut from the urchin's mouth toward the widest part of the urchin, then cut around the perimeter of the shell, as though you were removing the top of a pumpkin to make a jack-o'-lantern. Cut open all of your sea urchins this way and line them up on the baking sheet before you remove the tongues.

Gently free each urchin tongue—the five vibrant orange parts affixed to the outer shell—from the shell by slowly working the tip of a very small spoon between the shell and tongue. Place each tongue on a plate or board. Once all five tongues are free from the first shell, flip the urchin over a bowl to let all the water and other bits drain into it. Repeat the process with the remaining urchins.

CONTINUED

SERVES 4

4 large sea urchins

1 large egg

1¾ cups plus 2 tablespoons Dashi (page 177)

Kosher salt

4 scallions, trimmed, white and light green parts only

1 cup Confit Mushrooms made with black trumpet mushrooms, plus a little Confit Mushroom Oil (page 186)

CHAWANMUSHI

CONTINUED

Fill three shallow containers with ice water. Place the urchin tongues into one container of ice water and jostle briefly to release grit and impurities. Very gently transfer the tongues from that ice bath to a second ice bath, doing your best to allow anything that isn't a tongue to fall away between your fingertips. Then transfer again to the third bath, at which point the urchin tongues should be clean and free of impurities.

Arrange the tongues on a dry towel. Some tongues will be plump, orange, and gorgeous. Others will be less so. Reserve the ten or so most beautiful tongues for garnish on ice in a small plastic container, and set the others aside in a bowl for making the custard.

To make the custard, set up a pot with a steamer insert or a bamboo steamer large enough to hold four small bowls or ramekins over a wok. In a blender, puree the egg and the ugly urchin tongues until smooth. Add the dashi and continue to blend until perfectly smooth. Pass the mixture through a fine-mesh strainer into a bowl and season with salt to taste. Divide the custard base among four small bowls or ramekins. Wrap the bowls or ramekins tightly in plastic wrap, and steam them for 10 minutes, after which the custard should be fully set, but plenty jiggly.

To cook the scallions, toss the scallions in a little mushroom oil and grill (or broil) on one side for 1 to 2 minutes, until they are lightly charred. Allow to cool and thinly slice on the bias.

To assemble the dish, arrange the mushrooms, urchin tongues, and scallions evenly across the surface of the four small bowls or ramekins of warm chawanmushi (feel free to reheat the custards by steaming again before serving), then spoon a little of the black trumpet oil over the top. Serve within 30 minutes.

RAZOR CLAM

Parsley, Lardo, Grilled Bread Crumbs

Pork and clams are a favorite of mine, and I come back to the pairing so often that our cooks make fun of me for it. It may be a cliché, but that doesn't make it un-delicious. To defy the expectation a bit, we use lardo as the pork element in this dish, which adds nice, subtle richness without weighing things down or taking away from the flavor of the razor clams. Some people find them too full-flavored, in the clammy sense, but the bracing greenness of the parsley and the richness of the lardo provide balance in this preparation. Razor clams can often be found fresh at a good fish counter (or you can ask your fishmonger whether they can be special ordered), and many people make a hobby of digging them like regular clams. Preparing them is a fickle task. If you cook them for much more than a minute by any means, they can become tough, so serving them raw, with balancing accompaniments, is a good play. A note on the parsley purée: If your quantity of blanching water is insufficient in volume or temperature, the pot will lose the boil upon adding the parsley. Not only do you tempt the technical wrath of chef Thomas Keller in so doing, but you also risk a parsley sauce that is not vibrant green in color, which will be unacceptable. —*Mike*

Submerge the clams in clean, cold salted water for 30 minutes to encourage them to release their grit. Slip a sharp knife between the razor clam shell and its meat, following the shells all the way around to release the meat. For this recipe, you're looking to use just the foot, which looks like a little piece of white asparagus, and can be separated from the clam belly and strips with a flick of the knife. Place the feet on ice and discard the rest of the clam, which can be very sandy, or reserve for drying or making stock. Thoroughly wash four of the half shells for serving.

Set out the clam shells on a plate covered with a layer of crushed ice. With a sharp knife, slice the clam meat into small rings and season with salt. With a small spoon, drizzle a tablespoon of the parsley purée into each shell and scatter the clam slices over the purée. Sprinkle a light layer of the lardo and bread crumbs evenly over all the shells (it shouldn't be blanketed, just lightly covered). Serve immediately.

CONTINUED

SERVES 4

12 razor clams

Crushed ice for garnish

3 tablespoons finely diced Lardo (page 203)

½ cup Parsley Puree (recipe follows)

½ cup Grilled Bread Crumbs (recipe follows)

Finishing salt

RAZOR CLAM

CONTINUED

PARSLEY PUREE

MAKES 1 TO 2 CUPS

2 bunches flat-leaf parsley, plus more for garnish

Canola oil

Kosher salt

Prepare a large bowl of ice water. Bring a large pot of heavily salted water to a rolling boil. Pick the leaves from the parsley bunches, discarding the larger stems, and add to the boiling water. After 10 seconds in the boiling water, use a spider or fine-mesh strainer to lift the parsley up from the boiling water and plunge into the ice water. Wring the blanched parsley dry and coarsely chop it.

In a blender, combine the chopped parsley with an ice cube and 2 tablespoons of canola oil and process into a smooth puree, starting at low speed and turning up to high as the parsley is incorporated. This will require a little finesse and practice. Ensure that you have enough ice and oil that the parsley will catch the blade as you turn it up slowly from low to high speed. Otherwise, your blade will just spin and things won't come together. The resulting puree should be thick like paint. Season with salt to taste, and strain the puree through a fine-mesh strainer into a bowl.

The leftover puree can be stored, covered, in the freezer for a month and/or used to garnish other dishes like grilled fish, raw shellfish, or soup.

GRILLED BREAD CRUMBS

MAKES 1 TO 2 CUPS

6 slices high-quality sourdough bread

Extra-virgin olive oil

Kosher salt

Preheat the oven to 350°F. Brush the slices of bread with olive oil and grill or broil them until they take on a bit of char. Transfer the bread to a sheet pan and place in the oven, baking until the slices are completely dried out and no longer pliable, about 15 minutes.

Line a baking sheet with paper towels. In a food processor, pulse the grilled bread to achieve a very fine crumb and season with salt. Spread the crumbs out on the paper towel–lined baking sheet and bake for a few minutes to draw the excess oil from the crumbs.

Use immediately or store in an airtight container for up to 3 days at room temperature or in the freezer for 2 months and use for coating ingredients to be fried, adding body to meatloaf, or adding crunchiness to salads and other vegetable dishes.

GRILLED SQUID SALAD

Citrus, Castelvetrano Olive, Kalamata Olive, Confit Potato

SERVES 4

2 pounds squid, cleaned, with about 6 bodies and 6 tentacle bunches

Canola oil

Finishing salt

8 Confit Potato cylinders (page 185) made from russet potatoes, cut in half on the diagonal, at room temperature

½ cup Citrus Vinaigrette (recipe follows)

12 Castelvetrano olives, pitted and sliced

Kalamata Olive Crumb (recipe follows)

Flat-leaf parsley leaves for garnish

There've been many versions of this Spanish-inflected squid dish on our menu over the years, but they always include confit potato, olive crumb, and citrus. We just really love the texture of a perfectly cooked confit potato (it should be fudgy) alongside barely cooked, still-snappy squid, Your local fishmonger will be able to set you up with freshly caught, cleaned squid—especially in the summertime. If you must, you can use flash-frozen squid for this recipe; both squid and octopus suffer far less from freezing than fin fish do. —*Mike*

Butterfly the squid tubes by cutting from top to bottom on one side. With the pieces now lying flat, score each lightly in a crosshatch pattern. Toss the tubes and tentacles in canola oil to lightly coat. Separate the tentacles into clusters of three or four each, and leave the squid body whole.

Light a hot charcoal fire or get your gas grill ripping hot and give the squid tentacles a hard sear on each side for 2 to 3 minutes until they are browned. Grill the butterflied and scored squid bodies for 2 to 3 minutes until they've taken on some color and curled up nicely. Cut the bodies into bite-size pieces. Season everything lightly with salt.

To assemble the dish, lay three to five of the potato pieces on each of four plates. In a bowl, toss the grilled squid pieces in the vinaigrette and distribute them evenly across the four plates. Garnish with a few spoonfuls of the sliced olives, the olive crumb, and parsley leaves. Serve immediately.

KALAMATA OLIVE CRUMB

MAKES 1 CUP

4 cups Kalamata olives, pitted and drained

In a food dehydrator or a 350°F oven that has just been turned off, dry the pitted Kalamata olives overnight or until they are completely brittle. Chop the dried olives with a sharp knife until you've achieved a fine crumb.

Store the leftovers in a jar with a lid at room temperature for 1 week and use as a garnish for salads, bagels and cream cheese, or other crudos.

CITRUS VINAIGRETTE

MAKES 1⅓ CUPS

¾ cup extra-virgin olive oil

3 tablespoons fresh lemon juice

2 tablespoons fresh orange juice

¼ cup sherry vinegar

Kosher salt

Thoroughly whisk together the olive oil, citrus juices, and vinegar in a bowl to combine. Add salt to taste. Use immediately and store extra in a tightly sealed jar in the refrigerator for up to a month. This vinaigrette can be used as a dressing for salads or other vegetable dishes.

CURED SALMON

Scallion Tofu, Furikake, Yuzu Kosho

SERVES 4

SALMON CURE

2 ½ cups kosher salt, plus more for seasoning

1 cup sugar

Juice and finely grated zest of 2 lemons

Finely grated zest of 2 limes

Finely grated zest of 1 grapefruit

1 large piece kombu (see Glossary)

10-ounce salmon fillet, skin removed

Finishing salt

Green yuzu kosho (see Glossary) for garnish

½ cup Scallion Tofu Puree (recipe follows) for garnish

½ cup Furikake (recipe follows) for garnish

Micro mustard greens (see Glossary) for garnish

Finely grated zest of 1 lemon for garnish

This dish combines a traditional Japanese method with a decidedly Western approach to quick-curing fish. Curing fish with kombu helps to impart a savoriness that plays especially well with fully flavored fish, like salmon. You won't need much yuzu kosho—a spicy Japanese condiment of fresh chiles, salt, and yuzu zest—to garnish this dish, but you won't regret buying it. It is one of the greatest condiments on earth. We use both red and green yuzu kosho; the green is grassier and the red has more of a chile-forward flavor, but both are delicious. —*Mike*

To make the salmon cure, in a large bowl, combine the kosher salt, sugar, and citrus zests and massage aggressively with your fingers for several minutes in order to release the essential oils of the citrus.

Rinse the piece of kombu and lay it on a sheet pan. Place the salmon fillet on top of the kombu and cover it with a thick layer of the cure, patting the cure down a little bit to make sure it encases the fillet. Let cure for 15 minutes at room temperature. Dig the fillet out of the cure and rinse it under cold water, then pat it dry. Slice the fish crosswise into ¼-inch pieces and season with a sprinkle of lemon juice (you will not need it all) and finishing salt.

Load the yuzu kosho in a piping bag, squeeze bottle, or large ziplock plastic bag with a corner cut off. Lay the seasoned fish attractively on a large platter or four plates, then dot all over the plate and the fish with the Scallion Tofu Puree and the yuzu kosho. Finish with sprinkles of Furikake, micro mustard greens, and lemon zest. Serve within 30 minutes.

SCALLION TOFU PUREE

MAKES 3 TO 4 CUPS

2 tablespoons canola oil

4 bunches scallions, trimmed, white parts separated from green parts

1 large shallot, thinly sliced

2 cloves garlic, chopped

1 small waxy white potato, peeled and diced

⅔ block (9 ounces) firm tofu, diced

Kosher salt

In a large sauté pan over medium heat, heat the oil and add the scallion whites, shallot, garlic, and potato. Cook for 20 minutes, stirring often, until the vegetables have all but turned to mush.

Set up a bowl of ice water. Bring a small pot of salted water to a boil, add the scallion greens, and blanch for 10 to 15 seconds, until they have just started to go limp but retain their bright green color. Transfer them to the bowl of ice water. Squeeze them dry and set aside.

In a blender, puree the sauteed vegetables until smooth. Add the tofu and puree again until smooth. With the motor running, add the scallion greens (the puree should turn bright green) and salt to taste. Drain the puree through a fine-mesh strainer into a bowl, cover, and move it to the refrigerator to cool down a bit and maintain its vibrant color.

Once it has cooled, adjust the seasoning with more salt, if needed. To use, load the puree in a piping bag, squeeze bottle, or large ziplock plastic bag with a cor-ner cut off. Store any extra in an airtight container in the refrigerator for up to 1 week, using it as a dip or dressing for vegetables or drizzling on rice or noodle dishes.

FURIKAKE

MAKES ABOUT 1 CUP

10 sheets nori

¼ cup Fried Aromatics (page 184) made with shallots

2 tablespoons Fried Aromatics (page 184) made with garlic

2 tablespoon mixed black and white sesame seeds

Finishing salt

Holding a sheet of nori with tongs, wave it over a gas burner flame a few times until it becomes lighter green and fragrant, about 1 minute. (Or heat a large skillet on high heat and toast the nori on both sides for 30 sec-onds.) Repeat with the remaining sheets.

Cut the nori sheets into small pieces and process in a food processor until reduced to consistent, small flakes.

In a small mixing bowl, combine the nori flakes with the fried shallots, fried garlic, and sesame seeds. Work the mixture with your fingertips for a minute or two to break down the shallots and garlic and bring the furikake together. Season with salt to taste. Store in an airtight container at room temperature for 1 week. The extra is great for sprinkling on rice or noodle dishes.

BLACK BASS CEVICHE

Pique de Piña, Cilantro, Lime, Masa

SERVES 4

10 ounces black bass fillets, skin removed

¼ cup Pique de piña (recipe follows)

Fat pinch of kosher salt

Juice of 1 lime

1 cup finely chopped fresh cilantro

½ cup Pickled Red Onion (page 192)

1 jalapeño, seeded and finely minced

Masa Crisps (recipe follows)

This dish was created by one of our old chefs, and it has been on the menu for years, which is quite an achievement for a restaurant where the crudo menu changes constantly. The pique de piña, which is a spicy, pineapple-flavored vinegar popular in Puerto Rico, is a really cool move that we encourage you to try out. It's best used like a hot sauce, but it's also a fun addition to dressings or marinades. —*Mike*

Dice the black bass fillets into ¼-inch pieces and transfer to a stainless steel work bowl. Dress the bass with the pique de piña and salt. Toss the fish and allow to cure for a minute before transferring equal amounts to four bowls. Drizzle lime juice over the fish and scatter the chopped cilantro, pickled red onion, minced jalapeño, and masa crisps over the top. Serve within 30 minutes.

PIQUE DE PIÑA

MAKES 4 TO 5 CUPS

1 ripe pineapple, peeled, cored, and chopped

4 garlic cloves, crushed

1 jalapeño, quartered

3 to 4 teaspoons sugar

2 cups pineapple juice

2 cups water

Mix the pineapple with the garlic, jalapeño, sugar, pineapple juice, and water in a large jar or nonreactive bowl. Cover with a cheesecloth or towel and allow to ferment at room temperature until nearly fizzy and well soured, usually about 5 days (if it's warmer, perhaps less; colder, perhaps more).

In a blender, puree the mixture, then strain it through a fine-mesh strainer into a pot. Bring the mixture up to 160°F and hold it there for 10 minutes to pasteurize.

Chill thoroughly and use or store in an airtight container in the refrigerator for up to 1 month. The extra can be used in splashes to add sweet and sour spiciness to almost anything under the sun.

MASA CRISPS

MAKES 2 TO 3 CUPS

Canola oil for frying

1 cup masa harina (see Glossary)

½ cup water, or more as needed

Kosher salt

Fill a large pot with 3 inches of the canola oil and heat on high to 350°F (or bring a deep-fryer to 350°F). Line a plate with paper towels.

In a bowl, stir together the masa harina and water to achieve a wet, shaggy dough (masa absorbs water eagerly, so you may need to add more water). Slowly and carefully press the masa harina dough through a ricer or mesh strainer onto a plate or into a bowl, then carefully pour the masa bits into the oil. Fry the masa crisps until golden brown, 2 to 3 minutes, and then use a heatproof slotted spoon or mesh strainer to transfer them to the paper towel–lined plate. Season with salt to taste. Use immediately.

Leftovers can be stored in an airtight container at room temperature for 1 week and used to add a crunchy component to salads or vegetable dishes.

MUSSELS EN ESCABECHE

Grilled Bread, Chorizo, Chive

As much as we love a good bowl of steamed mussels, we just never saw the classic white-wine-and-garlic preparation being a part of our menu. However, there is a fantastic mussel farm, Bangs Island Mussels, a couple of miles from our restaurant, so we almost always have a unique preparation of them on the menu. This one, which is inspired by the incredible tinned mussels I tried on a trip to Barcelona, was on our opening menu at Eventide and remains a favorite. *En escabeche* refers to the Mediterranean and Latin American tradition of cooking fish or meat and then placing it in an acidic mixture, sometimes flavored with smoked paprika or another piquant spice. *—Andrew*

Place a large, heavy pot over high heat. When it is very hot, carefully add the mussels, onion, fennel, garlic, orange zest, chorizo scraps, and sherry. Cover the pot and give it a shake. After 5 minutes, uncover the pot and remove any mussels that have opened, placing them in a large bowl. Continue to cook the mussels until all have opened (any mussels that remain closed after 10 minutes should be discarded).

Strain the cooking liquid through a fine-mesh strainer into a smaller pot and bring to a simmer, stirring occasionally over medium-high heat for 3 to 5 minutes, until the liquid reduces to about ¾ cup. While the cooking liquid is reducing, pick all the mussels from their shells and remove their little wispy beards, if necessary. Place the mussels in a heatproof bowl.

In a blender, combine the mussel reduction with the xanthan gum and ¼ cup sherry vinegar. Turn on the machine to puree, then slowly stream in the paprika oil until you have a loose, saucy consistency (it will tighten up as it cools). Season to taste with additional sherry vinegar and salt. Pour the liquid over the mussels and let cool to room temperature.

To assemble the dish, grill or toast the crusty bread. Put the mussels in a large serving bowl or four separate bowls, spooning extra sauce over the top, then garnish with the chorizo scraps, chopped olives, and minced chives. Serve within 30 minutes, with the bread alongside to sop up the escabeche liquid.

SERVES 4

3 pounds mussels in shells

½ yellow onion, peeled, charred under a broiler, and coarsely chopped

½ bulb fennel with stalk, core removed and coarsely chopped

3 garlic cloves, crushed

Zest of 1 orange

4 ounces dry-cured Spanish chorizo, peeled and diced in ¼-inch pieces (scraps reserved)

1 cup dry sherry

Pinch of xanthan gum (see Glossary)

¼ cup sherry vinegar, plus more as needed

1 cup Paprika Oil (page 183)

Kosher salt

Good crusty bread for serving

Pitted and chopped Castelvetrano olives for garnish

Minced fresh chives for garnish

BONITO TATAKI

Chicharrones, Chile, Tomatillos

Bonito is a fickle little fish that rarely makes an appearance up here in New England. But when it does, usually in the fall, and you can get it really fresh, it is an absolute treat. Since it is a rich and oily fish, we love the tataki preparation, which is about cooking aggressively and quickly on one side to deepen the flavor, but leaving the majority of the fish raw. We then pair the bonito with assertive flavors like peppers or other nightshades that are around in the fall. —*Andrew*

Prepare a bowl of ice water large enough to hold the bonito. Preheat a charcoal grill or set a gas grill or grill pan or broiler to high heat.

Brush oil over the more darkly colored bloodline side of the bonito. Sear the bloodline side of the fish until it is deeply brown, 1 to 2 minutes. Remove it from the heat and carefully dip it in the ice bath to arrest the cooking. Place on a cutting board and pat dry. Chill completely.

Make a couple of artful streaks of chile puree across the center of a serving plate. Cut the bonito against the grain into ¼- to ⅓-inch slices with the grilled side resting on the cutting board. Make your knife strokes smooth and confident as you cut through the cooked fish; any hesitancy will result in raggedy cuts. Arrange the slices along the length of a plate, grilled-side up. Season the bonito with a squeeze of lime juice and salt. With a spoon, drop a few teaspoons of tomatillo jam around the fish. Garnish with pork rinds and cilantro leaves and serve within 30 minutes.

CONTINUED

SERVES 4

Canola oil

10 ounces bonito fillets

Chile Puree (recipe follows) for serving

Fresh lime juice

Finishing salt

Tomatillo Jam (recipe follows) for serving

7 ounces Puffed Pork Skin (page 190) or store-bought pork rinds (chicharrones)

3 sprigs cilantro, leaves picked

BONITO TATAKI

CONTINUED

CHILE PUREE

MAKES ABOUT 1 CUP

10 dried ancho chiles	Sugar
Water	Apple cider vinegar
Kosher salt	

With gloved hands, remove the stems, seeds, and ribs from the chiles. In a dry, hot pan, toast the chiles for 1 minute until they darken in color and become fragrant. Transfer the roasted chiles to a heatproof container and pour boiling water over them just to cover. Cover the container and let it sit for 30 minutes. Drain the chiles, reserving the soaking water. Put the chiles in a blender with a splash of the soaking water. Turn the blender on and drizzle in more soaking liquid, until the puree catches the blade and the mixture achieves a vortex. Blend on high for several minutes. Strain the mixture through a fine-mesh strainer into a bowl. Season with salt, sugar, and apple cider vinegar to taste. The excess can be stored in a sealed container in the refrigerator for 1 week or freezer for 3 months.

TOMATILLO JAM

MAKES 2¼ CUPS

5 tomatillos	2 tablespoons glucose (optional; see Glossary)
2 cups pickling brine (see Pickles, page 192)	Pinch of sugar
	Pinch of kosher salt

Remove the papery husk from the tomatillos. With a sharp knife, slice the rounded sides off of each tomatillo, leaving a cube to be finely diced into small, uniform squares. Save the scraps and place them in a small pot and add the pickling liquid just to cover. Simmer until the tomatillo scraps are completely broken down and tender, about 5 minutes. Transfer to a blender and puree until smooth. Add the glucose and blend again on high speed for a minute or two. The glucose helps bind the sauce and give it a sheen. Season to taste with a pinch of sugar and salt.

Fill a bowl with ice water. Bring a small pot of water to a boil and drop in the diced tomatillos, blanching them for 1 minute, until they just start to soften. They will turn to mush pretty quickly if you cook them too long, so be careful. Remove the tomatillos from the pot and dunk them in the ice water. Pat dry and fold the diced tomatillo into the tomatillo puree. Use immediately or store in a sealed container in the refrigerator for 1 month or the freezer for 3 months.

FLUKE CRUDO

Caramelized Crab, Sea Beans, Chile, Pickled Kombu

Fluke is a fixture on Eventide's menu. It is abundant, locally available, and makes delightful crudos and tartares. Be sure to slice the fish very thinly, because it can be a little too toothsome if left in large slices. To the extent that you can, avoid serving fluke sliced from the tail end of the fillet as crudo; there's a lot of connective tissue near the tail—it's great for cooking though! Buy sea beans at specialty stores (or find them on Maine's rocky coast). Be aware that sea beans can be woody and very bitter. If you can't find them at their height of freshness—crisp and salty—then it's better to leave them off of the dish. —*Mike*

Pull apart the sea beans into small, tender, bite-size pieces (they will come apart easily).

With a spoon, distribute the chile crisp and the caramelized crab across a large platter or four plates. Very thinly slice the fluke fillet and arrange in one layer over the chile crisp and crab. Season the fluke with a squeeze of lemon, a scattering of puffed sushi rice, and a sprinkling of salt. Scatter the pickled kombu and the sea beans over the fish for a briny, crunchy garnish. Serve immediately.

CONTINUED

SERVES 4

¼ pound sea beans

3 to 4 tablespoons Chile Crisp
(recipe follows)

1 cup Caramelized Crab
(page 185)

10 ounces fluke fillet

Fresh lemon juice for garnish

Puffed Sushi Rice (page 51)
for garnish

Finishing salt

Pickled Kombu (page 193)
for garnish

FLUKE CRUDO

CONTINUED

CHILE CRISP

MAKES 3 CUPS

10 to 15 dried chiles de árbol

10 to 15 dried Chinese red chiles

1 teaspoon freshly ground black pepper

1 tablespoon ground cumin

¼ cup ground Szechuan pepper

1 tablespoon dried mushroom powder

3 tablespoons ground Aleppo pepper

7 teaspoons Korean chile powder (gochujaru)

5¼ teaspoons kosher salt

1½ tablespoons sugar

2 black cardamom pods, split

3 star anise pods

3- to 4-inch piece of fresh ginger, peeled and thinly sliced

2⅓ cups Confit Mushroom Oil (page 186) made with maitakes

10 to 12 large shallots, peeled and thinly sliced (about 2 cups)

20 garlic cloves, thinly sliced

With gloved hands, tear open the dried chiles and remove the stems and seeds. In a large dry skillet over medium heat, toast the chile pieces for 1 minute until they are fragrant. Transfer them to a bowl to cool. Grind them to a coarse powder in a spice grinder, then transfer them to a large heatproof bowl.

Wipe out the pan and, again over medium heat, toast the black pepper, cumin, and Szechuan pepper for 1 minute, until they are fragrant, and put them in a separate small bowl to cool.

Grind the toasted spices and the mushroom powder in a spice grinder and add them to the bowl with the ground chiles. Add the Aleppo pepper, Korean chile powder, salt, sugar, cardamom, star anise, and ginger and mix well.

Set up a fine-mesh strainer over a heatproof container. Line a baking sheet with paper towels. In a large heavy pot over medium heat, warm the maitake oil. Add the shallots and garlic and cook, stirring frequently to make sure that what is closer to the walls of the pot doesn't cook faster than what's in the middle. Let it cook for 3 to 5 minutes, until the shallots and garlic begin to turn golden (don't let them get all the way to brown), then quickly and carefully pour the contents of the pot through the fine-mesh strainer, reserving the oil. Immediately shake the alliums in the strainer onto the paper towel-lined baking sheet in an even layer. Once cool, taste some. If they're too dark, they will likely be too bitter and you'll have to discard them, but if they are perfectly golden they'll be delicious. Well done! The crunchy shallots and garlic can be used immediately in the recipe or stored in an airtight container with a piece of paper towel folded in the bottom at room temperature for 3 days.

Pour the reserved maitake oil back into the pot and bring it to 375°F, then add it to the bowl with the dried spices and chiles, stirring to distribute everything. Allow to cool completely.

Discard the cardamom and star anise pods. Crush the shallots and garlic into small pieces (don't pulverize) with gloved hands, then add them to the cooled, spiced oil. Put the chile crisp in a large jar or bowl and cover for 24 hours before using it. This concoction, a loose mixture of crispy solids and oil, will keep indefinitely in the refrigerator. It is good on virtually anything you want to add depth and spice to.

THE GREAT WESTERN NORTH ATLANTIC BLUEFIN TUNA

If the thick-shelled, briny oysters and the glorious North American lobster represent Maine's two greatest gifts to us as oyster bar proprietors, then the bluefin tuna is a close third. From July to October, the western North Atlantic bluefin tuna's northern migration lands it in the Gulf of Maine, sometimes within a mile of Portland. It is only during this time, and from this fishery in the Gulf of Maine, that we take advantage of this beautiful resource.

Bluefin tuna is, as it should be, a controversial product. Overwhelming demand skyrocketed in the 1980s and 1990s and pushed all stocks of bluefin tuna—including the western Atlantic stock—to the brink of endangerment. In the early 2000s, conservation groups led the effort to heavily restrict the bluefin catch and attempt to rebuild the fishery. While efforts to conserve the Pacific, eastern Atlantic, and Southern stocks have been challenging and are only just recently showing signs of rebuilding, the locations of the breeding grounds and limited migratory pattern of the western Atlantic stock have allowed a smaller international group of fisheries to coordinate a successful rebuilding of the biomass. As a result, catch limits have actually increased and minimum size requirements have shrunk in the past five years. We have worked with the Gulf of Maine Research Institute (GMRI) as Sustainable Seafood Culinary Partners to support their important role in the overall conservation effort.

Every bit of the effort is worth it for these spectacular animals, whose culinary gifts are abundant and diverse. Because bluefin season coincides with the busy season at all four of our restaurants, we can take a whole, 200- to 450-pound beauty and work through it in under seven days. Receiving whole fish allows us to control quality from the dock to the plate, as well as utilize the breadth of products like loin, chu-toro, toro, collars, tails, ribs, scrapings, spinal jelly, and bloodline. We like to think that a local bluefin tuna will be more fully utilized by us than just about anybody in the world.

The dishes in the following pages showcase some of that variety. The chu-toro and toro dishes require bluefin tuna specifically, and since we insist that you use only bluefin from the western North Atlantic, this might be challenging if you are not on the East Coast. However, the tuna crudo, tuna tartare, and broiled collar can be made with yellowfin, big-eye, or albacore tuna, all of which are rated as sustainable in most parts of the world.

Tuna Loin Breakdown

1 Set up your work area with a long, thin slicing knife.

2 If your loin of tuna has the skin intact, remove it by resting the loin skin-side down and running your knife between the fillet and the skin.

3 Ease the skin away from the tuna loin and discard.

4 Cut straight down the loin at 1-inch intervals to create several large rectangles.

5 Laying the large rectangles flat on your cutting board, cut in uniform ¾-inch intervals.

6 You will have created what we call "blocks" at the restaurant.

7 Lay a block on your cutting board, cut a bite-size slice, and taste for freshness.

8 Use a very sharp knife to cut ¼-inch slices off your block.

9 Tile out your slices for a beautiful crudo!

TUNA CRUDO

Ginger Scallion, Tare, Radish

With ultrafresh tuna, a couple of great sauces, and crunchy radishes, this is the archetypal Eventide crudo. It's been on the menu since Day One. Depending on the season, we make it with bluefin, yellowfin, and big-eye tuna (but if you can source western North Atlantic bluefin, that's the best move). Our tip of the cap to David Chang for the ginger scallion sauce recipe. —*Andrew*

Cut the tuna against the grain into uniform ¼-inch slices. Tile the tuna slices on a large platter or four plates, season with salt, and drizzle with tare and then with a light layer of the ginger scallion sauce. Shower the radish slices over the top in a thin layer. Serve within 30 minutes.

SERVES 4

10 ounces of the freshest, best-quality, most local tuna you can get your hands on

¼ cup Tare (page 168)

¼ cup Ginger Scallion Sauce (recipe follows)

2 or 3 red or French breakfast radishes, sliced into very thin rounds

Finishing salt

GINGER SCALLION SAUCE

MAKES 2½ CUPS

3 bunches scallions, trimmed and thinly sliced into rounds

½ pound ginger, peeled and minced (to yield 1 cup)

½ cup canola oil

1 cup light soy sauce

1 tablespoon sherry vinegar

Splash of mirin

Pinch of kosher salt

Mix the scallions, ginger, canola oil, soy sauce, and vinegar in a jar or bowl, and season with a splash of mirin and a pinch of salt. If possible, let the flavors meld for a few hours or refrigerate overnight before using. Store in a sealed jar in the refrigerator for 2 weeks. The sauce can be used to dress noodles, rice bowls, and salads.

TORO CARPACCIO

Celery, Sesame, Yuzu

SERVES 4

TORO MARINADE

1 (12-ounce) can dry cider (we use Urban Farm Fermentory Dry Cidah)

1 garlic clove, minced

3 scallions, trimmed, white parts only, minced

¼ cup light soy sauce

¼ cup mirin

1 tablespoon kosher salt

1 teaspoon Asian sesame oil

8 ounces bluefin toro

4 celery ribs

1 tablespoon mixed black and white sesame seeds, toasted

½ cup Sesame Sauce (recipe follows)

Finishing salt

1 teaspoon yuzu juice

1 tablespoon Fried Aromatics Oil (page 184) made with shallots

In our quest to achieve total utilization of bluefin tuna, we found a way to deal with the textural curveballs you sometimes encounter in tuna bellies, which are called *otoro* in Japanese. There are bands of sinew that run the gamut from inedible to disruptive. There's little that can be done with the inedible sinew, but for the more delicate stuff, freezing and thinly slicing the tuna can be a great way to avoid textural pitfalls. Moreover, if you want to splurge on a pretty ritzy piece of tuna, this recipe will allow you to stretch it across many servings. And if you have a vacuum sealer, you could conceivably dominate a season's worth of potlucks with this recipe alone by buying a large piece of toro and sealing and freezing it. —*Mike*

To make the marinade, in a small pot, bring the dry cider to a boil and boil vigorously for 30 to 60 seconds to cook off the alcohol. Cool the cider to room temperature and whisk in the garlic, scallions, soy sauce, mirin, kosher salt, and sesame oil, taking care to ensure that the salt is dissolved. Transfer to an airtight container large enough to hold the tuna and put in the refrigerator to cool completely.

Once chilled, put the tuna in the marinade, making sure it's submerged. Allow it to marinate in the refrigerator for at least 1 hour, or up to overnight.

Preheat a charcoal grill or set a gas grill or grill pan to high heat. Remove the tuna from the marinade and pat dry. Over the hottest part of the grill, sear the tuna on each side for 1 minute. (The goal is to develop a little grill flavor while keeping the tuna completely raw inside.) Transfer the tuna to a plate and put it in the refrigerator to chill.

Once cooled completely, wrap the tuna in two layers of plastic wrap and freeze for at least 2 hours, or until it is hard enough to slice easily.

Peel the outside of each rib of celery to expose the stringy fibers that run the length of the stalk. With a paring knife, peel the fibers from the celery. Once you've cleaned up the celery nicely, use a mandoline or vegetable peeler to thinly slice it lengthwise into ribbons. Place the ribbons in ice water for at least 10 minutes, during which time they'll crisp up and curl up.

CONTINUED

TORO CARPACCIO

CONTINUED

In a small skillet over medium heat, toast the sesame seeds for 30 seconds until they are fragrant, then remove them from the pan.

Retrieve the tuna from the freezer, unwrap it, and let it temper for a couple of minutes. With a deli slicer or very sharp knife, thinly slice the tuna against the grain.

To assemble the dish, artfully lay out the tuna on a large platter or four plates. Dot the sliced tuna with the sesame sauce and scatter toasted sesame seeds over the top. Drain the celery ribbons well and transfer to a small work bowl. Season with finishing salt to taste and dress with the yuzu juice and shallot oil. Arrange the celery in an attractive tangle over the tuna and spoon the yuzu mixture over the fish. Serve within 30 minutes.

SESAME SAUCE

MAKES 2½ CUPS

1 cup white sesame seeds, toasted

½ cup shiro miso (see Glossary)

½ cup sake

1½ tablespoons soy sauce

1 tablespoon mirin

½ tablespoon sugar

1 tablespoon rice wine vinegar

1 tablespoon fresh lime juice

1 tablespoon cold water

1 tablespoon Asian sesame oil

2 tablespoons canola oil

Kosher salt

In a small skillet over medium heat, toast the sesame seeds for 30 seconds until they are fragrant, then remove them from the pan to cool.

Combine the sesame seeds, miso, sake, soy sauce, mirin, sugar, vinegar, lime juice, and water in a blender and blend until completely smooth. With the blender running, stream the oils slowly into the sauce to emulsify. Season with salt to taste.

To use, spoon into a piping bag, squeeze bottle, or large ziplock plastic bag with a corner cut off. Store extra sauce in an airtight container in the fridge for 2 weeks and use as a dressing for all types of other fish, grilled meats, and vegetable dishes.

CHU-TORO

Ramp Leaf–Almond Pistou, Pickled Ramp,
Garlic Chips

Though it probably wouldn't fly in terms of the formal Japanese codification of bluefin tuna, we use the term *chu-toro* for all medium-fatty bluefin tuna cuts from the back and sides of the fish. This tightly marbled and rosy-pink cut is our favorite part of the bluefin to serve raw, because it has such a luxurious balance of richness and tender, creamy, supple texture. It is different from the pale and deeply marbled belly (*otoro*), which can be intensely rich and sometimes sinewy, and the deep red loin (*akami*), which is lean and slightly metallic in flavor. Chu-toro stands out when served simply with some sea salt, but it also holds up beautifully against assertive flavors like the ramps, almonds, and fried garlic in this recipe. —*Andrew*

Slice the block of fish against the grain into ¼-inch pieces. Place a pool of the ramp pistou on the bottom of a large platter or on four plates. Arrange the fish artfully on the pistou and season lightly with salt. Garnish with dollops of ramp relish and the fried garlic. Serve within 30 minutes.

CONTINUED

SERVES 4

10 ounces chu-toro, trimmed into a uniform, pristine block

½ cup Ramp Leaf–Almond Pistou (recipe follows)

Finishing salt

½ cup Pickled Ramp Relish (recipe follows)

¼ cup Fried Aromatics (page 184) made with garlic

CHU-TORO

CONTINUED

RAMP LEAF-ALMOND PISTOU

MAKES 2½ CUPS

1 cup blanched and peeled almonds, toasted

1 pound ramp leaves, cleaned, bulbs saved for pickling (page 193)

½ cup water

½ cup Fried Aromatics Oil (page 184) made with shallots

2 tablespoons honey

Sherry vinegar

Kosher salt

In a large skillet over medium heat, toast the almonds for 60 seconds until they are fragrant and then remove them from the pan.

Preheat a charcoal grill or set a gas grill or grill pan to high heat. Grill the ramp leaves for 1 to 2 minutes on each side until they are dark green and smoky. Chop the leaves finely and puree in a blender with the almonds and water. With the blender running on high, slowly add the shallot oil until the mixture is thick and smooth. If it gets too thick for the blender, add more water a bit at a time to help create a vortex. Add the honey, sherry vinegar, and salt to taste. Let the mixture cool to room temperature.

Once cooled, you can use immediately, or store any extra mixture in an airtight container with a little shallot oil covering the surface in the refrigerator for up to 2 days. Or, pour in small containers and freeze for 2 months, thawing portions as needed. The excess can be used to add punch to soups, cooked fish dishes, and other crudos.

PICKLED RAMP RELISH

MAKES 1 CUP

½ cup Pickled Ramp bulbs, plus ½ cup ramp pickling liquid (page 193)

1 tablespoon cornstarch

1 tablespoon water

1 teaspoon finely chopped chives

1 teaspoon mustard oil (see Glossary; optional)

Chop the pickled ramps finely and place in a heat-proof bowl.

In a small bowl, stir the cornstarch and water together.

In a small pot over medium-high heat, bring the ramp pickling liquid to a boil, then turn down the heat to a medium boil. Whisking constantly, add the cornstarch and water mixture, a teaspoon at a time, until the mixture thickens enough to just coat the back of a spoon. Remove the pot from the heat, pour the mixture over the chopped ramps, and let it cool to room temperature. Stir the chives and mustard oil into the mixture.

Use immediately or store any extra relish in an airtight container in the refrigerator for up to 1 month, or freeze it indefinitely. The relish is a great addition to hot dogs, sandwiches, raw bar or cheese platters, or anything that benefits greatly from the addition of pickles.

TUNA TARTARE

Ramen Cracker, Umeboshi, Pickled Sea Vegetables

SERVES 4

10 ounces of the freshest, best-quality, most local tuna you can get your hands on

2 tablespoons Umeboshi Vinaigrette (recipe follows)

Kosher salt

Ramen Cracker (recipe follows), large enough to cover a large plate whole or in pieces

2 tablespoons Pickled Sea Vegetables (recipe follows)

Sliced scallion greens for garnish

We've done many versions of tuna tartare over the years, and we're pretty adamant that you need something crunchy to enjoy with any kind of tartare. These ramen crackers are nothing more than sheets of uncooked ramen noodle, but they have a wonderful noodle-meets-pretzel-or-bagel appeal. You can easily break the crackers up into bite-size pieces for a soigné little hors d'oeuvre, or (my preference) you can serve one enormous cracker on a plate that barely accommodates it. I like dropping off the larger version in front of large parties at the restaurant without any silverware. Eventually, everybody just starts cracking into it. —*Mike*

Slice the tuna into smaller pieces, and then chop with a sharp knife to make a coarse tartare.

In a stainless steel work bowl, dress the tuna with the umeboshi vinaigrette, tossing lightly and seasoning to taste with salt.

Plate the tartare on a large cracker, or make bite-size crackers with the tartare balanced on top, or plate the tartare and use the ramen cracker like croutons in a salad. Garnish with the pickled sea vegetables and sliced scallions, and serve within 30 minutes.

RAMEN CRACKER

MAKES 1 LARGE CRACKER OR 50 SMALL CRACKERS

2 teaspoons baking soda

1 cup water

3½ cups all-purpose flour

2 heaping tablespoons kosher salt, plus more to season

Canola oil for frying

Preheat the oven to 200°F. Put the baking soda on a small sheet pan or piece of foil, and bake for 2 hours. Let cool.

In a small bowl, combine the baking soda with the water and stir until the baking soda dissolves.

In a separate bowl, combine the flour and salt. Add the liquid to the dried ingredients and knead by hand until the dough comes together. Turn the dough out onto a lightly floured surface and knead until you have a stiff, smooth ball. Wrap tightly in plastic wrap. Allow to rest for 30 minutes.

Roll out the dough with a pasta maker or rolling pin to a uniform thinness that should allow you to see the grain of a wooden cutting board or counter through it. Depending on how you plan to plate the dish, either keep the sheet the same diameter as your frying pot for a larger appetizer or cut the dough into uniform cracker shapes about the size of a regular saltine for a bite-size snack.

Fill a large pot with 3 inches of canola oil and heat on high to 350°F (or bring a deep-fryer to 350°F). Line a plate with paper towels. Carefully slip the dough pieces into the oil in batches, making sure not to crowd the pot, and fry until golden brown, 3 to 5 minutes. Using a slotted spoon or wire-mesh strainer, transfer

the crackers onto the paper towel–lined plate and season lightly with salt. Let cool and store in an airtight container at room temperature for 1 week. They are great as a snack with cheese, dips, hummus, and more.

UMEBOSHI VINAIGRETTE

MAKES ABOUT 1 CUP

1 umeboshi (Japanese pickled plum), pitted

1 cup canola oil

5 tablespoons fresh lime juice

½ teaspoon fish sauce

Kosher salt

In a blender, combine the umeboshi, canola oil, lime juice, and fish sauce and puree. Season to taste with salt. Use immediately.

The extra can be stored in an airtight container in the refrigerator for 1 week and used to dress salads, vegetables, rice and noodle dishes, and a huge variety of crudos and cooked fish dishes.

PICKLED SEA VEGETABLES

MAKES 2 TABLESPOONS

1 pinch hijiki (see Glossary)

1 pinch wakame (see Glossary)

1 pinch Pickled Kombu (page 193)

Finishing salt

Confit Mushroom Oil (page 186) made with maitakes

1 pinch white sesame seeds

Place the hijiki and wakame in separate small heat-proof bowls. Pour boiling water over them, and let sit for 10 minutes. Drain the hijiki and wakame and combine with the pickled kombu in a small bowl. Season the sea vegetables with salt and a drizzle of maitake oil.

In a dry skillet, carefully toast the sesame seeds until they are uniformly golden brown, then dump them into the bowl with the sea vegetables and stir to combine.

CHAPTER 3

THE ULTIMATE CLAMBAKE

Whatever you think of the contemporary American culinary landscape, it's hard to deny that the last ten years have seen a great and productive reawakening of interest in the country's regional cuisines.

We have been trying humbly to contribute to that movement, alongside others who have helped lift up New England food and many other styles, like Cajun, Low Country, Appalachian, and Chesapeake cuisines, as well as the broader and cross-cultural contributions of the African diaspora, Native Americans, Latinxs, and many others who have shaped what we eat.

All of these different cultural niches share one commonality: the feast, where families, friends, and whole communities come together to break bread. To name a few of these feasts: the Cajun *boucherie* (pig butchering and all-day roast) and crayfish boil; the Low Country oyster roast and barbecue; the Appalachian pig roast; the Maryland crab boil; and cedar-planked salmon roasts in the Pacific Northwest.

Which brings us, of course, to New England's contribution: the clambake.

At its grandest, a New England clambake is a warm, loud, boisterous gathering of family and friends around a smoky and steamy heap of seaweed. The shellfish and fixings hiding underneath are basically picked from the fire and eaten right away, steps away from the ice-cold North Atlantic. The details of the experience vary only a bit from the sandy beaches of Narragansett Bay in Rhode Island to the rugged, rocky coastline of Maine.

The reality is, the same guiding principles can be used at any scale, in any place, including your home kitchen.

THE GRAND SEASIDE (OR BACKYARD) VERSION

Pulling off a classic clambake steps from the ocean is pure memory-making, not just because of the setting and the delicious food, but because it takes a family and friends to pull off. Everyone has a job, from gathering seaweed, to tending fire, to setting a beautiful table, to sitting off to the side, drinking and making unhelpful comments. And, of course, there's the viscerally pleasing experience of eating with your hands surrounded by people you love. It takes a little planning and a little fussing, but it's really a simple pleasure. We're going to show you how.

THE BASICS

The first thing to understand is that clambake is really a misnomer. If it didn't sound so awkward, a clambake would more accurately be called a clamsteam, because introducing a little moisture to the cooking equation frees shellfish from their shells and produces the most succulent results.

When we do clambakes, either at the restaurant or seaside, we add a base of sea or salted water to ensure consistent steam, but in many traditional clambakes—like those of southern New England, cooked in pits dug in the sand—people rely solely on soaked seaweed to provide the necessary moisture to produce the steam that cooks the shellfish. Seaweed is probably the single thing that holds the whole tradition together because it provides that critical moisture and imbues everything with a cohesive, umami-rich seaweed flavor.

THE EXTRAS AND ACCOMPANIMENTS

While clams, potatoes, and seaweed are a must in a clambake, you'll see an impressive variance by locale. In Rhode Island, where clams are king, god forbid you try to fit lobster into the equation. In Fall River, Massachusetts, which has a large Portuguese population, you are likely to find *chouriço* sausage in the mix and Portuguese sweet bread served on the side. In Midcoast and northern Maine, lobster is requisite, and you may also stumble across the otherworldly red snapper, also known as the state hot dog of Maine, from time to time. Here in southern Maine and at Eventide, our platter includes potatoes, salt pork, steamers, mussels, lobster, smoked sausage, eggs, and corn (when it's in season). But we also like to add rock crabs, wild oysters, periwinkles, or anything else we might gather along the shore. Every single version, no matter what, includes copious amounts of butter.

We love this basic formula, but we're also restless chefs, and we can't leave well enough alone, so we like to have a little fun with the fixings served with a clambake. Along with seasoned drawn butter, we serve bracing, spicy, and acidic condiments to dress the shellfish, pork, and potatoes. Those little touches include Salt Pork Sambal (page 171), Nori Vinaigrette (page 199), Maitake XO Sauce (page 170), any type of hot sauce, and Eventide Steamed Buns (page 162). And don't forget the egg, which is said to have become part of the tradition for an ingenious reason: as a timer. Lore says that when you crack the egg and it is perfectly hard-boiled, you know the rest of the bake is done. However, we've found that using a cooler (see page 101) helps everything turn out more evenly in the end. Along with that bit of wisdom, here are some other clambake mantras to keep in mind as you prepare for the adventure.

Observe fire safety. If you are building a fire outside, *please* don't start a forest fire. *Please* understand and comply with local and state fire regulations. *Please* obtain a fire permit, if required. We like to do our clambakes below the high-tide line, so the tide puts the embers out, but if you aren't below the tide line, *please* put the fire out with the kind of fanatical overkill that would make Smokey the Bear proud.

Choose a sturdy cooking vessel. Here are some of our favorite types of vessels:

- Custom 4 by 3-foot stainless steel tray: Our welder friend made us these monster trays for large-format catering events. They are the sturdiest and best of all the vessels we've tried, but they probably aren't realistic for using (much less storing) in a regular apartment or house.

- Roasting pans or 2-inch-deep hotel pans: These come in a variety of widths and are a good alternative for smaller-scale clambakes at the beach or at home.
- Lobster pot or other large pot: Pots usually limit how much stuff you can fit in, but you can use a pot to get good results.

Aim for the perfect experience, not perfect cookery. We've done thousands of clambakes in the restaurant, on the beach, and almost everywhere in between. Trust us, it's virtually impossible to achieve evenly cooked perfection with so many different things firing at once. Steamers and lobsters just don't cook at the same rates. That's not the point, anyway. Clambakes are meant to be casual, familial, and abundant, focusing on the beauty of nature and breaking bread with loved ones, rather than the flawless execution of every little morsel. Don't get us wrong, our process is calibrated to deliver delicious results, but the mussels might be cooked further than your anal retentive foodie friend might like. If someone complains, confiscate their butter or send them off to gather seaweed.

Provide starch. Serve some steamed buns, sticky rice, or flatbread with the meal, so people can stack, wrap, and combine ingredients. Making little composed sandwiches with funky and spicy sauces is a great twist to add to the feast.

Have a blast. Particularly if you're doing the outside version, you might as well swing for the fences. There's a bunch of down time, and you can really stretch things out as much as you want. Anything that you'd bring to a car camping trip or beach day—fishing rods, cribbage, Frisbees, guitars, slack lines, ingredients for s'mores, cannabis (if it's legal where you live, of course), camp chairs, footballs— are welcome distractions and good ways to make the best of the day.

Carry in, carry out. If you're doing it outside, have respect for your surroundings, for the love of all that is sacred. Carry out your trash. Leave no trace. Don't be a goon.

With all that in mind, you're ready to go!

GETTING IT DONE THE DRAMATIC WAY

There is nothing like cooking a clambake over an open fire on a breezy summer afternoon. While doing so steps from the water may feel like the most appropriate way, you can do it anywhere under the sky. As long as you do it safely, it doesn't matter if it's Uncle Jimmy's backyard, the sandy bend of a river, or a gravel parking lot.

Scope is the most important question when planning for a clambake, because the headcount will determine the cooking vessel size. If forty people are rolling through, you're going to need a pretty large, specialized vessel. If it's a more intimate setup, like a romantic, beachside dinner for two, a large pot will do. The only real key for our purposes is that the vessel be able to hold at least a couple inches of water and withstand some serious heat from the fire.

Here are our instructions for a clambake, starting with the tools and equipment you'll need to make it all happen:

- Enough firewood and/or charcoal to keep a fire going for a couple of hours (and beyond if you're hanging out for a while)
- A sturdy cooking vessel (see page 91)
- Mesh shellfish bags, which when filled with smaller items like steamers or potatoes, make removal easier and should be available at most seafood retailers (only necessary if you're cooking for a large group)
- A lid for your vessel or, in its absence, a large piece of soaked burlap or a soaked clean bedsheet to drape over the vessel and trap some of the steam
- Small bowls or ramekins for all of your butter and sauces

- Enough heavy-duty pot holders, fire gloves, or kitchen towels to lift your vessel safely off the fire
- A bucket of water, preferably seawater, but if not, then salted enough to taste like it
- A regular-size trash barrel (clean, of course) of waterlogged rockweed—a type of stringy and sturdy seaweed found on both coasts—preferably pulled from rocks on the beach around your cook site. If you're not on a beach, your seafood retailer should be able to procure it for you. The companies that ship lobsters and oysters will also sometimes ship seaweed if you ask nicely.
- A clean cooler for holding cooked food

And of course, no Eventide clambake would be complete without a giant white cooler brimming with ice and an assortment of tasty beverages. When stocking the cooler for a clambake, we tend to reach for crisp and crushable options that will pair well with the impending seafood deluge. You're likely to see cans of Bunker Brewing Company's Machine Czech-Style Pilz alongside go-to beers like Allagash White. For wine, we gravitate toward food-friendly whites like fresh, young Grüner Veltliner or briny, lip-smacking Picpoul. A proper summer celebration practically screams for bubbles, and so we always make sure to lay in several bottles of bright and lively sparkling rosé. We also can't think of a better opportunity than a clambake to try out our Tea with a Twist (page 243).

GATHER YOUR INGREDIENTS

Next, it's time to think about ingredients and scale them for whatever size party you're having. Here's a handy rule of thumb:

1 (1¼-pound) live lobster per person (and a couple extra if you want lobster rolls the next day)

½ pound live mussels per person

½ pound live steamer clams per person

1 ear of corn per person (optional, unless it's in season locally, in which case it is mandatory)

1 egg per person, plus a couple extras to use as timers

3 to 5 small potatoes per person (no more than 1 inch diameter)

½ cup (1 stick) unsalted butter per person, melted, clarified, or browned

Salty swine of your choice, like a big hunk of Salt Pork (page 202), sliced thick; thick-sliced slab bacon or cured ham; fresh or smoked sausage; whole hot dogs (we like red snappers, as mentioned, but any hot dogs will do); whole, fresh Spanish chorizo or its many cousins (like *chouriço*), or something else cured and delicious

Nori Vinaigrette (page 199), Salt Pork Sambal (page 171), Maitake XO Sauce (page 170), or the hot sauce of your choice, as well as plates of starchy accompaniments like Eventide Steamed Buns (page 162), crusty bread, flatbread, or sticky rice

½ lemon per person, arrayed around the table with the sauces

SCOPE OUT AND PREP YOUR SITE

If you're throwing a clambake seaside, make sure to research the tides! The incoming tide is relentless and unsympathetic to your culinary aspirations or your schedule. Beyond that, your first and most important challenge in setting up your cook site is ensuring that you can safely hold your cooking vessel—which will be significantly

heavier when full of water and product—on a level plane 4 to 6 inches above a fire. This can be accomplished in a number of ways. If your party, and therefore your vessel, is small, then you can set up on a Weber grill in your backyard. If your party and your vessel are really large, and you're on a beach, grab four large rocks and place them under the corners of your vessel, then shift them around until the setup is sturdy and level. Cinder blocks and fire bricks work well here, too. You may be waiting for us to call for digging a trench in the sand, but in Maine, that's rare. Our beaches are rocky, which is a pain for sunbathing and in-ground clambakes, but a pretty good thing for setting up a sturdy above-ground clambake.

Once you've leveled the vessel and feel confident it won't move or fall during cooking, pull it off and put it aside.

It's worth noting here to keep a sharp eye on the wind. If it is really cutting across the beach you're cooking on, you're looking at problems that include a fire going out, a fire turning into an inferno, or a vessel overturning in the wind. You can arrange more rocks around the edges of your vessel or even build a ring of wet seaweed piled around the fire to block some of the wind. Be careful, in any case.

BUILD YOUR FIRE

Once you've prepped your site, you must now summon and flex your bushcraft skills. Whether you're doing your clambake on a grill or on the beach, you need to build a fire robust enough to boil water evenly and consistently. You can accomplish

this by having an even bed of coals that is at least the same diameter as your vessel. Our guidance here is to start a base fire that is a little bigger than your instincts say it should be, so when it burns down to embers, you have enough to spread to the edges under your vessel. You just want to make sure it's ripping hot and loaded up to burn for a while. It's not a bad idea to get a bag of charcoal to throw on top of the embers to make the fire burn longer and more consistently.

Once you have your fire going, you should be heading out to gather your seaweed, if that's the route you're taking.

ASSEMBLE YOUR CLAMBAKE

First, put an even 1 to 2 inches of seawater (or fresh water salted to taste like seawater) in your vessel. Lay 3 to 4 inches of seaweed in the bottom of the vessel. Next, lay in your bags of potatoes, pork product, corn, and eggs in an even layer. Cover those with several inches of seaweed. Next, lay down your lobsters, steamers, and mussels. Make sure to put a loose egg on either side of the vessel, buried in the seaweed with the upper layers of food. Cover with enough seaweed so you can't see any of the ingredients below. Put the lid on if you have it, or lay the soaked burlap or cloth over the top.

LOAD IT UP

Lift the clambake onto the stones (this may be a two-person job), so it sits 4 to 6 inches above the fire, and ensure that the whole thing is sturdy and sound so it won't tip or fall off. While it's cooking, you're going to need to attend to other things, but make sure that you don't take your eyes off the prize. A few things to watch for:

- Be sure you have a strong-enough fire to boil the water and produce consistent steam. After you've had the pot over the heat for a little while, you should see steam starting to escape from the top of the rig, and it should feel hot to the touch. If it doesn't, load a bit more wood or charcoal under the rig.
- Make sure your system doesn't run out of water. If the fire is too hot, it can boil off the water completely and scorch the seaweed, which will produce a really unpleasant taste.

Periodically check the corners of your vessel to make sure there is plenty of water. If you see, smell, or feel like your vessel is low on water, just add a little by lifting the lid and pouring it over the top or just pouring it over the burlap or cloth.

- If your vessel is really wide, make sure the heat is evenly spread underneath, so that all the food gets cooked evenly. There's nothing worse than pulling a clambake off the fire and finding out that only half of the food is cooked.

POUR A DRINK AND GET READY TO FEAST

Prepping your table doesn't have to be complex, and you should do it the way you like it. Here are some of the steps we take:

- Grab and stage a folding table, a wooden picnic table, a piece of wood stretched over sawhorses, or another improvised table.
- Lay newspaper or butcher paper over the top of your table.
- Set out enough butter for each person to have their own tub (small bowl) to luxuriate in. If you need to melt butter without access to a stove, put butter in a lidded glass jar and set it in or on top of the steaming seaweed while your clambake is cooking.
- Set out enough pairs of Joyce Chen's scissors or Shanghai crab scissors or something similar for each person to cut open the lobster shells cleanly (trust us: you'll never use lobster crackers again) and provide a shell bucket or bowl for every two to four people for spent shells.
- Drop a pile of lobster bibs on the middle of the table.
- Keep paper towels nearby for the eating, and wet naps or wet towels handy for cleaning up after.
- Put out cups or bowls of warm seawater for dipping the steamers in (to remove grit) before dunking them in butter or sauce.
- Lay out small bowls of different sauces for dipping all the food.

UNVEIL THE CLAMBAKE

We wish we could give you a hard-and-fast time for how long to cook. But we know from experience that when working with varying conditions, fuels, and ingredients, you're going to have to rely on intuition and a few pieces of good advice to know when your clambake is finished. Don't even think about checking for doneness until you see that vigorous steam has been coming off the top of your cooking vessel for at least 20 minutes, and it is very hot to the touch. When you're ready to check, take a peek at the lobsters. They should be red. Not reddish or mottled red. You want bright, beautiful, Ferrari red. Next, crack the two eggs that you put on the top on either side of the vessel. The whites should be fully set and the yolk should be set. Make sure your clams and mussels are all open, and give a potato a poke with a knife to make sure it's tender. If some of the items are done but others aren't, you can use your heat-resistant gloves to pull those items off the bake and hold them in your clean cooler, which will keep them nice and warm until it's time to plate up. We call this the Down East crutch because it's our version of the Texas crutch—a means by which the cook balances the demands of service against the technical demands of food service. Once everything is done, you're ready to plate up!

TABLE AND ENJOY

Wearing your heat-resistant gloves, pull the whole shebang a safe distance from the fire and remove the covering to reveal the bounty within. You can either put everything in your cooler to hold until presentation, or we think it's great to just pull all the food directly out of the vessel with the gloves and lay everything out in the center of the table on top of the table covering. The only thing to note is to make sure things are spread out enough so everybody has access. Encourage everyone to take a bit of this and a bit of that, put it on a bun and sauce and butter it. Bragging rights go to those who find the most intriguing flavor combinations. This is not the time for niceties; there should be lots of eager reaching and perhaps even the judicious use of elbows. If you're not getting your hands dirty, you've got the wrong approach.

MAKE IT LAST

Having eaten your fill, it's time to let languor set in and enjoy the company around you. Push on into the night, or don't. Whiskey can help in clarifying the position.

THE EFFICIENCY APARTMENT VERSION

Is it the middle of winter? Are you quarantined in your Brooklyn walk-up? Does that dreamy summer vibe in Maine seem too far in the past or too far in the future? Not to worry. We promise that you can use all the same principles described in the Grand Seaside Version and still pull off a killer little clambake in your home kitchen, even on an electric stovetop.

THE BASICS

You'll have to make peace with the fact that some of the princely elements of the seaside clambake will be missing here, but other things remain constant. Foremost is the fun of it all. You're going to surprise your dinner guests with this simple offering, and the hands-on, family-style nature of it will by definition pull people closer together. That's why we do it every summer on the beach and why we felt compelled to serve this version of it at Eventide.

In terms of execution, the formula is also basically the same: combine the freshest, best ingredients you can find with steam, sweat the details a bit, and everything will work out stupendously.

THE EXTRAS AND ACCOMPANIMENTS

The clambake we serve in the restaurant includes potatoes, salt pork, steamers, mussels, lobster, smoked sausage, eggs, corn, butter, and Nori Vinaigrette (page 199). Feel free to add a few extra Eventide twists like Salt Pork Sambal (page 171), Maitake XO Sauce (page 170), any type of hot sauce, and Eventide Steamed Buns (page 162) to dial up the flavors and textures and give people some room to explore different combinations. You don't have to follow that approach exactly, but just look for ways to bring acidic, spicy, funky condiments and a carb wrapper of some kind to the table for that extra kick.

The vessel you choose to cook in is also important in this format. We suggest using a 12-inch bamboo steamer basket with a lid, set over a wok with a small amount of water in it to create steam. Woks are useful for this because their curved sides allow a steamer to sit inside but not touch the water in the bottom of the pan. You can use a straight-sided pot, too, but you need to make sure it is of the same diameter as the bamboo steamer so the steamer sits snuggly atop the pot. If you have a pot with a perforated steamer insert, you can just build the clambake right in the insert.

And we'll reiterate this again, to hammer it home: aim for the perfect experience, not the perfect cookery. It's virtually impossible to achieve evenly cooked perfection with so many different things firing at once. Our process is calibrated to deliver delicious results, but it's inevitable that one thing or another will get a little overdone. Try to keep that one thing or another from being the lobster and don't sweat the rest.

GATHER YOUR INGREDIENTS

If you do go the steamer basket route, each basket serves two people comfortably. If you need to serve four or six people, you can just stack multiple baskets on top of each other during steaming. Once you get to four baskets and beyond, it's best to set up multiple woks and split up the load.

For a single basket, here is your ingredient list (scale up as needed):

1 (1- to 1¼-pound) live lobster, or 2 fresh or thawed frozen (uncooked) lobster tails

½ pound live mussels

½ pound live steamer clams

1 ear of corn, shucked and cut in half

2 hard-boiled eggs (but not too hard)

10 Confit Potatoes (page 185) made with baby new potatoes or fingerlings

1 (2 by 2-inch) piece Salt Pork (page 202), sliced into ½-inch planks

¼ cup (½ stick) unsalted butter, melted, for serving

½ cup Nori Vinaigrette (page 199) for serving (optional)

½ cup Salt Pork Sambal (page 171) for serving (optional)

½ cup Maitake XO (page 170) for serving (optional)

4 Eventide Steamed Buns (page 162) for serving (optional)

For drinks, the same stuff that works for the Grand Seaside Version works here. Get light, crisp beers like a Pilsner (e.g. Bunker Brewing Company's Machine Czech-Style Pilz) or a wheat (e.g. Allagash White). For wine, we like fresh, young whites like a Grüner Veltliner or briny, lip-smacking Picpoul. Bubbles, like a sparkling rosé, are outstanding accompaniments, as are cocktails like our Tea with a Twist (page 243).

GETTING IT DONE

If you get a live lobster, place it on a clean work surface and dispatch it humanely by thrusting a sharp knife between its eyes. Pull the claws and tail off the lobster. Wash the mussels and clams. If you have it, lay the rockweed in the bottom of your steamer basket to create a bed for the shellfish. Put your lobster claws and tails atop the rockweed (save the bodies for Lobster Stew, page 126), in the middle, and arrange the mussels, clams, corn, egg, potatoes, and salt pork tightly around the lobster, keeping like ingredients together (mussels arrayed with mussels, clams arrayed with clams—you get the picture). Make it look nice so when you open the lid for your guest, it has that "wow" factor. Cover the basket with its top. (If you are stacking multiple baskets, you need to cover only the top basket.)

While you won't have the time or space in this version to sit languidly around the fire as the food cooks, once you have the basket(s) loaded, there's a nice opening for a drink with your guests. If for some reason you are worried that you may lose track of time after many pops, place the whole basket with the lid on in the refrigerator, where it will be fine for several hours.

When you're ready, fill your wok with 3 inches of water and a big pinch of salt (it should taste like seawater). Bring it to a boil over high heat and carefully place the steamer basket in the wok, so it sits sturdily above the water. Set a timer for 12 minutes. In the meantime, get your melted butter and any other sides and condiments set out on the table.

When the timer goes off, take the lid off the steamer basket and check the ingredients. If the lobster is bright red and all the mussel and clam shells have opened up, carefully remove the basket from the heat and set it on a cutting board or a large plate or platter, bring it to the table, and dig in.

CHAPTER 4

MODERN
SHACK FARE

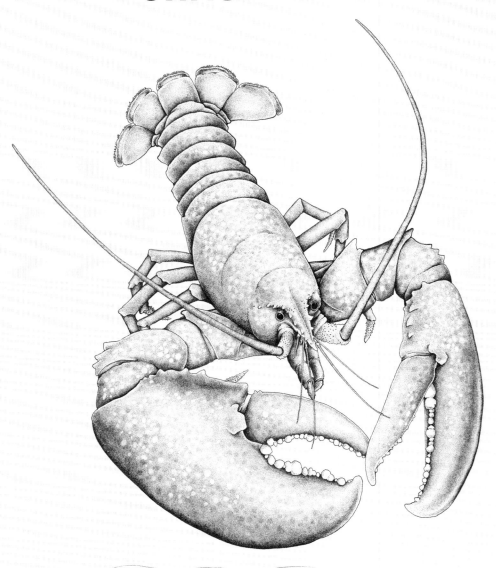

The Brown Butter Lobster Roll — 112

EVENTIDE STEAMED BUN, CHIVES, LOBSTER, BROWN BUTTER

Fried Oyster Bun — 117

TARTAR, TOMATO, PICKLED VEGETABLES

Crab Roll — 118

YUZU KOSHO MAYONNAISE

The Fish Sandwich — 120

TARTAR, TARE, ICEBERG LETTUCE

Smoked Tofu Sandwich — 123

ONION RINGS, JALAPEÑO MAYONNAISE

Eventide Burger — 125

TALLOW MAYONNAISE, ICEBERG LETTUCE, AMERICAN CHEESE

Lobster Stew — 126

GREEN CURRY, SALTINES

New England Clam Chowder — 128

SALT PORK, SALTINES

Broiled Black Cod — 131

SPICY MISO, HIJIKI, CITRUS

Broiled Jumbo Winter Point Oysters — 135

KOREAN BBQ SAUCE, DAIKON SLAW, CANDIED NUTS

Scallop Waffle-Yaki — 136

KABAYAKI, UMAMI MAYONNAISE, TEMPURA CRISPIES, PICKLED KOMBU, BONITO FLAKES, NORI, SCALLION

Grilled Swordfish Belly — 139

ROASTED PEPPERS, NIXTAMALIZED RYE BERRIES, CONFIT CHANTERELLES

Tempura Smelts — 143

CUCUMBER TARTAR, CUCUMBER SALT

Calçotes — 144

RAMPS, ROMESCO, TOASTED HAZELNUT

Braised Matsutake — 147

RAMEN BROTH, PICKLED SPRUCE TIPS, BUTTER

Halibut Tail Bo Ssam — 148

THAI BIRD CHILE SAMBAL, KOREAN BBQ, SMOKED OYSTER MAYONNAISE, HOISIN, PICKLES, CHILE OIL

Smoked Hake Brandade — 151

CUCUMBER SALAD, NUTRITIONAL YEAST

Broiled Albacore Collar — 153

KOJI-CALAMANSI VINAIGRETTE, GOMASIO, SUSHI RICE

Eventide's modern seafood shack approach is, by our estimation, a 90 percent low-brow, 10 percent high-brow affair. If we mess with that ratio too much, we start to get too far away for comfort from the classic shack experience and Maine's traditions. At the restaurant and throughout this book, you'll see us using fun ingredients and innovative techniques to elevate great products or traditional dishes, which can seem improvisational and even heretical, we suppose. But it's important to note that restraint is just as central to making Eventide work.

We want people to love and be surprised by what they're eating, of course, but we also want them to be focused on the moment and the people they're with and the breezy, familial warmth of it all. Immediacy is what Eventide is all about, and it's what the traditions we're trying to celebrate are all about, too.

UNTAMED MAINE

Maine's foodways are an amalgamation of many recognizable traditions: Native American, English, French-Acadian, and immigrant influences. But there's also something uniquely wild and untamed about Maine that has impacted the way we eat and cook here.

Maine was actually where the first English settlement in New England was established, thirteen years before the Pilgrims' 1620 landing at Plymouth Rock. Located near modern-day Phippsburg at the mouth of the Kennebec River (just across Casco Bay from Portland), the so-called Popham Colony was short-lived, at least in part because the settlers could not abide the harsh Maine winter. They left after little more than a year, only to come back a couple of decades later to stay permanently.

Ever since then, Maine has held on to its isolated, frontier nature. It remains among the ten least populated (1.35 million people), and ten least densely populated (43 people per square mile) US states. Ninety percent of the land is forested—the highest rate in the country. Huge swaths are barely inhabited, if even touched much by humans at all.

Ask ten Mainers, and nine of them would be fine if you bumped those numbers even further toward isolation. You'll never meet a people who embrace the wild solitude with such pride and respect. Our friend Don Lindgren, owner of Rabelais bookstore and dean of Maine's gastronomers, translates that idea into Maine's food traditions: "There's such a sense of immediacy in Maine, which refers to the fact that these amazing things are right here in front of us, at the water's edge or in the ocean, or in the fields or the kitchen garden. But aside from the place itself, there's also this idea that our cooking comes from something that people are engaged in the gathering or the growing or the hunting or the catching of, which you don't see a lot in America."

You can see that in all of the state's classic dishes. Pulling lobster traps or digging clams and having a dinner on the beach with a fire and a pot of water and some seaweed. Having a beanpot supper when you're out camping with friends. All of that stuff speaks to immediacy. You're the one involved in every part of the creation.

Maine is just one of those places where the local, seasonal, artisanal dynamic is ingrained. Mainers are born with respect for what the land and sea offer, and adopted Mainers are indoctrinated into it (if they didn't move to Maine specifically for the lifestyle). It seems everyone here grows, farms, fishes, hunts, forages, or is intimately tied to someone who does. And generations of families, like the Hennesseys of Winter Point Oyster Farm (our oyster spirit guides), have made their living close to the land and the sea.

The simple, one-pot chowders and stews, the steamed or stuffed seafood, the pies, and all the rest of traditional Maine cuisine make perfect sense in that broader context, born of close-to-the-land-and-sea necessity as they are. Building a restaurant with all of that in mind has been remarkably satisfying work.

SEAFOOD SHACKS AND THE GREAT ESCAPE

Escapism is also a foundational force in Maine's food traditions and our way at the restaurant, because it helped birth the legendary seafood shacks that dot New England's coast from Rhode Island to Maine.

Again, Don Lindgren helps put the pieces together: "People discovered Maine in large numbers when automobile culture blew up [in the first quarter of the twentieth century], and they could drive to this marvelous, beautiful, cool-in-the-summer state. People who visit can be one step removed from the digging or the fishing of amazing seafood by going to a shack, because most of the best ones are connected to people with boats."

As vacationers began to flock to the state, seafood businesses, many of them family-run, saw opportunities to create new revenue with direct-to-consumer counters or shacks. That's the story behind what is reputedly New England's oldest seafood shack, Woodman's of Essex in Massachusetts, where the original owners Chubby and Bessie Woodman are said to have first made the connection between a bucket of fresh-dug clams and sizzling fat in 1916. In Maine, Perkins Cove Lobster Shack, the granddaddy of steamed lobster huts, traces its roots to around the same time. As the tourism industry in New England grew through the 1950s, 1960s, and 1970s, many of the other legendary shacks opened their doors as well (see Our Top Seafood Shacks in Northern New England on page 7).

Today, throughout Maine and the rest of New England, you'll still find the same basic formula of a breezy, casual, seaside setting with raw and fried oysters and clams, steamed lobsters, chowders, fish and chips, and cold drinks. Why mess with a good thing?

Well, again, because we're restless chefs. There was so much room to take those ultra-simple, delicious seafood shack and Maine classics and build on them with technique and ingredients grabbed from every corner of the globe. You'll see what we mean.

THE BROWN BUTTER
LOBSTER ROLL

Eventide Steamed Bun, Chives, Lobster, Brown Butter

MAKES 4 ROLLS

4 Eventide Steamed Buns
(page 162)

¼ cup Brown Butter Vinaigrette
(recipe follows)

10 ounces Eventide Prepared
Lobster Meat (recipe follows)

Kosher salt

Minced fresh chives
for garnish

This is the signature dish that has really driven our good fortune and Eventide's success since it opened. We sell three to four times as many lobster rolls as we do any other food item because it is the item that everybody *must* try. We've won lobster roll competitions with it, it's been named the best sandwich in Maine by *People* magazine and a humorous array of celebrities from Alton Brown, Willem Dafoe, and Action Bronson (yes, it got a "f***, that's delicious") have fawned over it.

Good lobster rolls have always been one of my favorite things in the world. Like many New England families, mine gathered every summer and did lobster boils or bakes to celebrate the season. I had a reputation as the kid in the brood who always pestered the elders to buy extra lobsters so I could shell them for lobster rolls the next day.

There has never really been, at least to my knowledge, a codified approach to making a traditional Maine lobster roll. Mainers are happy to tell you that, no matter how you're making it, it isn't traditional and their grandma does it or did it better. That said—and I'm going to be very careful here—most Mainers will generally acknowledge three key tenets: first, there are two predominant and accepted styles of lobster rolls, hot and cold; second, a griddled, split-top hot dog bun is the perfectly suited vessel for the lobster; and third and most important, simpler is better.

Heeding these tenets, but determined to put forth a lobster roll that was outside the box, we developed a hot version served on a split-top Chinese-style steamed bun, embellished with deeply flavorful brown butter. Even with those twists, simple is still the name of the game.

We're including a very specific approach here for cooking the lobster in the recipe that follows for a very specific reason: it's the best way we've found to guarantee the lobster meat isn't overcooked. We slightly undercook the lobster meat because you'll be finishing cooking the lobster in the skillet with the brown butter. It's an art and a mandate to keep the lobster from overcooking! *—Andrew*

Note: You can purchase picked lobster meat as a substitute for this process, but the results won't be quite the same and you run the risk of overcooking the meat during the rewarming process.

CONTINUED

THE BROWN BUTTER
LOBSTER ROLL

CONTINUED

When you are ready to make the lobster rolls, place the buns in a steamer insert inside a large pot, or a bamboo steamer set over a wok, and steam for 5 minutes, until they are very hot, soft, and pliable. Remove the pot from the heat, but leave the buns in the steamer to keep warm.

In a skillet, combine the brown butter vinaigrette and lobster meat over medium heat, stirring frequently for 3 to 5 minutes, until just heated through. Season with salt to taste.

Retrieve the buns from the steamer and divide the lobster evenly among them. Top with chives and serve warm.

EVENTIDE PREPARED LOBSTER MEAT

MAKES 10 OUNCES

3 or 4 (1- to 1½-pound) lobsters

Dispatch the lobsters as humanely as possible by thrusting a sharp thin knife through the lobster shell between the eyes. Place the lobsters in a heatproof container large enough to hold them with ample space. Bring a second large pot of salted water to a boil (enough to cover the lobsters), pour the boiling water over the lobsters, and let the lobsters steep for 4 minutes. When the timer goes off, use tongs to remove the lobsters from the water to a large cutting board.

Wearing gloves or using a towel to avoid burning yourself, pull the claws off the lobster and put them back in the hot water for 4 minutes (set another timer). In the meantime, twist the tails off the lobsters and use kitchen shears to cut the shell along the length of the tail, so you can remove the meat easily. You will notice that the meat is slightly undercooked, which is what you want, since you'll be cooking it further in the brown butter later.

As with shrimp, lobster tails have a digestive tract running the length of the tail; it is easily removed by pulling back the long flap of meat that runs along the top of the tail. Once finished with the tails, use kitchen shears to cut along both sides of the knuckles and claws to

separate the shells and easily remove the meat. If you want to pick through the bodies and legs for meat, have at it (a rolling pin works to press the leg meat out), but we just reserve the bodies and shells for Lobster Stew (page 126). Lightly rinse all the shelled lobster meat under cold water. Tear the meat into good-size chunks and reserve for use in recipes. (Mainers don't cut lobster meat. We tear it so as to get the most possible surface area to draw in whatever you're dressing your meat with, such as butter).

Use immediately or transfer the torn meat to an airtight container; it will keep in the refrigerator for 3 to 4 days.

BROWN BUTTER VINAIGRETTE

MAKES ABOUT 2½ CUPS

2 cups (4 sticks) unsalted butter

½ cup nonfat dry milk powder

¼ cup fresh lemon juice

Kosher salt

In a saucepan over medium heat, melt the butter. Whisk in the milk powder and cook, stirring often, until the solids begin to brown and take on a nutty aroma. Pour the butter into a bowl and stir in the lemon juice and salt to taste. Use immediately or store in an airtight container in the refrigerator for 1 month. Use the excess to add a little luxury to any recipe that calls for melted butter.

Lobster Breakdown

1 Place your well-drained parcooked lobster on a clean surface. Have kitchen scissors and a plate ready for receiving the picked lobster meat.

2 Grabbing the body with one hand and the tail with the other, twist and pull to remove the tail.

3 Grabbing the body with one hand and a claw with the other, pull the claw backward to remove the claw. Repeat with the second claw.

4 Reserve the body and legs for Lobster Stew (page 126). Most of the meat will be found in the tail, knuckles, and claws.

5 Snap the claws from the knuckles. Using scissors, work from the base of the claws and knuckles to cut open the shells and remove the meat.

6 Using scissors, cut the soft underside of the tail on both sides where it meets the shell.

7 Pull back the soft underside of the shell to expose the tail meat.

8 Gently pull the tail out of the shell, keeping it intact.

9 Your finished lobster meat!

FRIED OYSTER BUN

Tartar, Tomato, Pickled Vegetables

We knew we wanted to have a fried oyster bun on our menu, but up until an hour or two before our soft opening, we hadn't even gotten around to testing one out. In a panic, we "asked" our opening sous chef, Ian Driscoll (aka "Teen Wolf"), to put something together. He had no idea what we were talking about, so Andrew just sort of shouted, "Kinda like po' boy style. Fry some oysters and put them on a bun with some tartar sauce and some pickles. Figure it out." He sure did! The dish, which has become one of our most popular items, hasn't changed a bit since. —*Mike*

Place the buns in a large pot set up with a steamer insert, or a bamboo steamer set over a wok, and steam for 5 minutes, or until they are very hot, soft, and pliable. Remove the pot from the heat, but leave the buns in the steamer to keep warm.

Fill a large pot with 3 inches of canola oil and heat on high to 350°F (or bring a deep-fryer to 350°F). Line a plate with paper towels.

Pour the masa harina into a large bowl or onto a tray and bury the oysters in it. Let them sit for 2 minutes, then transfer them to a plate, shaking off any excess masa. Slip half of the oysters into the hot oil and fry until they are golden brown, about 3 minutes. With a slotted spoon or wire-mesh strainer, remove the oysters from the oil and turn onto the paper towel–lined plate. Season with salt. Repeat with the remaining oysters.

Retrieve the buns from the steamer and slather the tartar sauce inside them, making sure to achieve wall-to-wall coverage. Tuck a couple of tomato slices and then three fried oysters into each bun. If the oysters are huge, you might need to use just two in each bun and snack on every third. Drape all the pickled stuff on top and enjoy immediately.

MAKES 6 BUNS

6 Eventide Steamed Buns (page 162)

Canola oil for frying

1 pound masa harina (see Glossary)

18 oysters, shucked

Kosher salt

1 cup House Tartar Sauce (page 174)

2 large, ripe red tomatoes, sliced

1 cup drained Pickled Daikon (page 193)

1 cup Pickled Red Onion (page 192)

½ cup Pickled Jalapeño (page 193)

CRAB ROLL

Yuzu Kosho Mayonnaise

MAKES 4 ROLLS

12 ounces fresh, cooked crabmeat

¼ to ½ cup Yuzu Kosho Mayonnaise (page 173)

4 Eventide Steamed Buns (page 162)

Lobster roll is king in Maine, and for good reason. But while tourists and Mainers alike argue about the various merits of each version of the lobster roll, the secret gem of seafood shack fare—the crab roll—often gets overlooked by outsiders. As many Mainers will say, "If the lobster roll is for tourists, the crab roll is for us."

Rock crab and Jonah crab, the two species used for Maine crab rolls, are basically bycatch from lobstering, but rarely do you see live or steamed whole crabs for sale. Historically, fishing families kept the crabs they pulled in, picked them at home, and sold the meat for additional income (many still do).

Our crab roll—aside from being on a steamed bun—is pretty traditional and has very little in it to get in the way of the sweet taste of the crab. We add yuzu kosho to the mayonnaise dressing for a little zing. How much mayonnaise you add is a matter of preference. If you like the crab salad creamier, by all means add more mayonnaise. We like just enough to add some richness to the crab and bind the mixture, but not so much that it shouts down the natural sweetness of the crab. —*Andrew*

Carefully inspect the crabmeat with your fingers to make sure not even a little bit of shell remains. (Don't trust your eyes; this needs to be a tactile search.) Starting with ¼ cup, mix the mayonnaise into the crabmeat and stir to incorporate. At this point, check to make sure it's dressed and seasoned to your liking, adding the rest of the mayonnaise if you like.

Place the buns in a large pot set with a steamer insert, or a bamboo steamer set over a wok, and steam for 5 minutes, or until they are very hot, soft, and pliable. Remove the pot from the heat, but leave the buns in the steamer to keep warm.

Divide the crab mixture among the four buns and serve immediately.

THE FISH SANDWICH

Tartar, Tare, Iceberg Lettuce

MAKES 4 SANDWICHES

4 cups water

1 tablespoon kosher salt, plus more to season

1 pound hake fillets (or cod, haddock, or pollock), skin and pinbones removed

Canola oil for frying

1 cup all-purpose flour

2 eggs

2 cups panko bread crumbs

4 Sesame Burger Buns, sliced open (page 163)

½ cup Fillet of Fish Tartar Sauce (page 174)

½ cup Tare (page 168)

1 cup drained Bread and Butter Pickles (page 193)

1½ cups shredded iceberg lettuce

Sometimes inspiration comes from funny, terrible places. A couple of years into Eventide's existence, we realized it was kind of absurd that we had never had a fish sandwich on the menu. For reasons we'll never be able to explain, we attempted to refamiliarize ourselves with the format by grabbing a bag o' fish sandwiches from a not-to-be-mentioned monolithic fast food restaurant. They were terrible—not at all what nostalgia had led us to believe.

We knew we could do a whole lot better, so we charged Graeme Miller, Eventide's sous chef at the time, with creating a new and better fish sandwich that would hit all the familiar notes of simple, classic New England fried seafood sandwiches. Our twist was borrowing from the Japanese *katsu*-style dishes, because they're slightly more refined than your average fry-up. Graeme knocked it out of the park with a spot-on classic tartar sauce and brined, pressed, and panko-crusted hake fillet slathered with *tare*. The result creates its own nostalgia. —*Andrew*

Pour the water and salt into a nonreactive container. Stir to dissolve the salt and create a brine. Cut the hake fillets in four equal portions and place them in the brine. Cover the container and put it in the refrigerator for at least 1 hour, or up to overnight.

Fill a large pot with 3 inches of canola oil and heat on high to 350°F (or bring a deep-fryer to 350°F). Line a plate with paper towels.

Remove the fish from the brine and pat dry with paper towels. Place a big piece of plastic wrap on your counter or a cutting board. Put a piece of hake on the plastic wrap and cover with another piece of plastic wrap. Pound gently with a meat mallet or a small pan until you have a ⅓- to ½-inch-thick piece of fish. Repeat with the remaining fillets and set aside.

Pull out three shallow bowls to set up your breading station. Set up a plate or rack nearby. In the first bowl, put the flour. Crack the eggs into the second bowl and beat them with a splash of water. In the third bowl, put the panko bread crumbs. Dip each fillet in the flour to cover and shake off the excess back into the bowl. Then dip in the egg to cover

CONTINUED

THE FISH SANDWICH

CONTINUED

and shake the excess back into the bowl. Finally, dip the fillets in the bread crumbs to cover and shake the excess back into the bowl. Set the breaded fillets aside on the plate or rack.

Set up a large pot with a steamer insert, or a bamboo steamer set over a wok, and steam the burger buns to freshen them up, about 3 minutes. Remove the pot from the heat, but leave the buns in the steamer to keep warm.

Carefully slip the fillets into the hot oil, working in batches if necessary to avoid overcrowding the pot. Fry the fish for 3 to 4 minutes, until the crust is golden brown and a cake tester or skewer slides through the fish without resistance. Using a slotted spoon or wire-mesh strainer, remove the fish from the oil and place on a paper towel–lined plate; sprinkle with salt.

Pour a light film of oil in a pan and heat over high heat. Pull the buns out of the steamer and lightly toast the cut sides for 30 to 60 seconds. Slather the bottom of each bun with an abundant amount of tartar sauce and place a piece of fried fish on top. Drizzle the fish with the tare, then top with the pickles, a good amount of shredded lettuce, and the top bun. Serve immediately.

SMOKED TOFU SANDWICH

Onion Rings, Jalapeño Mayonnaise

Rich and meaty, but entirely vegetarian, this sandwich has become a favorite among our guests. Marinade leftover after the tofu is marinated is great for any number of grillable or smokable foods. It will last a month in the fridge or many months in the freezer.

To make the smoked tofu, in a blender, puree the sugars, water, salt, soy sauce, garlic, jalapeños, lemon juice, and vinegar. Transfer to a large bowl. Cut each block of tofu into three thin squares about the size of the burger buns, place in the marinade, and refrigerate in a covered container for at least 1 hour, and preferably overnight. Drain the tofu. Preheat a smoker (see Glossary) with a water pan in it to 200°F. Smoke the tofu for 2 hours until it is slightly leathery on the surface. Remove and let cool.

To make the onions, fill a large pot with 3 inches of canola oil and heat on high to 350°F (or bring a deep-fryer to 350°F). Line a plate with paper towels. Pour the buttermilk in a large bowl and the masa in a separate large bowl. Soak the onions in the buttermilk for 5 minutes. Remove the onions from the buttermilk, allowing the excess to drip off, and dredge them in the masa. Make sure that the onions are coated individually, so they don't clump into a large mass. Let the onions sit in the masa for 5 minutes to 30 minutes (patience yields crispier onions). Fry the onions until golden brown, 3 to 5 minutes. Using a slotted spoon or wire-mesh strainer, transfer to a paper towel–lined plate and season with salt.

In a large pot set up as a steamer, or a bamboo steamer set over a wok, steam the buns to refresh them, about 3 minutes. Remove the pot from the heat, but leave the buns in the steamer to keep warm.

To prepare the sandwiches, in a large skillet, warm a thin film of oil over medium-high heat and add the smoked tofu, shaking the pan frequently until the tofu is warm all the way through, 3 to 5 minutes. Transfer to a bowl and wipe out the pan.

Pull the buns out of the steamer and, in the same pan slicked with oil over medium-high heat, lightly toast the cut sides. Smear the mayo on every available cut surface of bun. Place the tofu on the bottom buns and pile the onions, tomato slices, pickles, and lettuce on top. Add the bun tops and serve immediately.

MAKES 6 SANDWICHES

SMOKED TOFU

1 cup maple sugar (or substitute light brown sugar)

1 cup light brown sugar

1½ cups water

6 tablespoons kosher salt

1½ cups light soy sauce

1 cup garlic cloves, chopped

1 cup stemmed, seeded, and chopped jalapeños

¾ cup fresh lemon juice

¾ cup rice wine vinegar

2 (1-pound) blocks extra-firm tofu

ONION

2 cups thinly sliced onions in rings

Canola oil for frying

1 cup buttermilk

2 cups masa harina (see Glossary)

Kosher salt

6 Sesame Burger Buns, sliced open (page 163)

Canola oil

½ cup Jalapeño Mayonnaise (page 173)

2 ripe tomatoes, sliced

½ cup Pickled Jalapeño (page 173), drained

¼ cup Pickled Red Onion (page 192), drained

2 cups shredded iceberg lettuce

EVENTIDE BURGER

Tallow Mayonnaise, Iceberg Lettuce, American Cheese

I fought the idea of having a burger on the menu until we became overwhelmed by aged beef. We started buying whole sides for the restaurants without fully realizing the sheer mass of product we'd be dealing with. After you've exhausted yourself butchering and trimming, prepping lean cuts for rare beef salads, finding walk-in real estate for aging the rib section and the short loin, rendering the fat, and making charcuterie, you've still got a lot of beef left over. Anders Tallberg, our sous chef at Hugo's at the time, ground some fatty beef and made the first Eventide burger. It hasn't changed since.

Our burger blend changes based on what cuts are being used in the restaurants, but one thing is constant: it is absurdly fatty. We make our burger blend fatty because fat tastes good, it helps get a super-caramelized crust, and it helps us achieve full utilization of our beeves. If you're looking to re-create our blend, aim for at least 25 percent fat. Cooking Eventide burger patties over an open flame is not a good idea. This is a thinner, smashed-style burger, so cook it in a pan or on a griddle and beware of flare-ups! —*Mike*

Set up a large pot with a steamer insert, or a bamboo steamer set over a wok, and steam the burger buns to freshen them up, about 3 minutes. Remove the pot from the heat, but keep the buns in the steamer to stay warm.

While the buns are steaming, portion the ground beef into six equal patties (¼ pound each) and flatten each patty to about ⅓ inch.

Heat a griddle over high heat. Season the patties aggressively with salt on both sides and place on the hot griddle. You are cooking a smashed patty-style burger, so forget about medium rare. You want it cooked through and crispy on both sides, so use that sizzling beef fat to your advantage by letting the burger wallow in it. When the patties are crispy on one side, after 2 to 3 minutes, flip them carefully and top each patty with ¼ cup of the pickled onions and 2 slices of cheese. By the time the bottom side is done, 2 to 3 minutes, your cheese should be melted.

Remove the buns from the steamer and toast the cut sides in the beef fat remaining on the griddle. Place a burger on each bun's bottom side and pile the lettuce on top. Smear each top side with a good helping of the mayo and close the burger loop. Serve immediately.

MAKES 6 BURGERS

6 Sesame Burger Buns (page 163), sliced open

1½ pounds ground beef

Kosher salt

1 cup drained Pickled Red Onion (page 192)

12 slices American cheese

2 cups shredded iceberg lettuce

½ cup Tallow Mayonnaise (page 173)

LOBSTER STEW

Green Curry, Saltines

GREEN CURRY

½ small yellow onion, coarsely chopped

½ jalapeño, stemmed and coarsely chopped

¼ stalk of lemongrass, halved lengthwise, outer layers removed, chopped

2 garlic cloves, chopped

½ inch knob ginger, peeled and coarsely chopped

½ bunch cilantro, chopped

LOBSTER STOCK

10 ounces Eventide Prepared Lobster Meat (page 114), plus shucked bodies and shells

3 tablespoons canola oil

8 cups water

2 sweet potatoes, washed, peeled, and cubed

2 cups Dashi (page 177)

3 tablespoons Golden Mountain sauce (see Glossary)

¼ cup fish sauce

½ packed cup palm sugar (see Glossary) or light brown sugar

½ cup heavy cream

1 cup coconut milk

¾ cup drained Confit Mushrooms (page 186) made with maitakes

Kosher salt

Chive Oil (page 183) for garnish

Chile Oil (page 183) for garnish

Lobster stew is one of the pillars of Maine cooking. But really, *stew* is kind of a misnomer. The traditional version is a thin, rich, dairy-based broth with picked lobster meat and a slick of reddish butter on top. It usually consists of fewer than five ingredients: lobsters (with all the tomalley or liver), butter, milk or cream, and maybe a little nutmeg and brandy. We took this approach at Eventide for a while, but we got tired of people who expected a Frenchified bisque telling us it wasn't a stew. So we changed it.

Taking cues from *tom kha*, the classic coconut milk–based Thai soup, and enriching it further with umami-heavy Golden Mountain sauce and confit maitake mushrooms, we created this decadent stew. It looks and feels like a classic lobster stew but registers on the palate in a much more complex way. Serve with saltines (page 166). —*Andrew*

To make the curry, in a food processor, combine the onion, jalapeño, lemongrass, garlic, ginger, and cilantro and process to form a paste. Set aside.

To make the stock, clean the lobster bodies by pulling the top shell away from the body. Cut the lungs off (they look like four grey fingers on either side of the body), rinse the bodies and shells under cold water, and reserve.

In a large stockpot, heat the oil on high until nearly smoking. Add the reserved lobster bodies and shells, lower the heat to medium, and stir vigorously until the shells caramelize and turn a deep red color, about 10 minutes. Add the paste and sauté for 2 minutes, mixing everything together thoroughly. Add the water and scrape the bottom of the pot to remove all the caramelized, flavorful bits. Raise the heat to high and bring a boil; turn the heat down to a bare simmer and cook for 60 minutes. Turn off the heat and strain through a fine-mesh strainer into a new pot.

Add 1 cup of the diced sweet potato (pick the imperfect cubes) to the stock and cook at a simmer for 10 to 12 minutes, until they are tender. Puree with a blender to thicken the stock a bit. Add the dashi, Golden Mountain sauce, fish sauce, palm sugar, cream, coconut milk, and remaining diced sweet potato and simmer until the sweet potato is tender, about 10 minutes. Remove from the heat, stir in the confit mushrooms and lobster meat, and season with salt to taste. Ladle into six bowls and garnish with the chive oil and chile oil.

NEW ENGLAND CLAM CHOWDER

Salt Pork, Saltines

SERVES 4 TO 6

Kosher salt

5 pounds live chowder clams

2 pounds live steamer clams

2 (2-inch) pieces dried kombu

2 cups water

2 tablespoons unsalted butter

1 yellow onion, diced

1 pound medium-starch potatoes (like Yukon gold or Kennebec), peeled and diced

2 cups heavy cream

1 teaspoon freshly cracked or ground black pepper

Leaves from 1 to 2 thyme sprigs

¼ pound homemade Salt Pork (page 202) or store-bought bacon (optional)

2 or 3 sheets nori

Minced chives for garnish

Chive Oil (page 183) for garnish

Saltine Crackers (page 166) for serving

This is the one. The lobster roll gets all the glory, but New England clam chowder tells the most profound story of Yankee cooking. While entire books have rightfully been written on the topic, clam chowder is incredibly simple and pure at its core. Clam juice. Potatoes. Dairy. Everything else is just window dressing. Remember this when you're giving it a go in your kitchen, and don't mess it up too much.

This chowder is likely going to be thinner than the ones you may have encountered in a bread bowl. That's a good thing. It means you haven't squandered and sullied the gift of briny, steely gold that chowder clams give up with a paste of flour and butter. It's all about the broth, which deserves and should be given the fanatical attention usually reserved for ramen and pho broths. Keep it pure!

For this reason, we can't recommend strongly enough that you start with fresh, whole clams rather than canned clams and/or clam juice. When you sip the strained juice of steamed fresh clams, you will understand why. Better yet, next time you're on a summer beach vacation in New England, go dig some clams yourself. I can personally attest that wading in waist-deep water in murky bays, feeling for clams with your bare feet, is the ultimate family treasure hunt. Just make sure you look up local recreational shell-fishing rules, regulations, and closures if you plan to go on the hunt. —*Andrew*

Fill two separate bowls with cold, clean water that has been seasoned with kosher salt to taste like seawater. In a colander, rinse the exterior dirt from both types of clams and then submerge them separately in the bowls of water. Leave them to sit for 30 minutes to encourage them to release their grit. Drain the clams separately in a colander, rinsing them under running water, and shake them gently to drain. Rinse the pieces of kombu and set aside.

CONTINUED

NEW ENGLAND CLAM CHOWDER

CONTINUED

In a pot, combine the chowder clams, water, and 1 piece of kombu and bring to a boil. Turn down to a simmer, cover, and cook until the clams have just opened, 5 to 10 minutes. Remove the clams to a bowl, keeping the liquid in the pot. Add the steamer clams and the second piece of kombu to the broth, and repeat. Transfer the steamers to a bowl and strain the cooking liquid through a fine-mesh strainer into a separate bowl. Pick the meat from both types of clams, keeping the two types of clams in separate bowls and making sure to remove the muddy sheath from the siphon of the steamer clams. Place the clams in cold, fresh water and agitate them with your hands for a minute or so to remove any excess sand. Drain and coarsely chop the chowder clams but keep the steamer clams whole.

In a large pot, melt the butter over medium-high heat. When the butter is just sizzling, add the onion and potatoes and cook until they soften and start to brown, about 3 minutes. Add the strained clam juice, cream, black pepper, and thyme and bring to a boil. Turn the heat down to low and simmer until the potatoes are cooked through, about 10 minutes. Add the chopped clams and stir to incorporate and warm them.

Line a plate with paper towels. Cut the salt pork into either ¼-inch slices or 1 by ¼ by ¼-inch cubes (also known as lardons) and cook in a hot skillet for 3 to 5 minutes, stirring frequently, until nicely browned. Transfer to the paper towel–lined plate.

Holding the sheets of nori with tongs, wave them separately over a gas burner flame a few times until they become lighter in color and fragrant (or heat a large skillet on high heat and toast the nori on both sides for 30 seconds).

Ladle the finished chowder into four to six bowls, aiming for about two parts broth to one part chunky goodness. Add a couple of pieces of salt pork and a crushed half sheet of nori to each bowl. Garnish with chives and chive oil. Serve immediately with saltines.

BROILED BLACK COD

Spicy Miso, Hijiki, Citrus

We didn't have regular access to black cod, also known as sablefish, until a few years ago when Portland seafood wholesaler Browne Trading Company started carrying it. It's a wonderful fish and incredibly forgiving. If you've had bad luck overcooking fish, rendering it dry and flavorless, then this fish is for you. It also takes on cure and smoke marvelously.

The glaze is one of those sauces that can easily become a crutch. It does all of the hard work of a good barbecue sauce by delivering sweetness, acid, and heat. It serves as a great glaze for everything from broiled fish to fried chicken wings.

A dramatic, dark black sauce, hijiki puree adds a little visual theatre to the plate. But for those of us who are interested in eating it, there's a vegetal richness that's hard to place. . . . Its decidedly marine with enough sweetness to stand up to grilled and charred foods. Our vegan and vegetarian guests are big fans. —*Mike*

Portion the cod into four equal pieces, toss in the spicy miso glaze, and marinate in a covered container in the refrigerator for at least 2 hours, but preferably overnight.

Lightly rinse the cod under cold water, pat dry, and set on a lightly greased baking sheet skin-side up. Preheat the broiler to high with an oven rack in the uppermost position.

In a bowl, toss the daikon, carrots, and sesame seeds with the vinaigrette.

Put the baking sheet under the broiler and cook the cod until the skin is sizzling and crispy and a cake tester or sharp knife slides through the center of fish without resistance, about 6 minutes. Be careful not to burn the fish skin. If it gets too dark, too fast, pull it out of the oven and reduce the heat in the oven to 300°F. Return the baking sheet to the oven and let the fish finish cooking, which should take no more than a few minutes.

Swipe the hijiki puree with a spoon evenly across a platter or four plates and place a pile of the carrot-daikon mixture on top. Place the fish on the vegetables and garnish with scallion greens. Serve immediately.

CONTINUED

SERVES 4

1 pound black cod fillet, skin on

¼ cup Spicy Miso Glaze (recipe follows)

1 small 6-inch daikon radish, peeled and thinly sliced

2 carrots, peeled and thinly sliced

1 teaspoon sesame seeds, black and white mixed

1 tablespoon Citrus Vinaigrette (page 62)

½ cup Hijiki Puree (recipe follows)

2 tablespoons thinly sliced scallion greens

BROILED BLACK COD

CONTINUED

SPICY MISO GLAZE

MAKES 2 TO 3 CUPS

⅓ cup rice wine vinegar

⅓ cup mirin

8-inch piece ginger, peeled and sliced (1½ cups)

¼ cup red yuzu kosho (see Glossary)

2½ teaspoons Asian sesame oil

1½ teaspoons fresh lime juice

½ cup shiro miso (see Glossary)

In a blender, puree the vinegar, mirin, ginger, yuzu kosho, sesame oil, lime juice, and shiro miso. Use immediately and store any extra in a covered jar in the fridge for up to 1 week. Extra glaze can be used for other roasted and grilled proteins and vegetables.

HIJIKI PUREE

MAKES 2 TO 3 CUPS

½ cup dried hijiki (see Glossary)

¼ cup thinly sliced shallots

1 cup water

½ cup rice wine vinegar

¼ cup sugar

½ cup Fried Aromatics Oil (page 184) made with shallots

In a small saucepan, combine the hijiki, shallots, water, vinegar, and sugar and bring to a simmer over medium heat, then remove from the heat. Let the mixture cool for 5 minutes. Transfer to a blender, reserving a bit of the liquid. Puree on high until the mixture is smooth and has the consistency of pancake batter. Add some of the reserved liquid if you need to loosen things up a bit. With the blender running, slowly add the shallot oil until it is fully incorporated, giving the puree a luxurious texture and sheen. Cool the mixture to room temperature before using. Any leftover puree will keep in an airtight container in the refrigerator for up to 2 weeks. The excess makes a nice dressing for salads or vegetables.

BROILED JUMBO
WINTER POINT OYSTERS

Korean BBQ Sauce, Daikon Slaw, Candied Nuts

For years, the Hennesseys, proprietors of Winter Point Oyster Farm, tried to sell the jumbo oysters that had grown beyond normal "market" size. The bad boys were more than five inches long and between six and ten years old! When they asked me if the restaurants might have any use for them, I jumped at the chance.

When I lived in the Pacific Northwest, I periodically came across roadside shacks selling jumbo grilled oysters smothered with BBQ sauce or hot sauce. What could be more delicious? This homage to those spots was on the opening menu at Eventide and remained there for years until we finally used up the Hennesseys' backlog of jumbo Winter Points. It still makes an appearance when John Hennessey drags up new behemoths. Ask your fishmonger if they can request overgrown oysters from the oyster farmers they work with. This recipe can be made with regular large oysters but the dish won't be as grand! —*Andrew*

In a large pot set up with a steamer insert, or a bamboo steamer set over a wok, steam the oysters until they just barely start to open, 2 to 3 minutes. Remove the oysters from the steamer and let them cool for a few minutes until you can handle them. Pour the Korean BBQ sauce in a bowl.

Using an oyster knife, separate the oyster meat from the bottom shells and discard the top shells. Reserve any liquid and add it and the oyster meats to the Korean BBQ sauce, tossing to coat.

In a small bowl, toss the daikon with the vinaigrette and sesame seeds.

Preheat the broiler to high with an oven rack in the uppermost position.

On a baking sheet, make eight separate ¼-cup piles of salt. Place the oyster shells on the salt piles, which will hold them upright. Return the oyster meats to the shells and spoon the Korean BBQ sauce over them. Broil the oysters until the sauce browns nicely, 3 to 4 minutes. Transfer the oysters to a serving bowl with a 1-inch layer of kosher salt or uncooked rice in the bottom to hold the oysters upright. Place a little pile of marinated daikon on each oyster. Scatter the nuts and drizzle the chive oil and chile oil over the oysters. Serve immediately.

SERVES 4

8 jumbo oysters, preferably Winter Points with 5- to 8-inch shells

¼ cup Korean BBQ Sauce (page 168)

1 cup peeled and julienned daikon

1 tablespoon Citrus Vinaigrette (page 62)

1 teaspoon sesame seeds, white and black mixed

¼ cup chopped Candied Nuts (page 191)

1 tablespoon Chive Oil (page 183)

1 tablespoon Chile Oil (page 183)

2 cups kosher salt

Uncooked rice or kosher salt for nesting the shells

SCALLOP WAFFLE-YAKI

Kabayaki, Umami Mayonnaise, Tempura Crispies, Pickled Kombu, Bonito Flakes, Nori, Scallion

MAKES 8 WAFFLES

4 strips bacon, thinly julienned

TEMPURA CRISPIES

¼ cup tapioca starch

¼ cup potato starch

2 tablespoons rice flour

Canola oil for frying

Kosher salt

4 sheets nori

WAFFLE BATTER

½ pound (any size) scallops

3 eggs, separated

⅓ cup Dashi (page 177)

2 teaspoons light soy sauce

2 tablespoons Confit Mushroom Oil (page 186), made with maitakes

⅔ cup all-purpose flour

2 tablespoons Kabayaki Sauce (page 167)

2 tablespoons Umami Mayonnaise (page 173)

¼ cup Pickled Kombu (page 193)

½ cup bonito flakes

2 tablespoons trimmed and chopped scallions (green parts only) for garnish

For some reason, I am obsessed with the flavor of caramelized scallops. As many professional or prolific home cooks know, there are certain little treats or morsels that never make it to the dinner table because the person preparing the food hijacked them. The deeply browned end-cut of a roast or the stubborn crispy bits of chicken skin that get stuck to the pan are good examples. For me, with seared scallops, it's the little bits of caramel that cling to the spatula, or bread dipped in the leftover butter that remains in the pan after basting the scallops.

It's always been part of our mission to convert these kinds of culinary treats into something that can make it to the table. After trying unsuccessfully for years to harness the flavor of caramelized scallops, I had an epiphany one Sunday morning at home as I watched the waffles I was cooking for my kids slowly deepen in color. I realized that a scallop puree, worked into a waffle batter, could turn into something brilliant using all that heated surface area on a waffle iron. It worked spectacularly on its own and became an instant classic for the Eventide menu when we gave it the Japanese *izakaya* (Japanese pub) treatment where savory pancakes and fritters like *takoyaki* and *okonomiyaki* are buried in crunchy bits and savory sauces, turning them into the perfectly crushable late-night snack. —*Andrew*

Preheat the oven to 200°F. Line a baking sheet with paper towels.

Put the bacon in a shallow pan over medium heat and cook for 5 to 7 minutes until the fat has rendered out and the bacon is dark and crispy. With a slotted spoon, transfer the bacon to the prepared baking sheet and place in the oven for 10 minutes. The heat from the oven will melt excess grease onto the paper towels. Toss the greasy paper towels and set the bacon aside in a bowl.

To make the crispies, in a large bowl, mix the starches and flour. Whisk in ¼ cup water, and add more by the tablespoon after that until the mixture reaches the consistency of a very loose pancake batter.

CONTINUED

SCALLOP WAFFLE-YAKI

CONTINUED

Line a baking sheet with paper towels. Fill a large pot with 3 inches of canola oil and heat on high to 350°F (or bring a deep-fryer to 350°F). Dip a whisk in the batter and, immediately but carefully, lift it over the pot or fryer and drizzle the batter into the hot oil. The drops should disperse into small bits and bubble vigorously. Once they stop bubbling, after 1 minute or so, use a slotted spoon or wire-mesh strainer to transfer them to the prepared sheet. Season with salt. Work in batches until you've used up all the batter. Place the sheet in the oven for 10 minutes to remove excess grease. Transfer the crispies to a bowl and set aside.

Holding a sheet of nori with tongs, wave it over a gas burner flame a few times until it becomes darker and fragrant (or heat a large skillet on high heat and toast the nori on both sides for 30 seconds). Set aside. Repeat with the remaining nori sheets.

To make the waffle batter, in a food processor, puree the scallops until smooth. Add the egg yolks and puree until smooth. With the motor still running, drizzle in the dashi and soy sauce. Transfer the mixture to a large bowl and whisk in the maitake oil until smooth. Gently stir in the flour with a spatula, taking care not to overmix (lumps are okay!).

Preheat a waffle iron on the medium setting.

In a separate bowl, whip 2 of the egg whites into soft peaks with a whisk or with a stand or hand-held mixer (reserve the third white for another use). One-third at a time, use a spatula to very gently fold the whipped egg whites into the batter until just barely incorporated.

Pour in enough batter to cover the bottom of the waffle iron and cook on the medium setting for 5 to 7 minutes, until lightly browned and crispy. Transfer the waffle to a plate and repeat with the rest of the batter. (The waffles can be served immediately or made 2 or 3 days in advance and stored in a covered container in the fridge. To reheat them, fry them in a hot pan with canola oil or crisp them up in a toaster or oven.)

To serve, place the waffles on four separate plates or a large platter and drizzle the kabayaki sauce and umami mayonnaise over them. Sprinkle the bacon, crispies, pickled kombu, bonito flakes, and scallions over the waffles. Finally, crush the toasted nori sheets in your hands and sprinkle them over the waffles. Serve immediately.

GRILLED SWORDFISH BELLY

Roasted Peppers, Nixtamalized Rye Berries,
Confit Chanterelles

Swordfish is one of the most important fished species in the Northwestern Atlantic, and you can find it in about every grocery store and fish market in New England. Swordfish loin is what you'll see most often, but that's not the cut that appeals to us, because it can get dry and chalky when cooked. Swordfish belly is a different matter. Like bluefin tuna, swordfish store much of their fat in their belly muscles, which results in an incredibly dense, rich, and flavorful meat when cooked.

We use swordfish from northern waters, particularly the Gulf of Maine or around Nova Scotia, at their peak season in late summer to early fall. That's when they gorge on shrimp and krill and become fatty and orange-hued. You may hear fishmongers call them "pumpkin swords."

For this recipe, we use Maine rye berries—which is the whole grain before it is ground to rye flour—and we transform them with the traditional South American process of nixtamalization, which is the process of cooking grains in calcium hydroxide (i.e. slaked lime or pickling lime), typically applied to field corn to make it more digestible and turn it into hominy or masa. We just love the texture and flavor the nixtamalization process imparts on the rye berries. Caution: Be very careful with calcium hydroxide. Do not inhale the powder. Work with gloves when handling it. If you're wary of or can't find food-grade calcium hydroxide, you can just simmer the rye berries in 4 cups water in a small pot for 60 to 75 minutes until tender. You'll be missing out on that nixtamalized flavor though!
—*Andrew*

Cut the swordfish belly into four equal portions and let the fish rest for 30 to 60 minutes at room temperature.

Light a two-zone charcoal grill by gathering and lighting the coals on one side for direct cooking and leaving the other side cooler for indirect cooking (or preheat the oven to 300°F).

CONTINUED

SERVES 4

1 pound swordfish belly, skin and belly lining removed

4 to 6 sweet peppers (banana, Cubanelle, red Carmen, or bell) or 1 (16-ounce) jar roasted red peppers

2 cups Nixtamalized Rye Berries (recipe follows)

2 tablespoons unsalted butter

¼ cup Fish Stock (page 180) or water

Kosher salt

Fresh lime juice for seasoning

Canola oil for rubbing

¼ cup Confit Mushrooms (page 186) made with chanterelles for garnish

½ cup Puffed Beet Chips (page 190), torn into bite-size pieces for garnish

Micro basil or chopped regular basil for garnish

GRILLED SWORDFISH BELLY

CONTINUED

Grill the peppers directly on the coals (or directly over your gas flame of your stove) until the skin is charred but the peppers are not totally limp. Transfer from the grill to a bowl and cover with plastic wrap. When the peppers are cooled enough to handle, peel the skin off of them, reserving any liquid that has collected in the container. Rinse the peppers under cold water to get rid of any burnt flecks. Cut the peppers into ½-inch rings and set aside, separate from the reserved liquid.

In a pan, combine the rye berries with the butter, the fish stock, and reserved pepper juice and warm through over medium heat on your range or right on your grill. Season to taste with salt and lime juice. Keep warm.

Pat the swordfish dry and rub with canola oil. Season well on both sides with salt. Place on the hot section of the grill (or on a preheated grill pan or skillet over high heat on the stove) and char, 1 to 2 minutes per side. Move to the cooler part of grill (or to the preheated oven) and cook very gently until a cake tester or skewer slides through the center of the fish without resistance, 6 to 10 minutes.

To serve, use a slotted spoon to divide the warm rye berries equally among four plates. Put the grilled fish on top of the rye berries and garnish with roasted pepper rings, confit chanterelles, beet chips, and micro basil. Serve immediately.

NIXTAMALIZED RYE BERRIES

MAKES 3 CUPS

1 tablespoon food-grade calcium hydroxide

4 cups cold water

1½ teaspoons kosher salt

1 cup rye berries

In a large saucepan, mix the calcium hydroxide with the water and salt. Stir well with a whisk to combine. Add the rye berries to the pot and bring it to a simmer over medium heat, stirring frequently. Turn the heat to low and cook until the rye berries are just tender, 10 to 15 minutes. Remove from the heat and let cool in the solution.

Pour the rye berries and the solution into an airtight container and refrigerate for at least 4 hours or overnight. Drain the rye berries, discarding the liquid, and rinse them thoroughly in several changes of water, until the water draining from them runs clear. Rinsing is very important, as excess residual calcium hydroxide can be damaging to your digestive system. Refrigerate the berries in an airtight container for up to 1 week.

TEMPURA SMELTS

Cucumber Tartar, Cucumber Salt

They say what grows together goes together, and that's generally true. But sometimes fish from Maine and vegetables from California come together in a dish that's greater than the sum of its parts. Fresh smelt tastes and smells like cucumbers, so this combination works exceedingly well.

The success of this dish really relies on getting exceedingly fresh smelt. Most smelt you come across in markets are headless and gutted and have been soaked in a preservative, robbing them of their best qualities. We buy smelts only when they are running in the winter, and we can get them fully intact and can smell their cucumber-y freshness. They are rare, but we do not pass them up when we find them, and neither should you. —*Mike*

Place a smelt on a cutting board with its belly facing away from you, and use the tip of a knife to cut through the spine just behind the gills. Grasping the body in one hand, give a tug on the head to remove the viscera and the head in one go. Bonus points for those who leave the roe or milt sac in the belly cavity (it's delicious). You can also ask your fishmonger to clean your smelts for you. Repeat with the remaining smelts.

In a large bowl, combine the flours, tapioca starch, baking powder, and cornstarch and mix thoroughly.

Fill a large, heavy pot with 3 inches of canola oil and heat on high to 350°F (or bring a deep-fryer to 350°F). Line a plate with paper towels.

Dredge the cleaned smelts in the flour mixture, shake off the excess, and slip into the hot oil. Fry in batches until golden brown, 3 to 5 minutes, transfer them to the paper towel–lined plate, and season with the cucumber salt. Serve immediately with the tartar sauce.

SERVES 6 TO 8

2 pounds fresh head-on smelts

3 cups all-purpose flour

2 tablespoons rice flour

2½ tablespoons tapioca starch

1 heaping teaspoon baking powder

2 teaspoons cornstarch

Canola oil for frying

Cucumber Salt (recipe follows)

½ cup Cucumber Tartar Sauce (page 174)

CUCUMBER SALT

MAKES 2 TABLESPOONS

1 large unwaxed cucumber   1 tablespoon kosher salt

Peel the cucumber and dry the peel in a food dehydrator at 145°F or in a 350°F oven that has just been turned off, until it is completely brittle, which should take about 12 hours. Put the peel in a spice grinder and add the salt. Grind to a fine powder and store in a sealed container at room temperature. This will keep indefinitely.

CALÇOTES

Ramps, Romesco, Toasted Hazelnut

SERVES 4

ROMESCO

1 cup almonds

1 cup hazelnuts

5 cups dried guajillo chiles, stemmed, seeded, and torn into pieces

2 cups roasted bell peppers, drained and chopped

1 (15-ounce) can tomatoes, drained and chopped

¼ cup minced garlic

2 tablespoons smoked paprika

¼ cup sherry vinegar

1 cup extra-virgin olive oil

Kosher salt

RAMPS

2 to 3 pounds ramps or young spring onions

Extra virgin olive oil

Kosher salt

A *calçotada* is wonderful late-winter tradition in Catalan Spain, where freshly dug green onions are grilled over coals, wrapped in newspaper, and served with romesco sauce. Here in Maine, in the spring, we dip grilled ramps (wild green onions) in romesco sauce and eat them whole, which is just about as elementally sublime as you can get. We're fond of turning ramp-foraging trips into camping trips, just as an excuse to grill freshly dug ramps over a campfire. During the fleeting ramp season in Maine, which basically covers the month of May, we try to give our guests this little taste of tradition as well. This is best done outside with several *porróns*, a traditional Spanish glass wine pitcher that is often used to pour wine directly into one's mouth, filled with cava or some other light, fresh, young wine. —*Andrew*

Preheat the oven to 350°F.

To make the romesco, spread out the almonds and hazelnuts on a baking sheet and toast in the oven for 5 to 7 minutes, until they become fragrant and darken slightly in color. Transfer to a bowl. Set aside ¼ cup of the hazelnuts for the garnish.

In a large cast-iron pan over medium heat, dry-roast the chile pieces for 5 minutes, until they are aromatic and darken in color. Transfer to a heatproof bowl.

Pour in enough very hot water to cover the chiles, cover the bowl w plastic wrap, and let it sit for 30 minutes. With a slotted spoon, trans the chiles from the bowl to a blender. With the motor running, slowl pour in the soaking water until you have just enough for the mixture catch the blade and create a vortex. Blend for several minutes, add a bit more water, if necessary, to keep things moving.

Add the almonds, the remaining hazelnuts, roasted bell peppers, tomatoes, and garlic and blend until homogenous. Add the paprika ε vinegar and, with the blender running, stream in the olive oil. Seaso with salt to taste.

CONTINUED

CALÇOTES

CONTINUED

Cut off the hairy, woody roots on the bottom of the ramp bulbs. Gently rinse the ramps to remove any dirt or other material clinging to the leaves or bulb. Pat dry with paper towels or use a salad spinner.

Set up a charcoal or gas grill for high heat and warm the romesco sauce in a small pot on the grill as it warms up or on a burner over low heat. Brush the ramps with olive oil, season them with salt, and put them on the grill. Keep the ramps moving on the grill, taking care to keep them perpendicular to the grill grates so they don't fall through (you can also use a wire baking sheet rack on top of the grill grate for this, if you don't mind subjecting the rack to the grill). Try to focus most of the heat on the bulbs. They're done after no more than 2 to 3 minutes, when the bulbs and leaves are nicely charred and the bulbs have softened when squeezed. (To cook indoors, preheat a grill plate over high heat. Working in batches, place the ramps on the hot grill plate in a single layer and grill until the bulbs and leaves are charred and the bulbs have softened.)

Serve the ramps in a magisterial pile on a large plate or platter and place the pot of romesco alongside, encouraging your guests to dip the ramps into the romesco and lower them into their mouths. Make your peace with the inevitable shirt stains. Did we mention these are best served with several *porróns*?

BRAISED MATSUTAKE

Ramen Broth, Pickled Spruce Tips, Butter

Hot take: Matsutake mushrooms are the single greatest culinary gift that the woods of Maine—or the woods anywhere, for that matter—have to offer. Truffle snobs might disagree, but they will not get me off my pedestal. The insanely funky, slightly floral, and deeply pungent aroma of *Tricholoma magnilavere*, the species of matsutake that grows in the northern states east of the Rockies and Canada (and similar matsutake species that grow in the Pacific Northwest), is more intoxicating than the French and Italian tubers.

While we rejoice in watching the progression of mushrooms in summer and fall, from chanterelles to black trumpets to porcini to maitake, we await the month of October like no other. It means trips into the brisk New England fall air to pluck matsutakes from the ground. While we end up confiting the bulk of the harvest for the winter months, we keep fresh matsutakes on all of our menus until the frost finally ends their season. In good seasons, thanks to our own harvest along with that of our incredible local foragers, we have an abundance of matsutakes, in the hundreds of pounds, that most chefs could only dream of.

We use this mushroom in a multitude of ways, but our favorite preparation is to shave it thinly on a mandoline and melt the resulting mushroom "noodles" in a light broth of dashi. The result is sublime. There's really no substitute for these magical fungi, because of their unique aroma, but if you absolutely can't find them and you want to try this recipe, you can use this technique on cultivated king trumpet mushrooms. —*Andrew*

If the mushrooms have closed caps, shave them very thinly lengthwise on a mandoline. If the mushrooms have opened caps, separate the caps from the stems. Shave the stems and caps very thinly lengthwise on a mandoline.

In a small pot over medium-high heat, melt the butter. Add the sliced mushrooms, soy sauce, sake, and mirin and stir until the mushrooms soften, 2 to 3 minutes. Add the dashi and bring to a simmer, then remove from the heat and stir.

Divide the mixture among four bowls and garnish each with sprinklings of pickled spruce tips, pine nuts, and scallions. Serve immediately.

SERVES 4

2 pounds matsutake mushrooms, cleaned

2 tablespoons unsalted butter

2 tablespoons light soy sauce

1 tablespoon sake (filtered or unfiltered is fine, dry is best)

1 tablespoon mirin

1 cup Dashi (page 177)

¼ cup Pickled Spruce Tips (page 193) or a pinch of minced fresh rosemary

½ cup pine nuts, lightly toasted

2 tablespoons thinly sliced scallions, white and light green parts

HALIBUT TAIL BO SSAM

Thai Bird Chile Sambal, Korean BBQ, Smoked Oyster Mayonnaise, Hoisin, Pickles, Chile Oil

SERVES 6 TO 8

4½ tablespoons kosher salt

4 quarts water

1 (3- to 4-pound) fresh halibut tail, scaled and cleaned

1¼ cups Korean BBQ Sauce (page 168)

2 heads butter lettuce, washed, dried, and separated into full leaf lettuce cups

¼ cup Smoked Oyster Mayonnaise (page 173)

¼ cup homemade Hoisin Sauce (page 169) or store-bought

2 tablespoons Thai Bird Chile Sambal (recipe follows)

½ cup each of several types of pickles (such as Bread and Butter Pickles made with daikon, page 193; Pickled Jalapeños, page 193; and Kimchi, page 194)

1 cup leaves picked from a variety of seasonal herbs (such as mint, cilantro, basil, lemon balm, hyssop, and culantro)

1 tablespoon Chile Oil (page 183)

1 teaspoon white sesame seeds

2 tablespoons scallions, thinly sliced on the diagonal

Finishing salt

Cooking whole fish tails is one of our favorite parts of whole-fish utilization. We like to cut the bottoms of the fillets off with the tail because that area of the fish is usually sinewy and not great for crudos but is fantastic when cooked. If your local fishmonger is getting fresh, local fish, don't be afraid to ask them to cut the tails off the fish with a little meat attached and reserve for you.

The tail from a fish as big as a North Atlantic halibut (often 50 to 200 pounds, and 3 to 7 feet long) can serve a good-size crowd. Bo ssam, the Korean party spread that usually centers on pork, is a perfect setup for doing so. The cut is full of collagen, and when it's cooked gently on the bone, it comes out moist and luxurious. It needs some spice, brightness, and acidity, which the bo ssam setup more than provides with its array of *banchan*, or side dishes like pickles, sauces, herbs, and other fun condiments. Light beer, crisp wine, and bracing soju are perfect additions here, too, if that's your thing. You can also substitute store-bought sambal, pickles, or other condiments here. —*Andrew*

In a large, nonreactive container, dissolve the kosher salt in the water to create a brine. Submerge the halibut tail in the brine, cover the container, and place it in the refrigerator for at least 2 hours, or up to Preheat the oven to 250°F. Grease a rack and set it inside a large, deep roasting pan.

Remove the tail from the brine, pat it dry, and coat with about half of the Korean BBQ sauce to cover it all over in a thin layer. Place the tail on the rack inside the roasting pan. Pour an inch of hot water in the pan, keeping the fish above the liquid, and cover the pan with a lid or aluminum foil. Bake until the tail reaches 125°F on an instant-read thermometer at its thickest point, 60 to 75 minutes.

While the fish bakes, set out your lettuce cups, mayonnaise, hoisin sauce, sambal, assorted pickles, herbs, and chile oil in bowls and array them on a huge platter, a lazy Susan, or right on a large table.

CONTINUED

HALIBUT TAIL BO SSAM

CONTINUED

When the tail has finished cooking, remove the pan from the oven and let the tail rest for 15 minutes.

Preheat the broiler to high with an oven rack in the uppermost position.

Carefully peel back the skin from the top of the halibut tail to expose the flesh. Slather the entire top of the fish with most of the remaining Korean BBQ sauce, reserving about ¼ cup to put out with all the rest of your accoutrements. Broil the tail until the sauce browns nicely, 4 to 6 minutes.

Transfer the tail to a large serving plate and garnish with the sesame seeds, scallions, and finishing salt. While the fish is still hot, encourage people to use their forks to grab chunks of it, place them in their lettuce cups, and garnish however they see fit.

THAI BIRD CHILE SAMBAL

MAKES ABOUT 2 CUPS

½ cup apple cider vinegar

½ cup palm sugar (see Glossary) or light brown sugar

5 fresh Thai bird chiles, stemmed

⅓ cup chopped garlic

⅓ cup chopped shallots

Pinch of kosher salt

Canola oil for cooking

In a small pot, warm the cider vinegar and palm sugar over low heat until the sugar dissolves (this could take a little while). Set the pot aside, off the heat.

In a food processor, combine the chiles, garlic, shallots, and salt and process them to achieve a smooth paste. Add a little splash of water (¼ cup at a time) to help keep things moving. Process for 1 minute and salt to taste.

In a large pot, warm a splash of canola oil over low heat until it begins to shimmer. Carefully cook the chile mash until it has thickened and darkened a bit, about 10 minutes. Add the cider vinegar and palm sugar mixture and stir to incorporate. Use immediately or transfer to a glass jar or other lidded container and store in the refrigerator for several months.

SMOKED HAKE BRANDADE

Cucumber Salad, Nutritional Yeast

Traditional brandade includes salt cod and either potatoes (in the north of France) or white beans (in the south of France); it is either served as a spread with bread or fried as a croquette. We make ours with smoked fish and celeriac and go the croquette route. We balance the rich flavor with fresh heirloom cucumber salad dressed with a savory and herbaceous vinaigrette. The vinaigrette is a nod to a brand of Maine popcorn called Little Lads that is flavored with nutritional yeast and dill, the latter of which is a classic flavoring for smoked fish. The popcorn is hard to put down and a favorite of our staff. Kirby cucumbers, mouse melons, and Jamaican gherkins are small varieties of cucumbers often used for pickling, because they are firm and crunchy. We like the mix for their aesthetic appeal, but you could use just about any small cucumber. —*Mike*

To make the brandade, in a large pot, combine the celeriac, milk, and water. Add the salt and sugar and stir. Bring the mixture to a boil over medium-high heat and lower to a simmer. After 20 minutes, start checking the celeriac with a cake tester or sharp knife. It is done when it gives no resistance to the poking. Remove it from the heat and strain through a fine-mesh strainer, discarding the liquid.

Put the celeriac in the center of a large clean kitchen towel and gather up the edges with one hand. Using tongs in the other hand (it will be hot!), twist the celeriac until the towel tightens and liquid drains through the towel, getting rid of as much as you can.

Transfer the celeriac to a food processor and add the butter, a tablespoon at a time, with the motor running. Transfer the mixture to a stand mixer fitted with the paddle attachment and, on low speed, add the smoked fish. Mix for 10 to 20 seconds to incorporate. Taste and adjust the seasoning. Put the mixture in the refrigerator, cover, and thoroughly chill for at least 1 hour, or up to 5 days.

CONTINUED

SERVES 6 TO 8

BRANDADE

4 celeriacs (celery roots), peeled and coarsely chopped

8 cups whole milk

8 cups water

2 tablespoons kosher salt, plus more for seasoning

1 tablespoon sugar

2 cups (4 sticks) unsalted butter, at room temperature

1 pound smoked hake (or other white fish), skinned and flaked

1 cup all-purpose flour

2 eggs

2 cups panko bread crumbs

Canola oil for frying

1 pound mixed cucumbers (such as Kirby, mouse melons, or Jamaican gherkins)

¼ cup Nutritional Yeast Vinaigrette (recipe follows), plus extra for garnish

SMOKED HAKE BRANDADE

CONTINUED

Pull out three shallow bowls to set up your breading station. Set up a large plate or rack nearby. In the first bowl, put the flour; crack the eggs into the second bowl and beat with a splash of water; in the third bowl, put the panko bread crumbs. Using two large spoons or soup spoons, make large quenelles, or rounded spoonfuls, of the brandade mixture. Drop each quenelle into the flour to cover and shake off the excess back into the bowl. Then dip in the egg to cover, and shake the excess back into the bowl. Finally, dip the quenelles in the bread crumbs to cover and shake the excess back into the bowl. Set aside on a plate or rack.

Fill a large pot with 3 inches of canola oil and heat on high to 350°F (or bring a deep-fryer to 350°F). Line a plate with paper towels.

Slip the quenelles into the hot oil in batches, making sure not to crowd the pot. Fry until golden brown, 3 to 5 minutes. Using a slotted spoon or wire-mesh strainer, transfer to the paper towel–lined plate and season with salt.

Cut the cucumbers into bite-size pieces and transfer to a bowl. Add a generous splash of vinaigrette and toss to coat. Check the seasoning and adjust as necessary with salt.

Fill a shallow bowl with the cucumber salad, spooning more vinaigrette over the cucumbers. Lay the fried brandade over the top and serve.

NUTRITIONAL YEAST VINAIGRETTE

MAKES 1 CUP

½ cup nutritional yeast

½ cup extra-virgin olive oil

3 tablespoons dill, minced

2 tablespoons fresh lemon juice

Kosher salt

In a small bowl, combine the yeast, oil, dill, and lemon juice. Whisk together until blended. Season to taste with salt. Use immediately. Any leftovers can be stored in a covered jar in the refrigerator for 1 week.

BROILED ALBACORE COLLAR

Koji-Calamansi Vinaigrette, Gomasio, Sushi Rice

Since we get virtually all of our fish whole, we end up with a lot of collars, which run on either side of the base of the fish's head and includes pectoral fins. The flesh is difficult to extract raw because they are bony, but they have luscious flesh when cooked whole. Large and small alike, they are put to good use. While bluefin collars are typically too big to handle in one piece (we like to cut them into chops and serve them grilled), albacore or yellowfin tuna collars from 40- to 100-pound fish work beautifully for dramatic group dining presentations. Here we serve an albacore collar broiled with sushi rice, lightly dressed greens, sunflower gomasio (our twist on gomasio, a condiment traditionally made with just sesame seeds and salt), pickled ginger, and a tropical-tasting koji-calamansi vinaigrette. Ask your local fishmongers if they get whole tuna in and see if they'll save you the collars. Collars often get thrown away, so they should be happy to save, clean, and trim them for you. —*Andrew*

Rinse and dry the albacore collar and place in a large, nonreactive container. Pour over 1 cup of the vinaigrette, cover, and let marinate in the refrigerator for at least 4 hours, but preferably overnight.

An hour before you start cooking, remove the fish from the marinade and set it skin-side down on a baking sheet at room temperature. Spoon a thick coating of the marinade over the flesh side of the fish and discard the rest of the marinade.

Rinse the sushi rice thoroughly, until the water runs clear from it, and drain. Combine the rice and the water in a pot, bring to a simmer, cover, and turn the heat to as low as possible. Cook the rice for 30 minutes, until fluffy. Remove the pot from the heat, take off the lid, and let steam escape for a full minute. Fluff the rice with a spatula, set aside, and keep warm.

Preheat the broiler to high with an oven rack in the uppermost position. Put the baking sheet with the fish in the oven and broil the collar for 2 to 3 minutes, until the flesh is nicely browned. Turn the broiler off and bake the fish at 250°F until a thermometer in the thickest part of the fish reads 120°F, about 20 minutes. Pull the baking sheet from the oven and let the collar rest for a few minutes.

CONTINUED

1 albacore tuna collar, about 2 pounds

1½ cups Koji-Calamansi Vinaigrette (recipe follows), Umami Mayonnaise (page 173), or Korean BBQ Sauce (page 168)

1 cup sushi rice

1¼ cups water

3 small heads baby lettuce, red and green varieties, separated into individual leaves and washed

½ cup Sunflower Gomasio (recipe follows)

2 scallions, white and light green parts, trimmed and thinly sliced on the diagonal (about ½ cup)

½ cup Pickled Ginger (page 193)

BROILED ALBACORE COLLAR

CONTINUED

In a bowl, dress the greens with ¼ cup of the remaining vinaigrette.

Carefully move the collar to a plate or serving tray and garnish it with a sprinkling of sunflower gomasio and scallions. Serve within 30 minutes with the greens, pickled ginger, sushi rice, and the remaining gomasio and koji-calamansi vinaigrette arrayed in bowls around the plate or serving tray.

KOJI-CALAMANSI VINAIGRETTE

MAKES 2½ CUPS

½ cup barley koji (see Glossary)

½ cup calamansi vinegar (see Glossary) or another fruit vinegar (such as apple cider vinegar)

Juice of 1 lime

1 cup Fried Aromatics Oil (page 184) made with shallots

½ cup Fried Aromatics Oil (page 184) made with garlic

Kosher salt

In a blender, combine the barley koji, vinegar, and the lime juice and blend on high. Add a little cold water as needed to make sure it blends smoothly. Slowly add the oils until the mixture is emulsified. If the mixture gets too thick to blend at any point, add a little more water to keep the vortex moving. Season to taste with salt. Use immediately or store in an airtight container in the refrigerator for up to 2 weeks. Use any extra to dress salads or other vegetable dishes.

SUNFLOWER GOMASIO

MAKES ½ CUP

¼ cup shelled unsalted sunflower seeds

¼ cup white sesame seeds

1 sheet nori

1 tablespoon finishing salt

Preheat the oven to 350°F. On two separate baking sheets, toast the sunflower seeds and sesame seeds in the oven. Check after 10 minutes, then in 3- to 5-minute intervals thereafter, until both are deeply browned but not burnt (watch them like a hawk; the sesame seeds will cook faster than the sunflower seeds!). Remove from the oven and let cool to room temperature.

Holding the sheet of nori with tongs, wave it over a gas burner flame a few times until it becomes lighter green and fragrant, about 1 minute. (Or heat a large skillet on high heat and toast the nori on both sides for 30 seconds.)

In a blender or spice grinder, combine the seeds with the nori and salt and pulse until you have a sandy consistency. (Don't go too far, or you'll make tahini.) Use immediately or store in an airtight container at room temperature for up to 1 week and use any extra for garnishing meat, seafood, and vegetable dishes.

BASICS

If you've been paying attention to the recipes in this book, you've probably noticed that there are a bunch of ingredients that are used multiple times and condiments that seem to share a common lineage or technique. Maybe, you might critique, some of the dishes even seem formulaic—a superlative local protein, a fat, an acidic component, a crunchy component, maybe some heat. That's astute. You've discovered the heart of our cooking style, which might fairly be labeled "pantry foraging."

Your success as a pantry forager depends on how big and interesting your pantry is, and we are honestly very proud of ours. The amount of experimenting and refining and process designing we've done means we have a girthy toolbelt for building new ideas, tweaking dishes, and keeping our menu lively.

Only one of us, Arlin, the front-of-house guy, has culinary school credentials. So we've mostly learned technique in bits and pieces on the line. None of us has ever had the time or resources to decamp to Asia or Europe for culinary apprenticeships nor have we eaten in more than a handful of the World's Best Restaurants. But still, exploration is what we live for, whether in the kitchen testing recipes, eating at other restaurants, or being out on the water or in the forest.

And let's not forget cookbooks. It would be hard to overstate how much the simple act of studying them has influenced us. Like we said in the introduction, Eventide was opened in the former site of Rabelais Fine Books, the storefront of one of the world's great culinary cookbook collections. It was a rare place where cooks could go immerse themselves in the ancient and the new, talking about all of it with Don and Sam. We took full advantage and amassed huge personal collections of books of our own. Though we rarely use recipes as they exist in cookbooks (notable exceptions being David Chang's ginger scallion sauce and David Kinch's tonnato sauce—we are in your debt!), we are constantly learning new techniques and methods from books and translating them in the restaurant.

Our desire to keep learning was one thing that led us down the path to building an incredible pantry of pickles, vinaigrettes, XO sauces, oils, puffs, emulsions, and other combinations that you'll see in this chapter. We'd be remiss if we forgot to mention how deeply grateful we are to all the chefs and cooks who have worked for us at our restaurants. Many of the ideas, methods, and recipes listed in the following pages have been championed and developed by them.

We're also going to admit in advance to using food terms extremely liberally. When we say *XO sauce*, we don't mean specifically the Cantonese condiment of dried shellfish, ham, and aromatics that is caramelized slowly for hours. We mean *anything* caramelized slowly with aromatics to develop umami and depth of flavor. Vinaigrettes aren't always just mixtures of vinegar and oil, but loose and saucy condiments or dressings varied in texture that register high on the acidity scale. And pickles aren't just cucumbers, they are virtually any food product marinated in or cooked in an acidic environment. Some may call our rhetorical acrobatics BS, but it's just the way we've learned to codify things and easily communicate a general idea to guests. "Vegan XO" sounds way better than "fresh and fermented vegetables cooked slowly at low temperatures submerged in oil with various aromatics."

In terms of using the items in this chapter, focus on the power of subtlety, because the last thing you want to do is overshadow something beautiful like a piece of fresh, local, raw fish. Most of the ingredients in this chapter offer a lot of bang even in small doses, so start with a light touch and move up to your preference from there. Look for balance that hits all the right sweet, salty, acidic, and textural notes. Over time, using these cool tools, you'll get the hang of achieving that balance.

This chapter only scratches the surface of where we've been and how these methods and techniques have developed up to this point. We've probably had hundreds of different quick pickles on our menus, and we'll probably have hundreds more as we discover new stuff. We encourage you to riff and expand on these techniques and understand that if one of the dishes in our book calls for pickled daikon, but daikon isn't available or in season, use cabbage or watermelon radish. Just be flexible and it'll probably work beautifully.

The moral of the story is that cooking is easier when you have some of these killer staples in your fridge or pantry.

EVENTIDE STEAMED BUN

MAKES 28 SMALL BUNS

1½ cups plus 1 tablespoon water (355 grams), at room temperature

½ cup (100 grams) sugar

5 teaspoons (2 packets/ 17.5 grams) active dry yeast

3 tablespoons plus ¾ teaspoon (13 grams) nonfat dry milk powder

6½ cups (780 grams) all-purpose flour

1 tablespoon plus ¾ teaspoon kosher salt (12.5 grams)

½ teaspoon (2.4 grams) baking soda

⅔ teaspoon (2.7 grams) baking powder

1 cup plus 2 tablespoons unsalted butter (2¼ sticks/ 254.4 grams), at room temperature

These are great with everything: The Brown Butter Lobster Roll (page 112), the Crab Roll (page 118), the Fried Oyster Bun (page 117), the Ultimate Clambake (page 87), your mom's classic tuna sandwich, or a simple hot dog. —*Andrew*

In the bowl of a stand mixer fitted with a dough hook, mix the water, sugar, yeast, and milk powder on low speed. Let bloom for 5 to 10 minutes until the mixture is frothy. Add 3¼ cups (390 grams) of the flour and the salt, baking soda, and baking powder, and mix on medium-low speed for 5 minutes. Add the remaining 3¼ cups (390 grams) flour and mix on low speed until the dough begins to come together in shaggy strands, about 2 minutes. Add the butter and continue to mix on low speed until the dough becomes smooth, about 5 minutes (the dough should slowly bounce back if you poke it with a finger). Transfer the dough to a lightly greased bowl, cover, and let proof in a warm, draft-free place for 1 hour.

Punch down the dough and portion it into twenty-eight 1.7-ounce pieces. On a large work surface, use the palm of your hand to roll the pieces into tight little balls. With the heel of your hand, roll each ball into a log 3½ to 4 inches long.

Cut a piece of parchment paper to fit and place inside a bamboo steamer basket or a steamer insert for a large pot (feel free to use a couple to fit all of the dough logs), then grease the paper with canola oil or cooking spray. Arrange the dough logs in rows on the parchment, leaving about ½ inch between each. Cover with a lid or kitchen towel and let proof for 1 to 1½ hours, until the dough bounces back slowly if you poke it and the expanded logs nearly touch each other.

Fill your wok or pot with 1 inch of water and bring to a boil. Set the dough-filled steamer basket in the wok or the insert in the pot, cover, and steam for 10 to 12 minutes, until the buns have puffed and crowded together. Remove from the heat and slightly crack the lid, letting the buns rest inside for 3 to 5 minutes. Transfer the buns to a plate, rack, or cutting board.

Once the buns are cool enough to handle, separate them with a sharp knife and cut a slit in the tops. Use immediately or refrigerate in a ziplock bag for up to 2 weeks or freeze for up to 3 months.

To refresh the stored buns, place them in a steamer insert in a large pot, or a bamboo steamer set over a wok, and steam for 5 minutes, until they are very hot, soft, and pliable. Serve warm.

SESAME BURGER BUN

The Eventide burger was the first of the burger bun–style sandwiches that hit our menu. Since we are overly prideful and gluttons for punishment, we weren't about to just use a store-bought bun, so we asked Kim Rodgers, our pastry chef, to whip one up. She did so remarkably quickly, with astonishing results. "Easy," she told us. "It's just the steamed bun dough rolled and baked." This bun is now the vehicle for our burger (page 125), as well as our fish (page 120), and tofu (page 123) sandwiches. —*Andrew*

In the bowl of a stand mixer fitted with a dough hook, mix the water, sugar, yeast, and milk powder on low speed. Let bloom for 5 to 10 minutes until the mixture is frothy. Add 3¼ cups (390 grams) of the flour and the kosher salt, baking soda, and baking powder and mix on medium-low speed for 5 minutes. Add the remaining 3¼ cups (390 grams) of flour and mix on low speed until the dough begins to come together in shaggy strands, about 2 minutes. Add the butter and continue to mix on low speed until the dough becomes smooth, about 5 minutes (the dough should slowly bounce back if you poke it with a finger). Transfer the dough to a lightly greased bowl, cover, and let proof in a warm, draft-free place for 1 hour.

Punch down the dough and portion it into twelve 3.5-ounce balls. Line a baking sheet with parchment paper and grease the paper with canola oil or cooking spray. Arrange the balls evenly on the parchment paper with a few inches between them. Mist the dough with a spray bottle of water, then sprinkle with the finishing salt and sesame seeds. Cover with a towel and let proof for 1 to 1½ hours, until the dough again bounces back slowly if you poke it with a finger.

Preheat the oven to 400°F.

Bake the buns for 12 to 14 minutes, rotating the sheet once halfway through, until evenly browned. Use immediately, store in an airtight container for up to 5 days at room temperature, or freeze for up to 1 month.

MAKES 12 BUNS

1½ cups plus 1 tablespoon water (355 grams), at room temperature

½ cup (100 grams) sugar

5 teaspoons (2 packets/ 17.5 grams) active dry yeast

3 tablespoons plus ¾ teaspoon (13 grams) nonfat dry milk powder

6½ cups (780 grams) all-purpose flour

1 tablespoon plus ¾ teaspoon kosher salt (12.5 grams)

½ teaspoon (2.4 grams) baking soda

⅔ teaspoon (2.7 grams) baking powder

1 cup plus 2 tablespoons unsalted butter (2¼ sticks/ 254.4 grams), at room temperature

Finishing salt

Black and white sesame seeds for sprinkling

BISCUITS (HUGO'S)

MAKES 12 TO 20 BISCUITS

2 cups (240 grams)
all-purpose flour

⅓ cup (53 grams) potato flour

1½ teaspoons (9 grams)
kosher salt

¾ teaspoon (3.6 grams)
baking soda

1 tablespoon (14.3 grams)
baking powder

Pinch of chopped Fried
Aromatics (page 184), made
with garlic, or granulated garlic

2 tablespoons cold unsalted
butter, diced, plus 9 tablespoons
(156.2 grams) unsalted butter,
melted

2 tablespoons plus ¾ teaspoon
(28.8 grams) vegetable
shortening

1⅓ cups (320 grams)
cold buttermilk

Finishing salt

When we bought Hugo's, the deal was structured so that we were buying both the business and the restaurant's "good will." We've never been sure of what precisely *good will* referred to, but we like to joke now that it had to do with the recipe for superlative biscuits we inherited from Rob and Nancy. As Donny Carrasco on our team says, "If they're fluffy when you make 'em, they'll be fluffy when you bake 'em." Be paranoid about overworking the dough, and you'll get a beautiful result. —*Mike*

In a large bowl, sift together the flours, kosher salt, baking soda, and baking powder. Add the fried garlic and mix. Add the cold butter, 1 tablespoon of the melted butter, and the shortening to the bowl and work it into the flour with your fingertips until the dough has the texture of coarse meal. This will take 3 to 5 minutes to get right.

Start adding the buttermilk a little at a time, folding it into the flour mixture gently with a spatula until the dough comes together as a homogenous mass.

On a lightly floured baking sheet or board, roll the dough out to a thickness of 1 inch, then chill the dough for at least an hour but no more than 4 hours in the refrigerator.

Preheat the oven to 450°F. Line a baking sheet with parchment paper and lightly grease the paper with canola oil or cooking spray.

Cut the biscuits with a 2- or 3-inch cookie cutter, making sure the cutter stays floured so your cuts are nice and clean. Place the biscuits on the prepared baking sheet at least an inch apart. Brush each one lightly with the remaining 8 tablespoons melted butter and sprinkle with the finishing salt.

Bake the biscuits until golden brown and cooked through, about 20 minutes. They are best served while still warm but can be stored in an airtight container at room temperature for 3 days. Toast the biscuits to reheat before serving again.

SALTINE CRACKERS

**MAKES APPROXIMATELY
30 TO 40 CRACKERS**

½ cup plus 1 tablespoon
(355 grams) room-temperature
water

2 ½ teaspoons (1 packet/
8 grams) active dry yeast

¾ teaspoon (3.2 grams) sugar

Heaping ⅓ cup plus 2 cups
and 2 tablespoons (295 grams)
all-purpose flour

½ teaspoon (3 grams)
kosher salt

⅛ teaspoon (0.6 grams)
baking soda

⅛ teaspoon (0.4 grams)
cream of tartar

1 tablespoon plus ¾ teaspoon
(17.8 grams) unsalted butter

1 tablespoon plus ¾ teaspoon
(16 grams) vegetable shortening

Finishing salt

You wouldn't dare eat one of the chowders or stews in this book
without saltine crackers, now would you?

In a bowl, whisk together the water, yeast, sugar, and the heaping
⅓ cup (40 grams) of the flour, and let bloom for 5 to 10 minutes, until
the mixture is frothy.

Into a large bowl, sift together the kosher salt, baking soda, cream of
tartar, and the remaining 2 cups and 2 tablespoons (255 grams) flour
and pour into the bowl of a stand mixer fitted with a paddle attachment.
Add the butter and shortening. Beat on medium-low speed until the
dough has a sandy, crumbly consistency, about 3 minutes. Switch the
mixer attachment to a dough hook and add the yeast mixture to the
mixing bowl. Mix on medium-low speed until the dough is smooth, about
7 minutes.

Transfer the dough to a lightly greased bowl, cover, and refrigerate for
at least 1 hour, or overnight.

Grease two large baking sheets. Divide the dough in half. Working with
half the dough at a time, on a lightly floured work surface, press the
dough into a square and roll it out into a larger square about ⅓ inch thick.
As if you were folding a letter to put in an envelope, fold the bottom
third of the dough to the center, then fold the top half of the dough
over the first fold. Rotate the dough 90 degrees and roll it out again to a
thickness of ⅓ inch; repeat the folds. Repeat the rotating and rolling (not
the folding) one more time. You should come out with a large rectangle.
Fit the dough inside one of the prepared baking sheets; trim the dough to
fit snugly. Repeat the whole process with the other half of the dough. (If
you have a lot of scrap, you can knead it back together and roll it out
for a little runty separate pan of crackers). Let the pans of dough proof,
covered, for 15 to 30 minutes, until they've started to puff up a bit.

Preheat the oven to 325°F. Using a fork, poke the dough all over its
surface, to keep it from rising during the baking process. At this point,
you can also use a knife to score shallow lines across the dough in a
grid pattern the size of the crackers you want in the end (this will make
them easy to crack apart uniformly when they are baked), but we just
skip this step and break them haphazardly. Mist the dough with a spray
or two of water and sprinkle finishing salt over the top.

Bake one pan at a time for 25 to 30 minutes, rotating the pan halfway
through, until the crackers are firm to the touch and have a hint of
golden color. Cool completely on a rack or large board. Use immediately
or store in an airtight container at room temperature for up to 1 week.

KABAYAKI SAUCE

Kabayaki—often called eel sauce—occupies the middle ground between the deeply savory *tare* and the sweeter hoisin sauce. We love it on the Scallop Waffle-Yaki (page 136) and, obviously, on eel, as in our American Unagi (page 167). This sauce calls for fish carcasses (or bones), which you can get from your fishmonger. If it's not easy for you to grill or smoke the bones, as instructed below, broil them on high heat on a greased pan until they are deep brown and charred, 5 to 7 minutes per side. —*Mike*

Brush the fish bones with oil and season lightly with salt. Light a hot grill and grill the fish bones (a grill pan is useful if the carcasses aren't whole) on both sides until they are darker in color and charred in places. Alternatively, set up a smoker (page 203) and smoke the bones for 1 hour, or preheat a broiler on high with the oven rack at its highest setting, then broil the fish bones for 5 to 7 minutes on each side, until they are deeply brown and charred.

In a pot, combine the garlic, ginger, scallions, fish bones, water, mirin, sake, soy sauce, and sugar. Bring to boil over medium-high heat, then turn down to a simmer and cook for 45 minutes, stirring occasionally, until the sauce has reduced by half and thickened noticeably. Strain the mixture through a fine-mesh strainer into a smaller pot and return to medium heat. Reduce again by half, until the sauce is thick enough to coat the back of a spoon, about 10 minutes. Let cool and use immediately, or store in an airtight container in the refrigerator for up to 2 weeks.

MAKES 2 CUPS

2 pounds fish bones

Canola oil for brushing

Kosher salt

3 garlic cloves, minced

4- to 6-inch knob of ginger, peeled and minced

4 scallions, white and light green parts finely chopped

2 cups water

1 cup mirin

1 cup sake

1 cup soy sauce or tamari

½ cup sugar

TARE

MAKES ABOUT 2 CUPS

1 tablespoon canola oil

3 garlic cloves, minced

4- to 6-inch knob of ginger, peeled and minced

2 cups chicken stock

1½ tablespoons mirin

1½ tablespoons sake

1 tablespoon sugar

2 to 6 tablespoons soy sauce

Tare is the sauce that makes Japanese grilled skewers delicious. It can add depth to a bowl of ramen noodles, and it puts the *tare* in *teriyaki*. We've found many other uses for the roasted, savory, and umami notes that *tare* brings to the table, but we use it chiefly on our Tuna Crudo (page 77) and our Fish Sandwich (page 120).

In a large pot, heat the oil over medium-high heat and sauté the garlic and ginger until they start to brown. Add the chicken stock, mirin, sake, and sugar. Stir to scrape up any browned bits from the bottom of the pan as you bring the liquid to a boil; then lower the heat to a simmer. Cook, stirring occasionally, until the tare has thickened enough to coat the back of a spoon, 30 to 60 minutes. Turn off the heat and pour through a fine-mesh strainer into a bowl. Season with the soy sauce to taste, until the mixture is rich and savory to your liking. Use immediately or store in an airtight container in the refrigerator for up to 1 month.

KOREAN BBQ SAUCE

MAKES 3 TO 4 CUPS

¼ cup Fried Aromatics Oil (page 184) made with garlic

3 sweet onions (such as Maui, Vidalia, or Walla Walla), diced

1 head garlic, cloves separated, peeled, and smashed

1 large knob of ginger, peeled and thinly sliced

¼ cup salted black beans (see Glossary) or soy sauce

8 ounces palm sugar (see Glossary) or light brown sugar

1½ cups rice wine vinegar

½ cup gochujang (Korean chile paste; see Glossary) or mix equal parts red pepper flakes, soy sauce, and sugar

4 cups water

This recipe was originally developed for the Broiled Jumbo Winter Point Oysters (page 135), but has since become a widely used staple. It's a great complement to fish, meat, and vegetables alike. —*Andrew*

In a large pot, heat the garlic oil over medium heat. Add the onions, garlic, and ginger and sauté until softened, 5 to 7 minutes. Add the salted black beans and palm sugar and sauté for another 1 to 2 minutes, until the sugar has melted. Add the vinegar, gochujang, and water and bring to a simmer. Simmer for 30 minutes, stirring occasionally. Remove from the heat and let cool slightly.

In a blender, puree the mixture until smooth. Strain the mixture through a fine-mesh strainer into a lidded container. Use immediately or keep in a sealed container in the refrigerator for up to 1 month.

HOISIN SAUCE

Hoisin is one of those Asian flavoring additives that lives perfectly, almost impossibly, at the exact midpoint between salty and sweet. It's great to have in your pantry for adding to marinades, sauces, soups, and other things. This recipe for the classic Chinese pantry sauce was developed by the chefs at The Honey Paw, Eventide's sister restaurant, and later absorbed (stolen) by Eventide chefs.

In a large saucepan, heat the garlic oil over medium heat. Add the ginger and garlic and sauté until they soften, 3 to 5 minutes. Add the salted black beans, wine, soy sauce, vinegar, sugar, water, prunes, sesame oil, and five-spice powder. Bring to a boil, then turn down to a simmer. Cook for 30 minutes, stirring occasionally.

Remove from the heat and let cool slightly. In a blender, puree the mixture at high speed until smooth, then strain it through a fine-mesh strainer into a bowl. Use immediately or store in an airtight container in the refrigerator for up to 1 month.

MAKES 5 CUPS

¼ cup Fried Aromatics Oil (page 184) made with garlic

3 (6-inch) knobs of ginger, peeled and minced (about 1 cup)

3 heads garlic, cloves peeled and minced (about 1 cup)

¼ cup salted black beans (see Glossary)

⅓ cup Shaoxing wine

1 cup light soy sauce or tamari

½ cup rice wine vinegar

1¼ cups palm sugar (see Glossary) or light brown sugar

⅔ cup water

¾ cup pitted prunes

1¾ tablespoons Asian sesame oil

2¼ teaspoons five-spice powder

MAITAKE XO SAUCE

MAKES 4 TO 5 CUPS

2 pounds maitake mushrooms, cleaned

Canola oil for simmering

2 shallots, minced

1 (6-inch) knob of ginger, peeled and minced

10 cloves garlic, minced

¼ cup tamari or soy sauce

Rice wine vinegar

Kosher salt

I'd love to meet the Hong Kong cook who invented XO sauce. It seems like we'd all get along, because Eventide is a place where it makes pitch-perfect sense to transform scraps of charcuterie, dried fish, chiles, and aromatics into something amazing with hours of gentle cooking. Such a move is the loftiest aspiration of the French *garde-manger* (guardian of the pantry), and it is precisely what made me fall in love with professional cooking.

Often, XO sauces are the result of a bumper crop of something interesting, like wild porcini mushrooms. We also frequently over-order something highly perishable, like crab, and turn it into XO.

Through all of our experimentation, we've discovered that shellfish, cured meats, or mushrooms aren't mandatory for making an umami-rich XO, contrary to popular belief. We make other XOs by fermenting vegetables like carrots, onions, and ginger with apples. Once the vegetables have fermented and soured, we chop them coarsely or pass them through a meat grinder and caramelize them about as far as we can take them before they burn. Salty-sour and incredibly savory, it's like sofrito on steroids. This method works beautifully with just about any kind of mushroom. Basically, if you can caramelize it, you can make an XO with it. —*Mike*

Tear the mushrooms into small pieces and put them in a wide, heavy pot. Add the oil to cover and bring the mushrooms up to a simmer. The goal at this stage is to thoroughly cook the maitakes and caramelize them lightly and slowly. During the cooking process, the natural juices in the mushrooms will evaporate, and you'll see steam rising off the surface of the oil. The steam will dissipate just as the mushrooms start to take on some color. Maintaining a steady, low flame will help slowly build flavor, and it will safeguard against frying the mushrooms.

Once the maitakes have deepened in aroma and have taken on a bit of color, after 30 minutes to 1 hour, add the shallots, ginger, garlic, and tamari. Stir and continue cooking over low heat. The tamari, like the mushroom juice, will reduce and evaporate. Keep cooking until the steam has dissipated and the shallots, ginger, and garlic have browned lightly, 30 minutes to 1 hour.

Take the XO off the heat and allow it to cool to room temperature. Season the sauce with rice wine vinegar and salt to taste. Use immediately or store in an airtight container in the refrigerator for up to 1 month.

SALT PORK SAMBAL

If I'm not working on anything specific, sometimes I just poke around in the walk-in until I find a source of waste or excess. This sauce resulted from just such a search in the cooler at our Eventide Fenway location in Boston. We had been stockpiling Fresno chile pickles and salt pork scraps, so I decided to try to make something from them. As with many traditional preparations, we take plenty of liberties with what constitutes a "sambal." Think of it as a condiment that is spicy, salty, sweet, and sour—as such, it plays pretty well with just about everything.—*Mike*

In a blender, puree the Fresno pickling liquid and pickles until smooth.

In a wide, shallow pot or a Dutch oven, slowly render the salt pork over medium heat, breaking it up with a wooden spoon as you go. Once the salt pork is crispy and mostly rendered, strain off all the fat and return the crispy pork to the pan. Add the onion and continue cooking slowly until it becomes translucent, about 5 minutes.

Add the pickled chile puree, garlic, fish sauce, and palm sugar. Continue to cook over medium heat for about 30 minutes, until the mixture is jammy. Transfer to a work bowl to cool. Once cooled, season with salt and lime juice to taste. Use immediately or store in an airtight container in the refrigerator for up to 1 month.

MAKES 3 TO 4 CUPS

2 cups Pickled Fresno Chiles plus 2 cups of their pickling liquid (page 193)

1 pound homemade Salt Pork (page 202) or store-bought slab bacon, coarsely chopped

1 yellow onion, finely chopped

10 garlic cloves, minced

¼ cup fish sauce

¼ cup palm sugar (see Glossary) or light brown sugar

Kosher salt

Fresh lime juice for seasoning

HOUSE MAYONNAISE

MAKES ABOUT 4½ CUPS

3 eggs

1 tablespoon kosher salt

1½ tablespoons sugar

¼ cup fresh lemon juice

4 cups canola oil

Egg-based emulsions are a great complement to many kinds of seafood, and they provide the necessary lubrication for making sandwiches delicious. This is not up for debate. A slightly more controversial view, held by Arlin, is that mayonnaise can provide the acidity needed to cut through particularly rich dishes.

We end up deploying a lot of mayonnaise at Eventide, and yet we've rarely put just plain mayonnaise on anything. Egg-based emulsions are an incredible vehicle for carrying other flavors, and the permutations that we've concocted from our basic mayo recipe have to number in the thousands. We do this in two ways: by simply making our house mayo recipe and adding ingredients after the fact, and by swapping out a few ingredients of the house recipe and making the emulsion with those ingredients.

Here is our house mayonnaise recipe followed by a handful of variations that appear in recipes throughout the book. Pro tips: We like using eggs that have been poached in the shell at 145°F and chilled (we call these 145°F eggs). Not only does the resulting mayonnaise enjoy a longer shelf life thanks to the cooking, but it also makes the emulsion more temperature-resistant. We can serve this mayonnaise hotter than a mayo made with raw eggs.

Emulsions are way easier when all the ingredients and equipment are really cold. If the mixture starts getting too thick at any point, you are tempting it to break. Add a little ice-cold water to thin it out and get the rest of your oil in there. If you do break your emulsion (it will go from thick to super-thin very quickly), don't fear! Just dump the contents of your blender into a container, add a couple more chilled 145°F eggs or egg yolks to the blender with a little cold water, turn the blender on, and start very slowly incorporating the broken mixture back into the blender. We promise it works! —*Andrew*

Set up an immersion circulator to 145°F. Gently lower the eggs into the sous vide water bath, being very careful not to crack any shells. Let cook for 60 minutes, remove the eggs from the water, and place in an ice bath until thoroughly chilled.

Crack the eggs into a blender, then add the salt, sugar, and lemon juice. Puree until smooth. With the motor still running, slowly drizzle in the oil until the mayonnaise is thickened and emulsified. Use immediately or store in an airtight container in the refrigerator for up to 2 weeks.

If you don't have an immersion circulator, you can substitute 3 fresh eggs for the 3 chilled 145°F eggs and puree them in a food processor with the salt, sugar, and lemon juice. With the motor still running, slowly pour in the oil until you have a thickened and well-incorporated final product. This basic approach, pureeing the ingredients and then pouring in the oil to emulsify, also works for the preparations below, as do the storage instructions.

KATSUOBUSHI MAYONNAISE (MAKES 4 TO 5 CUPS):

Crack 3 chilled 145°F eggs into a blender, then add 1 tablespoon sugar and the juice of 4 limes. With the motor running, slowly add 4 cups Katsuobushi Oil (page 183). Season with kosher salt and fresh lime juice to taste.

UMAMI MAYONNAISE (MAKES 5 CUPS):

Crack 3 chilled 145°F eggs into a blender, then add 1 tablespoon sugar, 3 tablespoons black vinegar (or 1½ tablespoons balsamic vinegar), and 3 tablespoons light soy sauce. Puree on high, and with the motor running, slowly stream in 1 cup canola oil, 1 cup Confit Mushroom Oil (page 186) made with maitakes, and 2 cups Fried Aromatics Oil (page 184) made with shallots until emulsified. Season with kosher salt and fresh lime juice to taste.

SMOKED OYSTER MAYONNAISE (MAKES 5½ CUPS):

Crack 3 chilled 145°F eggs into a blender and add 1 tablespoon sugar, 3 tablespoons black vinegar (or 1½ tablespoons balsamic vinegar), 3 tablespoons light soy sauce, and ½ cup drained olive oil-packed smoked oysters. Puree on high, and with the motor running, slowly stream in 1 cup canola oil, 1 cup Confit Mushroom Oil (page 186) made with maitakes, and 2 cups Fried Aromatics Oil (page 184) made with shallots until emulsified. Season with kosher salt and fresh lime juice to taste.

TALLOW MAYONNAISE (MAKES 4 CUPS):

In a small pan over low heat, melt ½ cup rendered beef fat until it is liquified, then whisk it together with 2½ cups canola oil. In a blender, combine the oils with 1 tablespoon xanthan gum (see Glossary) and puree for 1 to 2 minutes, until fully incorporated. Transfer to a bowl. Crack 3 chilled 145°F eggs into the blender and add ½ cup gochujang (Korean chile paste; see Glossary), ¼ cup fresh lemon juice, and 1 teaspoon kosher salt. Puree on high and slowly drizzle in the oil until fully emulsified.

YUZU KOSHO MAYONNAISE (MAKES 2 CUPS):

Combine 2 cups House Mayonnaise with 1 tablespoon red or green yuzu kosho (see Glossary) and mix well. Season with kosher salt and fresh lime juice to taste.

JALAPEÑO MAYONNAISE (MAKES 2 CUPS):

Roast 4 jalapeños over an open flame on a gas stove or under a broiler, until their skins are blackened and they are becoming limp. Transfer them to a covered container and let them steam for 10 minutes. Wearing gloves, remove the stems, blackened skin, and seeds with your fingers. Lightly rinse the peppers under cold water, then pat dry and mince them. Whisk together with 2 cups of House Mayonnaise, ½ teaspoon ground coriander, kosher salt, and fresh lemon juice to taste.

HOUSE MAYONNAISE

CONTINUED

MAPLE CHINESE MUSTARD (MAKES 3 TO 4 CUPS):

In a blender, combine 1 chilled 145°F egg with 2 tablespoons rice wine vinegar, 1 tablespoon ground turmeric, 2 teaspoons kosher salt, and ¼ cup maple sugar (or light brown sugar). Puree on high, then with the motor running, drizzle in 1 cup plus 2 tablespoons canola oil until emulsified. In a large bowl, combine the emulsion with 1 tablespoon yellow mustard, 1 cup Dijon mustard, and ¼ cup maple syrup and whisk to combine.

HOUSE TARTAR SAUCE (MAKES 3 TO 4 CUPS):

In a food processor, combine ⅓ cup Pickled Red Onion (page 192), ⅓ cup Pickled Cucumbers (page 192 or store-bought), and ⅓ cup cornichons with 3 tablespoons drained capers and pulse until you have a chunky mixture. In a large bowl, combine the mixture with 2½ cups House Mayonnaise, ¼ cup paprika, 2 tablespoons fresh lemon juice, 1½ teaspoons kosher salt, and a handful of mixed finely chopped dill and flat-leaf parsley. Whisk to combine. Season to taste with kosher salt and fresh lemon juice.

FILLET OF FISH TARTAR SAUCE (MAKES 3 TO 4 CUPS):

In a food processor, combine ⅓ cup Bread and Butter Pickles (page 193) and ⅓ cup cornichons and pulse until you have a chunky mixture. In a large bowl, combine the mixture with 2½ cups House Mayonnaise, ¼ cup diced yellow onion, a big pinch of finely chopped dill, and ¾ teaspoon MSG (optional). Whisk to combine. Season to taste with kosher salt and fresh lemon juice.

CUCUMBER TARTAR SAUCE (MAKES 1 TO 2 CUPS):

Peel one English cucumber and slice lengthwise into quarters, then scoop out the seeds and discard. Dice the cucumber uniformly. Combine the cucumber and ¼ cup Pickling Liquid (page 192) in a vacuum-sealing bag and seal on full pressure. Set aside for 30 minutes. Cut open the bag and drain the liquid, then scoop the diced cucumber into a bowl. Alternatively, use 1 whole store-bought dill pickle, diced, or the equivalent in chips or spears. Add 1 cup of House Mayonnaise and whisk to incorporate. If you don't want to go the vacuum-sealing route, make cucumber pickles using the method on page 193 and dice 1 to use for this recipe.

NAM PHRIK

5 shallots, thinly sliced

10 garlic cloves, thinly sliced

Canola oil for frying

4-inch knob of ginger, peeled and thinly sliced

½ cup fresh lime juice, plus more as needed

½ cup fish sauce, plus more as needed

1 tablespoon palm sugar (see Glossary) or light brown sugar

5 Thai bird chiles (or other fresh chiles, such as jalapeño, cayenne, or serrano), stemmed and seeded

If we're playing fast and loose with definitional requirements for dashi (opposite), then we're probably outright misusing the term *nam phrik*. At Eventide's sister restaurant, The Honey Paw, nam phriks— Thai spicy chile sauces—are deployed with far greater attention to tradition and regional variations than at Eventide, where, broadly, we understand them as Southeast Asian–inflected relishes. This spicy, sweet nam phrik pao was the first version we experimented with, and it's been a mainstay ever since. Enjoy it the way you would any spicy sauce: on eggs, with rice, or to goose up soups or sauces. —*Mike*

Set up a fine-mesh strainer over a heatproof container. Line a baking sheet with paper towels.

In a heavy pot, combine the shallots and garlic with enough oil to cover by 2 or more inches. Heat the pot on medium-high heat until your ingredients begin to sizzle and fry, stirring frequently to make sure that what is closer to the walls of the pot doesn't cook faster than what's in the middle. Let it cook until the ingredients begin to turn golden (don't let it get all the way to brown), then quickly and carefully pour the contents of the pot through the fine-mesh strainer, reserving the oil in a sealed jar to cook with later on (it should stay good for 3 months in the refrigerator). The oil will prove to be a valuable ally in any future cooking projects.

In a blender, combine the fried shallots and garlic with the ginger, lime juice, fish sauce, palm sugar, and chiles and blend to a uniform paste. The resulting sauce should be spicy, salty, funky, and sour. Adjust the flavor with additional lime juice and fish sauce as needed. Use immediately or store in a sealed jar in the refrigerator for 3 months.

VARIATION:

We've made many variations on this theme, and most of them are based on having an overabundance of one product, like mussels. To the shallot and garlic frying step, add 2 cups of cooked mussel meat (making sure there's enough oil to cover by 1 to 2 inches). Then follow the steps above to grind the ingredients into a paste in a blender, and you'll have something with a whole different layer of savoriness to use as a flavor enhancer or hot sauce/ dipping sauce. Use immediately or store in a sealed jar in the refrigerator for 3 months.

DASHI

We use the term *dashi* quite vaguely to refer to a savory infusion that always includes kombu seaweed and also gets its flavor from a dried and/or smoked ingredient. Dashis differ from stocks in a couple of respects: first, they spend no more than an hour on the stove, whereas stocks are often cooked for much longer; and second, they are valued for their clarity and cleanliness, whereas stocks are prized for their depth of flavor and rich texture. We take a lot of scraps of meat, fish, and vegetables and salt, dehydrate, and smoke them to make the ingredients for dashis. It's a great way to show off our pantry. —*Mike*

Combine the katsuobushi and kombu in a large bowl, pour in the water, cover, and store in the refrigerator for at least 2 hours, or overnight.

Pour the seaweed-water mixture into a pot over medium heat and bring to just below a simmer (you'll see a few wisps of steam, but no turbulence). Hold the dashi at this very low simmer for 30 minutes. Place the bonito flakes in a fine-mesh strainer set over a nonreactive container. Slowly pour the simmered mixture over the bonito into the container. Season to taste with tamari and salt. Use immediately or store in a covered container in the refrigerator for 1 week or freeze for 3 months.

This method lends itself to endless experimentation. Here are a couple of variations.

MAKES 2 QUARTS

2 cups katsuobushi flakes (see Glossary)

1 (6-inch) piece kombu (see Glossary)

2 quarts water

¾ cup bonito flakes (see Glossary)

Tamari or soy sauce

Finishing salt

VEGAN DASHI:

Combine 2 quarts of water, 1 tablespoon of daikon bushi (page 181), and one 6-inch piece of kombu in a medium pot and follow the recipe as above.

SCALLOP DASHI (OR ANY DRIED SEAFOOD DASHI):

Combine 2 quarts of water, ⅓ cup dried scallops (we always dry scallop feet for this purpose; you can buy dried scallops online or at an Asian market), and one 6-inch piece of kombu in a medium pot and follow the same process as above.

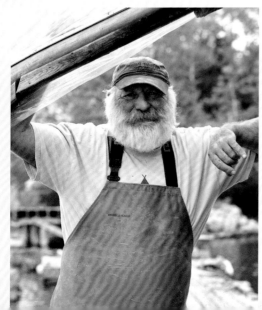

FISH STOCK

MAKES 6 TO 8 CUPS

3 pounds fish bones and scraps (from your fishmonger)

Water

1 (6-inch) piece of kombu

Fresh herbs (such as parsley, dill, thyme, or tarragon; optional)

Our stock-making program has been so influenced by dashi that we've pared down all of it to its simplest form. There was a time when we assiduously chopped mirepoix, made cute little sachets, and chose specific herbs for specific stocks. Now we follow a much simpler protocol. —*Mike*

In a large pot, cover the fish bones and scraps with water by 1 to 2 inches. Bring to a boil over high heat and allow to boil hard for 10 seconds (this is important because it helps coagulate proteins, blood, and anything else that might cloud up your finished product). Skim off any scum that rises to the surface as the water boils. After skimming, turn the heat down as low as it will go. Add the kombu to the pot, and simmer for 1 hour.

Carefully strain the stock through a fine-mesh strainer, taking care not to let any fish chunks or other material fall into the strainer by holding them back with a spoon (this will help keep the stock clear). If you want to add an herbaceous note to your stock, place a good handful of your choice of herbs in the strainer before you strain the stock through it. Let the stock cool and use immediately, or store in an airtight container in the refrigerator for up to 3 days or freeze for up to 3 months.

DAIKON BUSHI

Daikon bushi is an invention of ours that is basically salty, smoked, dehydrated daikon. It's inspired by Japanese katsuobushi—salted, fermented, smoked, and dried skipjack tuna. This ingredient was an enormously gratifying discovery. It's basically a vegan bouillon base that delivers far more flavor than we had any right to expect. Initially, it was a really delicious work-around for vegetarian and vegan dishes, but we find ourselves reaching for it even for meat and seafood dishes. You can use it to season directly, by grating the bushi like you might Parmesan cheese. Or steep the bushi in liquid to make a powerful infusion—but beware, it's salty. Start with a pint of broth, stock, or water, add a teaspoon-size chunk of bushi, steep for 5 minutes, then taste and add more if needed.

In a large, nonreactive container with a lid, bury the daikon radishes in just enough of the salt so they are completely encased, reserving the remaining salt. Cover the container and put it in the refrigerator for 1 week. The radishes will have released a good deal of liquid by this point—drain it off and add additional kosher salt to completely re-encase the daikon, reserving the remaining salt. In another week, repeat the draining and salt repacking process. Any remaining salt can be put to regular kitchen use. Sometime during the next few days to a week, you should notice that the daikon are very withered and no longer releasing liquid. At this point, rinse the daikon under cold water and set them on a rack to rest overnight.

The next day, cold-smoke the radishes. Set up a Weber grill and start a small fire on one side of the grill with about six handfuls of hardwood charcoal. When the smoke has subsided and the coals are glowing, about 10 minutes, add an equal amount of wood pellets or wood chips on top of the fire and put the grill grate on. Fill a heatproof bowl with ice. Place your ice bowl and the radishes on the grill grate as far away from the fire as possible. Cover the grill.

Smoke the daikon until they've browned slightly, then remove them from the smoker, split them in half lengthwise, and put in a dehydrator until they turn completely brittle. You cannot over-dehydrate the daikon bushi. Set your dehydrator on a medium-high setting and forget about them for several days. You can also dry them out in an oven. Turn your oven on to 350°F and let it run for a few minutes, then turn it off and leave the oven door slightly ajar for a couple of minutes. Place the daikon in the oven on a baking sheet, close the door, and leave it overnight.

The daikon bushi will keep indefinitely covered at room temperature.

MAKES 8 OUNCES

2 large (8- to 12-inch) daikon radishes, trimmed and peeled

3 (3-pound) boxes kosher salt

Special Equipment:

Cold smoking setup (see Glossary)

FLAVORED OILS

We appreciate good olive oil. Really, who doesn't? That said, we don't really think it makes a ton of sense to rely on it in a place where an olive tree wouldn't last more than three months. As a result, we use olive oil sparingly. Butter, animal fats, and canola oil, the latter of which is made from the hardy rapeseed, make a lot more sense in our local seafood shack context. Canola oil, like many other neutral ingredients in our repertoire, is something we're always looking to experiment with as a base layer for flavor. Flavored oils give life and visual appeal to vinaigrettes, bring depth of flavor to emulsions, and often make a wonderful cooking medium.

Generally speaking, we use two methods to doctor canola oil: infusing it with spices or blending in herbs. There is a third way we acquire flavored oil and that is by taking advantage of the oil that is by-product of other projects, like the Confit Mushroom Oil we get when we confit maitake mushrooms (page 186).

CHILE OIL

MAKES 5 CUPS

8 cups canola oil

½ cup Korean red pepper flakes (gochugaru), or 2 tablespoons red pepper flakes

¼ cup salted black beans (see Glossary)

2 tablespoons black peppercorns

1 tablespoon Szechuan chiles

3 cinnamon sticks

10 star anise pods

In a large pot, combine the oil, pepper flakes, salted black beans, peppercorns, chiles, cinnamon, and star anise. Over medium heat, bring the mixture to 200°F. Remove from the heat and whisk to distribute the flavors. Let cool at room temperature for 4 hours.

Strain the oil carefully through a fine-mesh strainer into a heatproof bowl. (To keep a clear, vibrant finished product, you want to pour mainly just the oil, not the sediment, through the strainer by holding back the solids with a spoon.) Use immediately or store the strained oil in an airtight container in the refrigerator indefinitely.

Note: After straining, you can fish out the cinnamon sticks and star anise from the sediment, discard them, and puree the remainder. We call this chile mash, and it is a great addition to marinades, vinaigrettes, or braising liquids. Store it in an airtight container in the refrigerator for up to 1 month.

PAPRIKA OIL:

Combine ½ cup good-quality smoked paprika with 8 cups of canola oil, and prepare as in the main recipe.

TURMERIC OIL:

Combine ½ cup good-quality ground turmeric with 8 cups of canola oil, and prepare as in the main recipe.

KATSUOBUSHI OIL:

Combine 2 cups thick-cut katsuobushi (see Glossary) with 4 cups canola oil, and prepare as in the main recipe.

CHIVE OIL

MAKES 2 CUPS

1 large bunch chives (or any vibrant green herb like scallions, parsley, oregano, or basil), coarsely chopped

2 cups canola oil

Set up a large bowl of ice water. In a blender, puree the chives with the oil for 1 to 2 minutes to really extract all the chlorophyll from the herb. Pour the puree into a small pot and bring it up to 216°F over medium-high heat. Pour into a heatproof container and place the container in the ice water to chill it completely. Use immediately or strain the oil through a fine-mesh strainer and store in an airtight container in the refrigerator for up to 2 weeks.

Note: When we want an herb oil, most of the time we're after that vivid green color to provide some visual appeal to a dish. But since the oils retain quite a bit of the flavor of the herb, we're also careful to make sure the herb oil makes sense with the profile of the dish. Think complementarity. For example, if a dish is anise-heavy, use tarragon oil. If it's allium-heavy, use chive oil. And so on.

FRIED AROMATICS
AND FRIED AROMATICS OIL

**MAKES ABOUT ½ CUP OF
CRUNCHY SHALLOTS,
GARLIC, OR GINGER AND
2 CUPS OF OIL**

10 large shallots, 3 heads
of garlic, or 3 large knobs of
ginger, peeled and thinly
shaved on a mandoline

Canola oil for frying

You're not The Flash. You're not Spider-Man. Your clairvoyance cannot prevent you from burning aromatics like shallots, garlic, and ginger! But if you can get this technique down, the beautiful crunchy bits and versatile flavored oils you'll have as a result will definitely become part of your rotation as recipe bases and garnishes. —*Mike*

Set up a fine-mesh strainer over a heatproof container. Line a baking sheet with paper towels.

In a heavy pot, combine the aromatics with enough oil to cover by 2 inches or more. Heat the pot on medium-high heat until your ingredients begin to sizzle and fry, stirring frequently to make sure that what is closer to the walls of the pot doesn't cook faster than what's in the middle. Let it cook until the aromatics begin to turn golden (don't let them get all the way to brown), then quickly and carefully pour the contents of the pot through the fine-mesh strainer, reserving the oil. Immediately shake the aromatics in the strainer onto the paper towel–lined baking sheet in an even layer. Once cool, taste some. If they're too dark, they will likely be too bitter, and you'll have to discard them.

The crunchy aromatics can be used immediately or stored in an airtight container with a piece of paper towel folded in the bottom at room temperature for 3 days. The oil can used immediately or kept in the refrigerator indefinitely.

CARAMELIZED CRAB

Fresh crabmeat is such a special thing. It doesn't last long, but we found that by slowly caramelizing it in a generous amount of canola oil, you can extend the refrigerated life of fresh crab many times over. The caramelized crab achieves the same depth of flavor and complexity that you'd expect from a caramelized onion. And the oil can be used in many various culinary applications—stir-fries, crab mayonnaise, or even vinaigrette.

In a heavy pot, warm the crabmeat and oil until it begins to simmer. Maintain this temperature for 3 hours, stirring once every 10 minutes or so. When the crab is deeply browned and aromatic, season with salt and you're done. Store the crabmeat and oil in a lidded container in the refrigerator; it will keep for 3 months.

MAKES 2 CUPS

8 ounces picked crabmeat

12 ounces canola oil

Kosher salt

CONFIT POTATOES

When done properly with good potatoes, this super-simple preparation yields a satisfyingly fudgy and delicious ingredient that can be used in a multitude of ways, most notably in crudos, but also in salads, fried in oil or butter as a breakfast treat, or just eaten cold with sea salt. For the recipes in this book, use the baby fingerlings for the clambake (see page 87) and russet (baking) potatoes for the Grilled Squid Salad (page 62). —*Mike*

Rinse and scrub the potatoes vigorously under cold running water in a colander. Drain the potatoes. If using baby new potatoes or fingerlings, leave them whole. If using russet potatoes, use an apple corer to punch width-wise cylinders out of the potatoes. Toss the potatoes with the salt and let sit for 1 hour.

In a pot, combine the potatoes and the oil. Bring the oil up to 200°F over medium-high heat and cook for about an hour, until the potatoes yield no resistance to a cake tester or skewer. Remove from the heat and let the potatoes and oil cool to room temperature before using. The potatoes can be packed in an airtight container and covered in their cooking oil to store in the refrigerator for up to 2 weeks. Extra oil can be used for subsequent batches of confit potatoes, vinaigrettes, frying, or any other oil needs.

MAKES ABOUT 5 POUNDS

5 pounds baby new potatoes or fingerlings, or 4 large russet potatoes

¼ cup kosher salt

4 quarts canola oil

CONFIT MUSHROOMS AND CONFIT MUSHROOM OIL

MAKES ABOUT 10 CUPS

3 pounds fresh mushrooms (such as maitake, shiitake, chanterelles, black trumpet, crimini, or porcini)

3 tablespoons kosher salt

12 cups canola oil

Confit mushrooms are an essential element of our pantry. This method of preserving allows us to process the huge amounts of beautiful local mushrooms that pop up in the late summer and fall so that we can properly store them and use them through the winter. As an additional benefit, the resulting oil from mushroom confit contains an obscene umami depth and adds great complexity to vinaigrettes and emulsions.

Confit maitake mushrooms play an important role in our Lobster Stew (page 126), so we keep them stocked year-round (wild in the fall and locally cultivated the rest of the year). The recipe makes enough to get you through the winter (maybe), and the method works for most mushrooms. Feel free to add a tablespoon of any number of flavoring ingredients—fish sauce, soy or tamari sauce, or garlic, flavored vinegars, citrus zests, and spices—to the initial salting of the mushrooms. —*Andrew*

Trim the mushrooms at their base, discarding the trim. For maitakes, pull the remaining feathery mushrooms into bite-size pieces. If you're using other mushrooms, remove their stems and cut them into bite-size pieces. Rinse the mushrooms gently in a colander until they are free of grit or dirt. Drain the mushrooms and place them in a large bowl. Add the salt to the bowl and toss to coat. Let rest for at least 1 hour.

In a large pot, combine the mushrooms with the oil and heat over medium-high heat to 190°F. Adjusting the heat as necessary, hold the mixture at this temperature for 1 hour. Cool the mixture thoroughly and strain the oil into a large bowl.

Use the mushrooms immediately or place them in a lidded container, ladle enough oil over them to cover, and store in the refrigerator for up to 1 month. For added longevity, put the mushrooms in a vacuum-seal bag, add mushroom oil to cover, seal, and freeze. They will keep indefinitely this way if they are properly sealed. The additional oil without mushrooms can be stored in a lidded container in the refrigerator indefinitely.

POTATO CHIPS

I generally operate under the assumption that nori makes all things better. One day, I put nori powder on chips and, just as I suspected, it only improved them. Adding citric acid to the seasoning mix gave a nice vinegar contrast to the seaweed flavor. Too often, these chips are my breakfast. —*Andrew*

Peel and thinly slice the potatoes with a mandoline. We prefer chips that are just shy of super-thin, as there is some charm in a slightly sturdier potato chip. As you slice, transfer the raw chips to a bowl of cold water to keep them from turning brown while drawing out some of their starch.

Toast the nori sheets by holding them with tongs, one at a time, and waving over the flame of your gas stove, until they stiffen up, become lighter in color, and start to get aromatic. (Or heat a large skillet on high heat and toast the nori on both sides for 30 seconds.) Cut the sheets into small pieces and grind them to a fine powder in batches in a spice mill or a powerful blender. Set aside.

Drain the potato slices and pat them as dry as you can with a towel or paper towels.

Line a baking sheet with paper towels. Fill a large high-sided pot with 3 inches of canola oil and heat on high to 300°F (or bring a deep-fryer to 300°F). Slip the raw potato slices, a few at a time, into the hot oil. The oil will bubble vigorously. Adjust the burner strength to maintain 300°F. When the chips are uniformly golden and have stopped bubbling, after 5 to 7 minutes, they are done.

With a slotted spoon or wire-mesh strainer, remove the chips from the oil and transfer to the prepared sheet pan. While the chips are still hot, dust them with the nori powder and salt to taste. If you're not serving them immediately, let them cool and transfer them to an airtight storage container at room temperature for up to 3 days, but they are best eaten right away.

SERVES 6 TO 8
(ONE LARGE BOWL)

1 pound russet potatoes (about 2 large potatoes)

4 sheets nori

Citric acid (optional)

Canola oil for frying

Finishing salt

PUFFED SNACKS

Who among us doesn't love Cheetos, pork rinds, Funyuns, prawn crackers, and other crunchy, salty snacks? They're especially tasty with good seafood and good drinks, and we've developed methods to puff just about anything. Below you will find two methods for making puffed snacks. The first technique involves mixing a flavorless starch base with a flavoring agent according to a 90 percent tapioca flour, 10 percent rice flour, 100 percent flavoring agent ratio. The other way to go about puffed snacks is via the funky, collagen-based route, with ingredients such pork skin, fish skin, fish swim bladder, beef tendon, and bacon rinds.

STARCH-BASED PUFFED SNACKS

MAKES ENOUGH FOR 5 TO 10 PEOPLE TO SNACK ON

2 cups tapioca flour

2½ tablespoons rice flour

2 cups plus 2½ tablespoons liquid, grated, or finely minced flavoring agent, such as hot sauce, beet juice, mustard, Parmesan cheese, nori, lobster, or shrimp

Kosher salt

About 1 cup water

Canola oil for frying

In a food processor, combine the flours and flavoring agent and turn on the machine to incorporate them. Add a good pinch of salt and slowly stream in the water until the mixture has a light gluey consistency (you may not need it all). This is your puffed snack batter.

Grease a plate small enough to fit inside a steamer basket and spread a portion of the batter sufficient to barely coat the surface of the plate (the thinner, the better). Place in the steamer. Cover and steam for 20 minutes, then transfer the cooked dough from the plate to a cooling rack. Repeat these steps to use up all of your batter. Allow the cooked dough to cool and dehydrate on the rack for 12 hours at room temperature, or if your local humidity is high, in a dehydrator or in an oven that was first preheated to 350°F and then turned off before inserting the dough. (In Maine in the winter, we can simply let the steamed snack batter sit on a rack overnight, but it's impossible in the summer.) The dough is suitable for frying when it's brittle and snaps when you bend it. Once it's dehydrated, the dough will keep in a ziplock bag at room temperature for up to 1 month. Your aim should be to fry the puffed snacks just before you serve them.

Line a baking sheet with paper towels. Fill a large pot with 3 inches of canola oil and heat on high to 350°F (or bring a deep-fryer to 350°F). Cut or break the dough into large potato chip-size pieces and slip them into the hot oil in batches. They should pop, sizzle, and expand within seconds of hitting the oil. Stir them for 10 seconds to achieve maximum puff and crisp. Remove from the oil with a slotted spoon or wire-mesh strainer and transfer the puffed snacks to the paper towel–lined sheet and season lightly with salt. These are best if served immediately but if making ahead for use in another recipe, they can be stored in an airtight container at room temperature for 5 days.

PUFFED BEET CHIPS:

Mix 1 cup tapioca flour and 1 tablespoon rice flour. Add ½ cup red beet juice, ½ cup red wine vinegar, and ½ teaspoon salt and mix well. Add enough water (about ½ cup) so the mixture has a gluey consistency and prepare as above.

CONTINUED

PUFFED SNACKS

CONTINUED

PUFFED PORK SKIN

MAKES ENOUGH FOR 5 TO 10 PEOPLE TO SNACK ON

8 ounces pork skin

Canola oil for frying

Kosher salt

Cut the pork skin into manageably large pieces and steam or simmer it in salted water for 2 hours until it is overcooked and a cake tester or skewer will slide right through it. Remove it from the pot and let it cool completely on a wire rack, then use a knife, dough knife, or other implement to scrape off every bit of meat and fat you can until you have a thin, translucent layer of outer skin.

Preheat the oven to 350°F and then turn it off. Lay the skin out on a rack set on a baking sheet and put it in the still-warm oven to partially dehydrate until it is brittle. It's really hard to give guidance on exactly how long it should stay in to dry, but several hours is usually needed. You'll have to keep a close eye on the process. It's done when you can lift up the skin and snap it in half.

Line a baking sheet with paper towels. Fill a large pot with 3 inches of canola oil and heat on high to 350°F (or bring a deep-fryer to 350°F). Cut or break the dried pork skin into large pieces, then slip the pieces into the hot oil in batches. They should pop, sizzle, and expand within seconds of hitting the oil. Stir them for 10 seconds to achieve maximum puff and crisp. Remove from the oil with a slotted spoon or wire-mesh strainer, transfer the puffed snacks to the paper towel–lined sheet, and season lightly with salt. These are best if served immediately but if making ahead for use in another recipe, they can be stored in an airtight container at room temperature for 5 days.

Note: Your butcher can get pork skin for you, or it can be found at most supermarkets.

CANDIED NUTS

Candied nuts are a versatile thing to have around to snack on, garnish crudos, or add to salads. If you take stock of our various menus at any time, you are bound to find three or four different variations of this candied nut recipe. Below is the basic method, but you can doctor it by adding various salts, sugars, spices, citric acid, and other ingredients after frying. This recipe uses peanuts, but the method works beautifully with hazelnuts, cashews, walnuts, pecans, and just about any nut you can think of. While this recipe keeps it neutral, to spice these nuts up, you can add a teaspoon of dried red pepper, smoked paprika, or other spice or spice mix when you remove the nuts from the hot oil and toss them with the salt.
—*Andrew*

In a small pot, combine the water and sugar and heat over medium heat, stirring until the sugar dissolves. Add the peanuts and simmer for 15 to 20 minutes, until the nuts soften a bit. Strain the nuts through a fine-mesh strainer. Transfer the nuts to a wire rack and let dry for 1 hour.

Fill a large pot with 3 inches of canola oil and heat on high to 350°F (or bring a deep-fryer to 350°F). Fry the dried peanuts until they turn a deep golden brown, about 3 minutes. Using a heatproof slotted spoon or wire-mesh strainer, transfer the nuts from the hot oil to a large metal bowl and toss them with salt to taste. Keep them moving for a minute or so, because as the sugars cool and dry, the nuts have a tendency to stick together. Once the nuts are completely cool, use immediately or store them in an airtight container at room temperature for up to 2 weeks.

MAKES 1 CUP

1 cup water

1 cup sugar

1 cup blanched and peeled peanuts

Canola oil for frying

Finishing salt

PICKLES

Pickles are not optional. We've talked at length in this book about the importance of balancing sweetness, salinity, and acidity. A properly deployed pickle will get you two-thirds of the way to a perfect bite.

The method we're using here makes a quick, vinegar-driven pickle. Everything that we pickle using this technique gets cooked lightly in the hot pickling liquid. The brief cooking breaks down the vegetable enough for the pickle brine to penetrate. At Eventide, we like to use mandolines and Japanese rotary slicers to render fruits and vegetables thin, uniform, and better able to take on pickling liquid. That said, a sharp knife will do just fine. Our basic pickling liquid is two parts water, one part rice vinegar, one part sugar, and salt to taste.

Consider saving your pickling liquid, because you can reuse it to make another batch of pickles. And with each subsequent round of pickles, you'll concentrate even more flavor into it. Not only that, but every time you read our exhortations to you to balance a sauce or dish with sweetness and acidity, just reach for your pickling liquid. This recipe is one of the most useful morsels in this entire book. —*Mike*

PICKLED RED ONION

MAKES 2 TO 3 CUPS

PICKLING LIQUID

1 cup filtered water

½ cup rice wine vinegar

½ cup sugar

Pinch of kosher salt

2 red onions, peeled and thinly sliced

To make the pickling liquid, in a nonreactive pot, combine the water, rice vinegar, sugar, and salt and bring the mixture to a rolling boil over medium-high heat.

Put the red onions in a nonreactive heatproof container, pour the hot brine over them, put a lid on it, and let the pickles cool to room temperature, then transfer to the refrigerator. The pickles will be at their best the next day, but you can start snacking on them once they are cold. The pickles will last indefinitely in the refrigerator if kept submerged in the pickling liquid.

PICKLED BEETS:

Replace the red onion with 1 cup peeled, thinly sliced beets. Simmer the beets in the pickling liquid for 10 minutes, then transfer to a lidded storage container and refrigerate.

PICKLED CARROTS:

Replace the red onion with 4 large carrots, peeled and thinly sliced into rounds, and prepare as in the main recipe.

PICKLED CUCUMBERS:

Replace the red onion with 2 large unwaxed cucumbers, thinly sliced into rounds, and prepare as in the main recipe.

PICKLED DAIKON:

Replace the red onion with 1 large 8- to 12-inch peeled and thinly sliced or julienned daikon and prepare as in the main recipe.

PICKLED GINGER:

Replace the red onion with 1 cup peeled, julienned ginger. Simmer it in the pickling liquid for 10 minutes instead of just pouring the hot liquid over it.

PICKLED JALAPEÑOS OR FRESNO CHILES:

Replace the red onion with 6 stemmed jalapeños or Fresno chiles, sliced thinly into rounds, and prepare as in the main recipe.

PICKLED KOMBU:

Take several sheets of dried kombu and rinse them well under cold water, then place them in a bowl. Reconstitute them by covering them in water for 20 to 30 minutes. Drain and julienne the kombu. Prepare as in the main recipe, replacing the red onion with the julienned kombu.

PICKLED RAMPS:

Replace the red onion with 1 cup trimmed ramp bulbs and prepare like the Pickled Ginger.

PICKLED SPRUCE TIPS:

In the spring, after the winter thaw, spruce trees sprout tiny, electric-green shoots from the tips of existing limbs. Replace the red onion with 1 cup of these tender spruce tips and prepare as above. Make sure the spruce tips are picked in spring when they are young and fresh, about 1 to 2 inches long. If you pick them while they're really young, you don't even need to heat the pickling liquid.

BREAD AND BUTTER PICKLES

MAKES 3 CUPS

1 pound pickling cucumbers or peeled daikon radish, thinly sliced

Filtered water

4 teaspoons kosher salt

½ teaspoon mustard seed

⅛ teaspoon celery seed

⅛ teaspoon black peppercorns

½ cup thinly sliced onion

½ cup apple cider vinegar

½ cup sugar

½ teaspoon ground turmeric

⅛ teaspoon calcium chloride (such as Pickle Crisp and related products, see page 249)

Place the cucumbers in a large nonreactive container and cover them with filtered water. Add the salt and stir well to dissolve it. Cover and let the container sit at room temperature for a few hours, or overnight.

Combine the mustard seed, celery seed, and peppercorns in a dry pan over medium heat and lightly toast for 30 to 60 seconds until fragrant.

Use a wire-mesh strainer or slotted spoon to remove the cucumbers from the soaking water into a bowl and store in the refrigerator. Pour the soaking water into a pot with the onion, vinegar, sugar, turmeric, toasted spices, and calcium chloride. Bring the mixture to a simmer. Remove the mixture from the heat and pour into an airtight heatproof container. Thoroughly chill the mixture.

Drain the cucumbers and mix with the chilled mixture in the airtight container, then return to the refrigerator. They will be ready to eat in 24 hours, but they'll be better after a few days. Store in the refrigerator for several months.

KIMCHI

KIMCHI BASE

5 jalapeños, stemmed and
coarsely chopped

3 bunches scallions,
white and light green parts,
coarsely chopped

1 cup fish sauce

1 cup light soy sauce

1 cup gochujang (Korean chile
paste; see Glossary)

10 garlic cloves, peeled

5 tablespoons kosher salt

4 quarts filtered water

1 large head green
cabbage, outer layers
removed and reserved,
cored and thinly sliced

1 large carrot, peeled and
julienned

1 large (8- to 12-inch) daikon
radish, peeled and grated

Our kimchi-making has been an evolving enterprise. The version here is savory and sour, but it's not loaded down with sugar or too much gochujang. We think it's better that way, because it complements what you serve with it, rather than overpowering it. This recipe serves a crowd and stays good in the refrigerator for a long while. The brine can be used in many different ways, including Kimchi Ice (page 33).

To make the kimchi base, combine the jalapenos, scallions, fish sauce, soy sauce, gochujang, and garlic in a food processor and puree until smooth.

In a large nonreactive container, dissolve the salt in the water. Add the base puree to the brine and mix well.

Add the sliced cabbage, carrot, and daikon to the brine, cover with the reserved cabbage leaves, and weigh down with a plate. Cover the container and let stand at room temperature for 3 to 5 days, until the vegetables taste pleasantly sour.

Store the kimchi in its brine in the refrigerator for several months. When serving, use a slotted spoon to remove the solids.

COLESLAW

People don't beat a path anywhere for coleslaw. There's a good reason for all of this: coleslaw is not the star player, and it never will be. But, coleslaw can play a supporting role, rounding out a meal as a side dish or a condiment. This recipe is lighter on mayonnaise and sugar than many out there, because we prefer slaw that provides freshness and crunch. This one has both in spades. —*Mike*

Mix the mayonnaise, fennel seed, black pepper, celery seed, sugar, 2 tablespoons of the salt, the mustard oil, onion powder, dried mustard, vinegar, and shallot oil together in a large jar with a lid, and let sit for at least 1 hour, or up to overnight, in the refrigerator.

In a large colander, toss the green and red cabbage and carrot with the remaining ½ cup of salt, and let sit for 15 to 20 minutes in the sink or over a bowl to drain. Rinse and drain the vegetables and give them a few good squeezes to wring out as much moisture as you can. Transfer the vegetables to a large bowl, dress with 1 cup of the dressing to start, then add more per your preference on creaminess. Let sit in the refrigerator for a couple of hours so the flavors can meld. Serve in a large bowl and store the leftovers, covered, in the fridge for 1 week.

2 cups mayonnaise, homemade (page 172) or store-bought

¼ teaspoon ground fennel seed

¼ teaspoon freshly ground black pepper

1 tablespoon whole celery seed

2½ tablespoons sugar

2 tablespoons plus ½ cup kosher salt

1¼ teaspoons mustard oil (see Glossary)

2 teaspoons onion powder

1½ teaspoons dried mustard powder

½ cup rice wine vinegar

2½ teaspoons Fried Aromatics Oil (page 184) made with shallots

1 small head green cabbage, outer layers removed, cored, and thinly sliced

½ head small red cabbage, outer layers removed, cored, and thinly sliced

1 large carrot, peeled and thinly sliced or shaved

GREENS SALAD

We find it enormously satisfying when we can convert people to foods they had previously shunned. This salad, in its simplicity, has done just that for many a hater of roughage. Serve it with slices of raw tuna (sliced as for the Tuna Crudo on page 77), and you've got the most popular staff order in the restaurant. —*Mike*

In a large bowl, combine the lettuces and greens with a generous splash of dressing and toss to coat. Arrange the pickled vegetables on top of the salad. Serve immediately.

SERVES 4 TO 6

6 cups assertive, spicy lettuces and salad greens (such as baby mizuna, baby mustards, or Red Frill)

Nori Vinaigrette (recipe follows)

½ cup Pickled Red Onions (page 192)

½ cup Pickled Carrots (page 193)

½ cup Pickled Cucumbers (page 193)

NORI VINAIGRETTE

MAKES ABOUT 1½ CUPS

10 sheets nori

½ cup rice wine vinegar

½ cup canola oil

¼ cup light soy sauce

2 tablespoons mirin

Toast the nori sheets by holding them with tongs one at a time, and waving them over the flame of your gas stove, until they stiffen up, become lighter in color, and start to become aromatic, about 1 minute. (Or heat a large skillet on high heat and toast the nori on both sides for 30 seconds).

Cut the nori sheets into small pieces. In a powerful blender or spice mill, grind the nori in batches to a fine powder.

In a bowl, combine the nori powder, vinegar, oil, soy sauce, and mirin and mix well. Use immediately or store in an airtight container in the refrigerator for 2 to 3 days.

BAKED BEANS

SERVES 6 TO 8

2 pounds dried Swedish brown, Marfax, or yellow eye beans

12 cups water

Pinch of baking powder

Kosher salt

¾ cup backstrap molasses

¾ cup maple syrup

3 tablespoons dried mustard powder

1 yellow onion, peeled

1 jalapeño, cut in half lengthwise

2 or 3 (2-inch) chunks homemade Salt Pork (page 202) or store-bought slab bacon (optional, but recommended)

There is some debate about the origins of baked beans. Bostonians will try to claim the dish as their own, but any good Mainer knows that baked beans really originated in eighteenth-century logging camps in northern Maine in what were known as "bean holes." Traditionally, beans were soaked overnight and then buried in cauldrons in wood-fired pits and cooked all day while the loggers worked. You still see signs in rural Maine grange halls and Lions Clubs advertising "bean hole suppers—all are welcome."

I'm a bit of a weirdo when it comes to baked beans, and I take my baked bean cookery very seriously. It's a trait that provokes quite a bit of scorn from my non–New England (people from New Hampshire included) peers. But I think a good pot of beans is deeply satisfying and a meal unto itself in the winter months. I like to start soaking my beans on Saturday morning, then put them in the oven late Saturday night so I can enjoy them with my family Sunday afternoon. —*Andrew*

Soak the beans in the water overnight in a large bowl.

Drain the beans and place them in a large pot. Cover the beans with fresh water by 2 to 3 inches, add a pinch of baking powder, and bring to a boil. Lower the heat to allow the beans to simmer, uncovered, and cook until completely tender, but still intact and plump, about 1 hour. (As John Thorne, a wonderful Maine food historian and author, would say, "cook the beans until a sharp breath will split them.") Season the beans and their cooking liquid very lightly with salt, then let cool. Drain the beans, reserving the cooking liquid.

Preheat the oven to 200°F.

Transfer the drained beans to a bean pot or heavy ovenproof pot with a lid. Add the molasses, maple syrup, dried mustard, and enough of the reserved cooking liquid to cover the beans. Stir until just incorporated. Add the onion, jalapeño, and salt pork; cover and bake for 6 to 8 hours, or overnight.

Open the pot and see where you are. The beans should have achieved a fudgy consistency and the liquid should have thickened to coat the back of a spoon. If the sauce is too thin, smash a couple beans against the side of the pot and stir them in. Season with salt to taste. Increase the oven temperature to 350°F and cook with the lid off until the sauce reaches the desired consistency and the top of the beans and chunks of pork get a nice crust on them.

Remove the onion and jalapeño and serve in a large bowl, storing leftovers in a covered contained in the fridge for up to 1 week.

SALT PORK

MAKES 2 POUNDS

5½ teaspoons kosher salt

2 teaspoons sugar

½ teaspoon pink salt
(see Glossary)

2 teaspoons freshly ground
black pepper

½ bunch thyme

5 garlic cloves, crushed

4 shallots, thinly sliced

2 yellow onions, thinly sliced

3 pounds skinless pork belly

Salt pork is bacon without the smoke (the French call it *petit sale*, meaning "a little salted") and it's a staple of New England cuisine. You won't have to look too far to find applications for it. If you end up having to buy salt pork at the grocery store, note that it's usually cured, but uncooked. You can skip the curing step below and cook it using the instructions we've laid out. —*Andrew*

In a small bowl, combine the kosher salt, sugar, pink salt, pepper, thyme, garlic, shallots, and onions and stir together. Massage the mixture with your hands to coax flavor from the aromatics. Place the pork belly on a work surface and rub it all over with the salt mixture. Seal the belly in a large vacuum-seal bag, or wrap it tightly in several layers of plastic wrap. Place in a large airtight container and store in the refrigerator for 7 days. Be sure to "overhaul" (flip) the belly every other day, to redistribute the cure. Remove the pork from its wrapping, rinse under cold water, and pat dry. At this point, your pork belly will be what Hormel or an American Revolution reenactor might call salt pork. For almost all of our recipes, we like to take it one step further and cook the salt pork.

To slow cook, set the temperature of the immersion circulator to 165°F. Seal the rinsed and dried pork in a large vacuum-seal bag and cook it in the immersion bath for 12 hours. Chill completely in an ice bath. If you don't have an immersion circulator, put the pork in a braising pan, add well-salted water to cover, put the lid on, and braise the pork in a 200°F oven for 6 hours. Remove from the pan and let cool.

The pork can be used immediately or kept in an airtight container in the refrigerator for up to 10 days or the freezer for up to 3 months.

LARDO

Lardo, the cured fat from a pig's back that is a popular Italian treat, has to be the simplest charcuterie project ever, and it's a great product to have in your pantry. The only hard part is sourcing the fat, but most good butchers should be able to get it for you. You can grind lardo and whip it to make a spread for crackers and crudités, you can dice it up and cook it lightly in a pan to make bacon-like crispies for sandwiches or salads, or you can put it to its best use: sliced into super-thin ribbons and eaten with crusty bread, so it melts in your mouth. Now that we think about it, it's so delicious it's actually kind of dangerous to have around. —*Mike*

Rinse the pork fatback and pat it dry. Bury it entirely in kosher salt in a nonreactive glass or plastic container, surrounding the fatback by at least 1 inch on all sides. Cover the container and place it in a dark, cool place (between 50° and 60°F) for 3 months. Pull the fatback out of the salt and rinse it well. Use immediately or store in an airtight container in the refrigerator for up to 3 months, cutting off pieces to use as necessary.

MAKES 1 TO 2 POUNDS

2 pounds pork fatback

Kosher salt, for packing

COLD-SMOKED FISH

MAKES 3 TO 5 POUNDS

2 pounds kosher salt

4 cups filtered cold water

3 to 5 pounds salmon fillets, skin on

1 pound sugar

Herbs and spices, such as fresh or dried dill, or anything else that fits your fancy (optional)

We find limitless opportunities for using cold-smoked fish of all kinds, including scraps that would otherwise go to waste. There are thousands of creative ways to cold smoke fish. The internet is rife with recommendations and most cookbooks will tell you to erect a structure involving hotel pans, perforated hotel pans, ice, and aluminum foil. We're going to recommend something better. You'll need cool weather, something like a Weber grill and an A-maze-n Smoker (see Glossary). Virtually any type of seafood in this book can be smoked using the following method, though this recipe is for salmon fillets.

Fillet whatever fish you are using, leaving the skin on and not bothering with the small pinbones to start. You'll eventually remove them, but they are finicky and it's easy to damage the flesh of the fish if you try to remove them when the fish is raw. They will be much easier to get rid of after the curing process is finished. —*Mike*

In a container large enough to hold the fillets, add ¾ cup salt to the clean, cold water, whisking vigorously until it starts to collect at the bottom. You can only get about a 26 percent salt concentration in the brine. Salt collected at the bottom is fine.

Score the skin of the fish several times, just deeply enough to penetrate to the flesh, to help it absorb the cure more evenly. Slip the fillets into the brine, skin-side up. Place a piece of plastic wrap across the surface of the brine to keep the fillets submerged. For a fillet that is roughly 1 inch thick, you'll want to brine for 1 hour. If it's thicker, go longer, and if it's thinner, go briefer.

While the fish brines, in a nonreactive bowl, mix the cure by mixing the remaining salt with the sugar. At this point you can add all sorts of herbs or spices.

In a second nonreactive container large enough to hold the fillets, place a ½-inch layer of the cure mixture on the bottom. Remove the fish fillets from the brine, pat them dry, and lay them skin-side down onto the cure. Cover each fillet with at least another ½ inch of the cure, cover the container, and allow the fish to cure at least overnight, or up to 24 hours, in the refrigerator.

After the fish has been curing for 24 hours, fill a large, nonreactive bowl with ice water. Dig the fillets out of the cure, brushing off any excess cure, and slip them into the ice bath. Allow the fillets to soak for as long as you brined the fillets (that is, 1 hour for a 1-inch-thick fillet).

Remove the fish from the water, pat it dry, and carefully remove the pinbones. Run your hands over the flesh and feel for the bones, then remove them carefully with fish pliers or small pliers.

Transfer the fillets to a wire rack placed on a baking sheet. Transfer the sheet to the refrigerator and chill, uncovered, for 12 hours. This step serves to build a pellicle (a coating of protein) on the surface of the fillets, which will later help the fish take on the smoke. After 12 hours, the fillets should be shiny and tacky to the touch, almost as though they had been lightly candied. Chill them an hour or two longer if this doesn't happen after 12 hours.

Set up a Weber grill and start a small fire on one side of the grill with about six handfuls of hardwood charcoal. When the smoke has subsided and the coals are glowing, after about 10 minutes, add an equal amount of wood pellets or wood chips on top of the fire and set the grill grate in place. Fill a heatproof bowl with ice. Place the ice bowl and the salmon fillets on the grill grate as far away from the fire as possible. Cover the grill.

Smoke the fish until you're happy with the color—the darker the color, the more smoke taste your fish will have. Your focus here is on smoke penetration, because you're not cooking the fish. If you love smoked foods, go for a deeper reddish brown, which will take 3 to 4 hours (in which case you'll probably need to add some charcoal and wood chips to the fire halfway through). If a little smoke goes a long way for you, pull the fish after an hour.

You can eat the fish right away, but we suggest wrapping the finished fillets tightly in plastic wrap and storing them in the refrigerator. The smoked fish is best after a couple days, when the flavors will have had time to meld and mellow. The fish will keep in the fridge for up to 2 weeks, or much longer if it has been vacuum-sealed. You can also wrap them tightly in two layers of plastic wrap, or vacuum-seal them, and freeze them for up to 3 months.

SMOKED SHELLFISH

**MAKES 25 OYSTERS,
CLAMS, OR MUSSELS**

10 cups filtered cold water

4 teaspoons kosher salt, plus
more for salting water

25 live oysters, clams, or
mussels

1 tablespoon plus 1 teaspoon
light brown sugar

Extra-virgin olive oil or a
mix of Chile Oil (page 183),
Confit Mushroom Oil
(page 186) made with maitakes,
and Fried Aromatics Oil
(page 184) made with shallots

Oysters, clams, and mussels are excellent for smoking and a great
thing to preserve in jars for use at home as appetizers on a shellfish
platter or additions to salads or other dishes. —*Andrew*

In a large bowl, mix 8 cups of the water with a few big pinches of salt.
Jostle your shellfish in the water to purge impurities. After 3 minutes,
pour the shellfish into a colander and rinse well with cold water.

Set a fine-mesh strainer over a bowl. In a pot set up as a steamer or in
a wok that will hold a bamboo basket, add the remaining 2 cups of water
and the 4 teaspoons of salt. Bring to a boil and turn down to a simmer.
Put your shellfish in the steamer, cover, and steam until all the shells open,
2 to 3 minutes. (Steam for another minute if a bunch haven't opened.)
Discard any shells that haven't opened at this point. Strain through the
fine-mesh strainer, reserving the liquid. Pick the meat from the shells,
and rinse with cold water.

Measure the reserved cooking liquid; you should have approximately
2 cups. Strain it through a fine-mesh strainer into a nonreactive bowl.
Add the brown sugar and stir to dissolve. Add the shellfish, making sure
it is covered completely; cover the bowl and refrigerate overnight.

Drain the shellfish, transfer to a wire rack set on a baking sheet, and
allow to dry out, uncovered, in the refrigerator for 24 to 48 hours until
you achieve a pellicle (shiny and tacky to the touch, almost as though
they had been lightly candied).

Set up a grill and start a small fire on one side of the grill with about six
handfuls of hardwood charcoal. When the smoke has subsided and the
coals are glowing, after about 10 minutes, add an equal amount of wood
pellets or wood chips on top of the fire and set the grill grate in place.
Place the shellfish on the grill grate as far away from the fire as possible.
Cover the grill and hot-smoke at 140°F for 4 hours. Add more coals
and wood pellets or chips to the fire to increase the heat to 160°F for
another 1 hour of smoking.

Transfer to a container with a lid and add twice as much extra-virgin
olive oil as you need to cover the shellfish. If you want to punch it up
instead, cover the shellfish with chile oil, then add equal parts confit
mushroom oil and fried aromatics oil to double the amount of oil. You
can serve immediately, but the smoked shellfish will be better if it sits
in the oil for at least 12 hours. Cover the container and store in the
refrigerator for up to 1 month.

SALTED MACKEREL

This salted mackerel can be used as a replacement for anchovies in any recipe.

Using kitchen scissors, snip the spine of the mackerel crosswise just below the head behind the gills. Holding the body firmly with one hand, use the other hand to pull the head off the fish and the entrails will all come out with the head. You can also ask your fishmonger to remove the heads from the fish for you.

Rinse the fish and the cavity well under cold water and use a finger to scoop out any remaining entrails. In a nonreactive container, toss the fish with a generous coating (about 1 cup) of the salt, transfer to a wire rack, and let sit in the refrigerator overnight. They should release lots of liquid.

Drain the fish in a colander and pat dry. Clean and dry your container. Place a generous 1-inch layer of salt on the bottom. Pack each of the mackerel cavities with the salt. Add the fish to the container, layering the fish and covering with salt until everything is encased. Cover the fish with plastic wrap and put a lid on the container. Let sit at room temperature for 2 months.

Take the fish out of the salt and rinse well under cold water. The fish should feel firm. Use your fingers to carefully pull the fillets from the bones (they should come away easily and intact). Pull the transparent film off the skin side of the fillets with your fingers or a paper towel and discard.

Pack the fillets in a large jar and cover with shallot oil. You can use immediately or you can put a lid on the jar and they will store in the refrigerator indefinitely.

MAKES 1 TO 1½ POUNDS

5 pounds Atlantic mackerel (about 5 to 7 whole, cleaned and scaled fish)

About 2 pounds kosher salt

2 cups Fried Aromatics Oil (page 184) made with shallots

DESSERTS

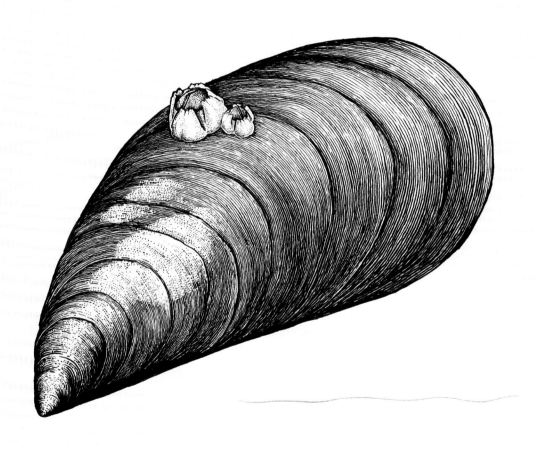

Desserts aren't usually the first thing that comes to mind when reminiscing about classic seafood shack meals. Maybe it's because the menus are so often a hit parade of American nostalgia: pies, cobblers, brownies, cookies, shortcakes, and bread puddings. These are some of the most ubiquitous and well-loved desserts in the country, and although mass-produced facsimiles can be found everywhere, including many seafood shacks, the best New England spots make their own.

Like savory seafood shack fare, these common desserts aren't meant to break new culinary boundaries. Cutting-edge technology isn't typically deployed, and abstract flavor combinations are not typically sought. As such, we always knew we wanted to have a really stripped-down set of dessert options at Eventide. However, true to our whole approach, we wanted to bring together that classicism with a touch of our team's refinement, creativity, and whimsy.

Kim Rodgers was our last hire before we opened Eventide. An art school graduate with very little kitchen experience, she got the job as a prep cook mostly out of our panicked desperation that we hadn't hired enough people. Headline: Kim was the best hire we ever made. Seven years later, she heads up the baking and pastry department for all our restaurants magnificently.

We've charged Kim with creating a wide range of desserts and baked goods, from fussy and abstract plated creations at the progressive Hugo's, to bánh mì buns and steamed bao at The Honey Paw, to, right in the middle, the Maine classics that make up the Eventide dessert menu. Kim and her team absolutely nail the whole spectrum. For Eventide in particular, they are adept at taking familiar forms or flavors and, by dint of stubbornness, creativity, and relentless organization (and maybe some masochistic tendencies, because this work is exacting!), reimagining them as the best versions of themselves, nostalgia intact.

In the recipes that follow, you'll find some cool tricks for boosting flavor and new methods that are widely applicable to what are very likely some of your favorite desserts. You'll notice that we include the weight of ingredients in this chapter. Pastry and dessert-making is such a precise form of cooking, and we believe the best results come from weighing ingredients. You can buy a cheap and reliable

digital food scale online for around twenty dollars. If you don't want to use a scale, we've also provided the volume measurement for every recipe.

Here are some pro tips to help you along:

- For cookies and whoopie pies, spray cooking spray around the edge of your baking tray before lining with parchment to help keep the parchment in place.
- When making cookies or cakes, pay attention to the bottom of the mixing bowl when you are scraping it down. Butter likes to hide there, which can cause streaking and uneven baking.
- Make sure all of your refrigerated ingredients are brought to room temperature for at least 30 minutes before making cookies or cakes. For pies, you want cold ingredients straight from the refrigerator.
- In a pinch, you can quickly temper eggs by placing them in warm water until they reach room temperature. But leave them in the shell!
- To soften butter in a hurry, dice 1 cup (2 sticks) into ½-inch cubes and microwave it in a glass bowl in 10-second increments until soft but not fully melted. But it's best to just leave it out on the counter overnight.

ICE CREAM SANDWICHES

MAKES ABOUT 9 ICE CREAM SANDWICHES

1 quart vanilla ice cream, store-bought or homemade (recipe follows)

18 cookies of your choice (recipes follow)

Ice cream sandwiches have become the cornerstone of our Eventide dessert menu but were borne out of necessity in the beginning. We didn't have a proper ice cream machine when we opened, and our baking space was miniscule, so we scrambled for something that was delicious, easy, and efficient to make ahead and store. Ice cream sandwiches were the perfect answer.

Fast-forward to today: our ice cream sandwich production line would make a PhD materials-handling engineer proud. We have engineered a system that is legendary for its elaborateness, involving silicone and ring molds, winter parkas, and individual smoothing of each sandwich with a gloved finger. If you want to chase the Platonic ideal of ice cream sandwiches, give the restaurant a call. For the rest of you content with feasible and delicious, read on.

The workhorse vanilla ice cream we provide is a good match for all the cookies to follow, but we encourage you to try out different ice cream combinations of your own. We push the limit of sugar content in our cookies but balance the flavor out with a generous amount of salt and dark chocolate. The higher the sugar content, the softer the cookie will be when it freezes. That, along with slight underbaking, has proven to yield the best textured sandwich once frozen. —*Kim Rodgers*

Pair the cookies by size, scoop a generous ⅓ cup of ice cream onto one of them, then top with the matching cookie and lightly smoosh the whole thing together. Using a butter knife, smooth the ice cream around the edges so that it is flush with the edges of the cookies. Place the cookies on a baking sheet or in a large ziplock bag and freeze for 2 to 3 hours until frozen solid.

If you're not serving the sandwiches within a day or two, wrap the sandwiches tightly in parchment paper and put them back in the freezer in the ziplock bags or a covered container for longer keeping. The sandwiches should keep for up to 1 month in the freezer.

VANILLA ICE CREAM

MAKES 1 QUART

1 cup (189 grams) whole milk

1 cup (189 grams) heavy cream

⅛ vanilla bean, or ⅛ teaspoon vanilla extract

¼ cup plus 1 teaspoon (55 grams) sugar

1 tablespoon (4 grams) nonfat dry milk powder

¼ teaspoon (1.5 grams) kosher salt

3 egg yolks

Special equipment:

Ice-cream maker

Fill a large mixing bowl with a good amount of crushed ice and a little bit of water, and set aside.

In a small pot, combine the milk and cream. Split and scrape the vanilla bean and add both the pod and seeds to the pot. Heat over medium-low heat as you prepare the dry ingredients.

In a mixing bowl, whisk the sugar, milk powder, and salt until completely combined. Then whisk the dry ingredients into the warm milk and cream mixture in the pot. Place the bowl the dry ingredients were in over the prepared ice bath. Increase the heat in the pot to medium and continue to whisk until you see the tiniest bubbles around the rim of the pot and bits of steam curling off the surface. Remove from the heat immediately.

Put the egg yolks in a bowl. Whisk about ¼ cup of the hot liquid into the yolks. Repeat, adding ¼ cup liquid at a time, until you have added enough of the hot liquid to the yolks that the outside of the bowl feels hot to the touch. Then pour the yolk mixture into the pot and whisk thoroughly to combine. Return the pot to medium-low heat. Whisk constantly until the liquid reaches 185°F (the mixture should coat the back of a spoon), then immediately pour it through a fine-mesh strainer into the bowl over the ice bath. Using a spatula, stir the mixture until cool.

Cover the bowl with plastic wrap, pressing it down to contact the surface to prevent a skin from forming. Transfer the bowl to the refrigerator and chill completely, for at least 2 hours and up to 6 hours. Freeze the mixture in your ice-cream maker according to the manufacturer's instructions. The ice cream needs to freeze hard enough that it will hold its shape but still be scoopable. It will keep in the freezer for 1 month.

Note: Mixing the nonfat dry milk powder with the larger granules of sugar ahead of time will help prevent the milk powder from clumping on the surface and allow it to dissolve more quickly.

CONTINUED

ICE CREAM SANDWICHES

CONTINUED

CHOCOLATE CHIP COOKIE

MAKES ABOUT 18 COOKIES

½ cup (1 stick/110 grams) unsalted butter, softened

½ cup (100 grams) granulated sugar

2½ tablespoons (31 grams) maple sugar or brown sugar

⅔ cup (130 grams) packed light brown sugar

1 egg, at room temperature

Heaping ½ teaspoon

(3.5 grams) kosher salt

⅛ teaspoon (0.5 grams) vanilla extract

1⅓ cups (181 grams) all-purpose flour

⅔ teaspoon (3.2 grams) baking soda

⅔ teaspoon (2.7 grams) baking powder

⅔ cup (125 grams) dark chocolate chips

In a stand mixer fitted with a paddle attachment, cream together the butter and sugars on high speed for 3 minutes, scraping down the bowl with a spatula halfway through.

Turn the mixer speed to low and add the egg; mix until fully incorporated, about 1 minute. Scrape down the sides of the bowl and the paddle. Add the salt and vanilla and mix on medium-high speed for 10 minutes. Scrape down the bowl and the paddle again.

In a medium bowl, whisk together the flour, baking soda, and baking powder. Sift them into the stand mixer bowl and mix on low speed until everything is almost combined. Add the chocolate chips and mix on low speed until they are distributed throughout the dough (don't overmix!). Use a spatula to fold the mixture a couple of times to make sure there are no streaks and everything is incorporated. Cover the dough and chill for 1 hour.

Preheat the oven to 350°F. Spray a baking sheet(s) with cooking spray and line with parchment paper.

Scoop 2 heaping tablespoons of the dough onto the prepared baking sheet(s), about 6 inches apart. Flatten the dough balls slightly with the heel of your hand. Bake one sheet at a time for 12 minutes, rotating halfway through, until the cookies are starting to lightly brown on the edges but remain soft and slightly under-baked in the center.

Transfer the cookies to a rack and let cool to room temperature, then pair the cookies by size on a sheet pan, cover with plastic wrap, and freeze (if you're hurting for room in your freezer, you can also pair the cookies up and freeze them in large ziplock bags).

HONEY-ROASTED PEANUT BUTTER COOKIE

MAKES ABOUT 18 COOKIES

½ cup (1 stick/110 grams) unsalted butter, at room temperature

⅔ cup (170 grams) creamy unsweetened peanut butter

2 tablespoons plus 1 teaspoon (49.5 grams) honey

⅔ cup (130 grams) packed light brown sugar

1 egg, at room temperature

Heaping ½ teaspoon (3.5 grams) kosher salt

⅛ teaspoon (0.5 grams) vanilla extract

1⅓ cups (181 grams) all-purpose flour

⅔ teaspoon (3.2 grams) baking soda

⅔ teaspoon (2.7 grams) baking powder

¼ cup (30 grams) chopped unsalted roasted peanuts

In a stand mixer fitted with a paddle attachment, cream together the butter, peanut butter, honey, and brown sugar on high for 3 minutes, scraping down the bowl with a spatula halfway through.

Turn the mixer speed down to low and add the egg; mix until fully incorporated, about 1 minute. Scrape down the sides of the bowl and the paddle. Add the salt and vanilla and mix on medium- high speed for 10 minutes. Scrape down the bowl and the paddle again.

In a medium bowl, whisk together the flour, baking soda, and baking powder. Sift them into the stand mixer bowl, and mix on low speed until everything is almost combined. Add the chopped peanuts and mix on low speed until they are distributed throughout the dough (don't overmix!). Use a spatula to fold the mixture a couple of times to make sure there are no streaks and everything is incorporated. Cover the dough and chill for 1 hour.

Preheat the oven to 350°F. Spray a sheet pan(s) with cooking spray and line it with parchment paper.

Scoop 2 heaping tablespoons of the dough onto the prepared sheet pan(s), about 6 inches apart. Flatten the dough balls slightly with the heel of your hand. Bake pans one pan at a time for 7 to 8 minutes, rotating the pan halfway through, until the cookies are lightly browned on the edges, but still soft and slightly under-baked in the center.

Transfer the cookies to a rack and let cool at room temperature, then pair the cookies by size on a sheet pan, cover with plastic wrap, and freeze (if you're hurting for room in your freezer, you can also pair the cookies up and freeze them in large ziplock bags).

Note: We make our own peanut butter so that we can control how much sugar and oil we add to our recipes, which we found allowed us to get a better and more consistent cookie. If you aren't able to find a no-sugar-added peanut butter, you should cut the brown sugar in the recipe below down by one-third to one-half.

CONTINUED

ICE CREAM SANDWICHES

CONTINUED

BROWN BUTTER SUGAR COOKIE

MAKES 14 COOKIES

1 cup (2 sticks/220 grams) unsalted butter

½ cup (100 grams) granulated sugar

2 ½ tablespoons (31 grams) maple sugar

⅔ cup (130 grams) packed light brown sugar

1 egg, at room temperature

1 tablespoon (15 grams) whole milk, at room temperature

⅔ teaspoon (4 grams) kosher salt

⅛ teaspoon (0.5 grams) vanilla extract

1 ⅓ cups (181 grams) all-purpose flour

⅔ teaspoon (3.2 grams) baking soda

⅔ teaspoon (2.7 grams) baking powder

1 cup plus 2 tablespoons (221 grams) turbinado sugar

Melt the butter in a small pan over medium heat until fragrant and lightly browned. Immediately remove from heat (be careful not to overcook, as it will continue to brown off the heat). Allow the solids to settle and decant the clarified butter off the top with a ladle. Let this re-solidify before using.

In a mixer fitted with a paddle attachment, cream together the room-temperature brown butter, granulated sugar, and maple sugar on high for 3 minutes, scraping down the bowl and paddle halfway through. Add the egg, mixing for a minute or so on low speed to fully incorporate. Scrape down the sides of the bowl and the paddle. Add the salt and vanilla extract, mix on low, stream in the milk, and then beat for another minute to incorporate. Scrape down the sides of the bowl and the paddle and beat on high for 10 minutes.

In a bowl, stir together the flour, baking soda, and baking powder; then sift into the stand mixer bowl. Pulse or mix on low speed until incorporated. Scrape down the bowl and the paddle and mix on low speed until everything is homogenous, no more than 60 seconds. Use a spatula to fold the mixture a couple of times to make sure there are no streaks and everything is incorporated. Cover and chill the dough for 1 hour.

Preheat the oven to 350°F. Spray a baking sheet(s) with cooking spray and line with parchment paper.

Scoop 2 heaping tablespoons of the dough and gently press the top of the dough ball into the turbinado sugar. Place on the prepared baking sheet(s) about 6 inches apart. Flatten the dough balls slightly with the heel of your hand.

Bake the pans one at a time for 10 to 12 minutes, rotating the pan halfway through, until the cookies are set but slightly underbaked in the center.

Transfer the cookies to a wire rack and cool at room temperature, then pair the cookies by size on a sheet pan, cover with plastic wrap, and freeze (if you're hurting for room in your freezer, you can also pair the cookies up and freeze them in large ziplock bags).

VARIATIONS:

To turn these cookies into snickerdoodles, press the dough into a mixture of cinnamon and sugar instead of turbinado sugar just before baking. To make funfetti cookies, press the dough into sprinkles instead of turbinado sugar just before baking.

TRIPLE CHOCOLATE COOKIE

MAKES ABOUT 18 COOKIES

10 tablespoons (1¼ sticks/ 137 grams) unsalted butter, at room temperature

½ cup (100 grams) granulated sugar

2 heaping tablespoons plus 1½ teaspoons (51 grams) maple sugar

1 cup (200 grams) packed light brown sugar

1 egg, at room temperature

1 teaspoon (6 grams) kosher salt

Dash of vanilla extract

2 tablespoons (30 grams)

buttermilk, at room temperature

1 cup plus 2 tablespoons (145 grams) all-purpose flour

½ cup (36 grams) cocoa powder

⅔ teaspoon (3.2 grams) baking soda

⅔ teaspoon (2.7 grams) baking powder

⅓ cup (63 grams) dark chocolate chips

⅓ cup (63 grams) milk chocolate chips

In a stand mixer fitted with a paddle attachment, cream together the butter and sugars on high for 3 minutes, scraping down the bowl with a spatula halfway through. Turn the mixer speed down to low and add the egg; mix until fully incorporated, about 1 minute. Scrape down the sides of the bowl and the paddle. Add the salt and vanilla and, with the mixer on low speed, stream in the buttermilk, then beat for

another minute to incorporate. Increase the speed to medium-high and beat for 10 minutes. Scrape down the bowl and the paddle again.

In a medium bowl, whisk together the flour, cocoa powder, baking soda, and baking powder. Sift the mixture into the stand mixer bowl and mix on low speed until everything is almost combined. Add both chocolate chips and mix on low speed until they are distributed throughout the dough (don't overmix!). Use a spatula to fold the mixture a couple of times to make sure there are no streaks and everything is incorporated. Cover the dough and chill for 1 hour.

Preheat the oven to 350°F. Spray a baking sheet(s) with cooking spray and line with parchment paper.

Scoop 2 heaping tablespoons of the dough onto the prepared baking sheets(s), about 6 inches apart. Flatten the dough balls slightly with the heel of your hand.

Bake the pans one at a time for 9 to 10 minutes, rotating the pan halfway through, until the cookies are lightly browned on the edges, but still soft and slightly underbaked in the center.

Transfer the cookies to a rack and let cool at room temperature, then pair the cookies by size on a sheet pan. Cover with plastic wrap and freeze (if you're hurting for room in your freezer, you can also pair the cookies up and freeze them in large ziplock bags).

WHOOPIE PIE

MAKES 15 WHOOPIE PIES

Heaping ¼ cup (50 grams) chopped dark chocolate or dark chocolate chips

½ cup (1 stick/110 grams) unsalted butter, at room temperature

1 cup plus 2 tablespoons (220 grams) packed light brown sugar

1 egg, at room temperature

1⅔ cups plus 2 tablespoons (243 grams) all-purpose flour

1 teaspoon (4.8 grams) baking soda

1½ teaspoons (6 grams) baking powder

⅔ cup (50 grams) cocoa powder

⅛ teaspoon (0.5 grams) vanilla extract

1 teaspoon (6 grams) kosher salt

1 cup (225 grams) buttermilk, at room temperature

5 cups Italian Buttercream (recipe follows)

Whoopie pies are usually found among the curiosities that live on the payment counter at every convenience and general store in Maine. With such cultural cache in Maine, I knew that we had to have whoopies on the opening menu at Eventide. We match a fairly traditional cake with a classic Italian buttercream, which makes the dessert pretty decadent. Italian buttercream can be used for all manner of cookies, pies, and pastries. It has been said that this buttercream disappears rapidly in spoonfuls if it's left around too long. —*Andrew*

Put the chocolate in a small bowl set over a pot of gently simmering water. Stir until the chocolate is completely melted, then set aside.

In a stand mixer fitted with a paddle attachment, beat the butter and brown sugar on medium speed until light and fluffy, about 3 minutes. Turn the mixer to low speed and add the egg; then increase the speed to medium and mix for 1 minute, until incorporated. Scrape down the bowl and the paddle with a spatula, then turn the mixer down to low and slowly pour in the melted chocolate. Once incorporated, stop the mixer, scrape down the bowl and paddle, and then beat again on medium speed for 5 minutes. Turn the mixer off.

Meanwhile, sift the flour, baking soda, and baking powder into a bowl and set aside.

Add the cocoa powder, vanilla, and salt to the butter mixture, then pulse the mixer on low until just incorporated. Increase the speed to medium and beat for another 5 minutes. Turn the mixer down to low again, add one-quarter of the flour mixture, and mix until almost incorporated, 30 to 60 seconds. With the mixer still running, add one-third of the buttermilk and mix until almost incorporated, 30 to 60 seconds. Continue alternating the two until everything has been added, scraping down the bowl and paddle in between additions. Once finished, use a spatula to make some final folds of the mixture to ensure there are no streaks and everything is incorporated.

Preheat the oven to 350°F. Spray two baking sheets with cooking spray and line with parchment paper.

CONTINUED

WHOOPIE PIE

CONTINUED

Spoon 2 tablespoons of the batter onto the prepared sheet pans for each cake, leaving 6 inches in between them. Bake the sheets one at a time for 10 minutes, rotating halfway through. Test for doneness by gently pressing on the center of a cake. It should bounce back immediately. If it doesn't, return the pan to the oven for another minute and then test again.

Let the cakes sit on the sheets at room temperature until they are cool enough to handle, then transfer them to a rack to cool completely. These cakes can be used immediately or stored in a covered container at room temperature for 3 days or wrapped tightly in plastic wrap and frozen for up to 1 month.

To assemble the whoopie pies, pair the chocolate cakes by size. Put the buttercream into a piping bag fitted with a large round piping tip. If you don't have piping tools, you can fill a ziplock bag and then cut a corner off. Flip half of the cakes over so the bottoms are facing up. Pipe a circle, following along the inside edge of the bottom of the cake, and then fill in the center. Each cake should take about ⅓ cup of the buttercream. Top with the other halves and gently press them together. Serve immediately or store in an airtight container at room temperature for 3 days. If you're worried about the pies sticking together, wrap them individually in plastic wrap.

ITALIAN BUTTERCREAM

MAKES ABOUT 5 CUPS

2 egg whites (from extra-large eggs; or 3 whites from large eggs), at room temperature

3 tablespoons plus ½ cup (138 grams) sugar

Kosher salt

2 tablespoons plus 2 teaspoons (40 grams) water

⅛ teaspoon vanilla bean seeds plus a small length of pod, or ⅛ teaspoon (0.5 grams) vanilla extract

1 cup (2 sticks/220 grams) unsalted butter, cubed, at room temperature

Vanilla extract as needed

In a stand mixer fitted with a whisk attachment, beat the egg whites on low speed until they are nice and frothy, 1 to 2 minutes. With the mixer still running, gradually sprinkle in 3 tablespoons (38 grams) of the sugar and a pinch of salt, then turn the mixer up to medium speed and whip until medium-soft peaks form, 4 to 5 minutes. Test this by stopping the mixer and lifting the whisk attachment out of the meringue: the peaks should mostly hold their shape, and the point of each peak should fold back on itself. If your meringue comes to medium-soft peaks before your sugar syrup reaches the proper temperature (see next step), leave the mixer running on low speed until it does.

While the egg whites and sugar are being whipped, in a small pot, combine the remaining ½ cup (100 grams) sugar and the water in a small pot and stir together gently, taking care to not leave any sugar granules on the side of the pot (they will burn). Add the piece of vanilla bean pod. Heat over medium heat until the mixture reaches 245°F or has just begun to bubble toward a boil. Remove the pot from the heat and use tongs to discard the vanilla pod.

Turn the mixer to medium speed and gradually pour a thin stream of the hot sugar syrup into the bowl, taking care to not hit the whisk to avoid splatter. After all the sugar syrup has been added, increase the speed to high and whip until the mixture cools down to room temperature, about 5 minutes. Add the vanilla bean seeds and ½ stick (55 grams) of the butter, mixing just until incorporated (this will help to pull the meringue off of the whisk's wires into the bowl). Stop the machine, gently tap the whisk against the side of the bowl to knock off any remaining meringue, and replace with the paddle attachment.

Turn the mixer to medium speed and begin adding the remaining 1½ sticks (165 grams) butter, about a spoonful at a time, making sure each one is fully incorporated before adding the next. When all the butter has been added, stop the mixer and scrape down the bowl and paddle. Then start the mixer again on medium-high speed and beat until the buttercream is white in color and light and fluffy in texture, about 2 minutes. If it looks shiny or waxy with a yellow tinge after 2 minutes, keep beating!

Taste the buttercream, and add small amounts of salt and vanilla extract to taste, beating to incorporate after each addition, until you get the flavor you desire. Be careful! A little can go a long way, but the right amount of salt should balance the sweetness.

Use immediately or make this ahead of time and hold it in the refrigerator in a covered container for up to 1 week. Just pull it out an hour or two before you want to use it and beat it for 30 to 60 seconds with the paddle attachment until it looks creamy instead of grainy and stiff.

Note: Timing is everything! We recommend measuring out all of your ingredients and gathering all of your equipment/tools before you begin. It will make following this recipe a whole lot easier. If the meringue turns into a broken mess once all of the butter has been added, it means your butter was too cold. Don't worry! Let it keep beating and the friction will slowly warm the mixture, bringing it back together. Alternatively, if it becomes soupy, the meringue might have been too warm when you added the butter. Just pour the mixture out onto a baking sheet in a thin layer, cover with plastic wrap, and chill until it re-solidifies. Then break it into chunks, put it back into the stand mixer bowl, and beat with a paddle again.

BLUEBERRY LATTICE PIE

Maine's sweet little wild blueberries are one of the world's greatest products, so it would be criminal negligence not to include this pie in the book. Served warm, with the vanilla ice cream (page 213) on top, it is an incredible taste of summer. Almost every restaurant in Maine will have some form of this (and apple pie) pie on the menu, so who are we to buck the trend? —*Andrew*

In a large nonreactive bowl, mix the blueberries with 1 cup (200 grams) of the sugar, 2 tablespoons (29 grams) of the lemon juice, and ½ teaspoon (3 grams) of the salt. Let sit for about 30 minutes, stirring occasionally. Pour into a colander and let drain for 10 to 15 minutes, until the berries are clumped in a mass and not swimming in liquid.

Spray cooking spray in a deep-dish 9-inch pie plate and generously flour a work surface. Divide the pie dough in half, and re-wrap one half and return it to the fridge. Roll out one half into a circle about 1 inch wider than the rim of the pie plate. Center the dough over the plate and lay it down, gently pushing down in the center first, then moving to the corners, and finally up the sides of the dish, pressing it firmly to avoid trapping any air bubbles underneath the crust. Drape the excess dough over the edge of the pie plate, wrap the whole thing tightly with plastic wrap, and chill in the refrigerator for 1 hour.

Dust the work surface with more flour and roll out the second portion of dough to the same size as the first. Transfer to a baking sheet, wrap tightly in plastic wrap, and chill for 1 hour.

Transfer the dough to a lightly floured work surface. Using a fluted pastry wheel or sharp knife, cut the dough into 1-inch strips. Transfer the pieces back to the baking sheet, wrap in plastic wrap, and chill in the refrigerator again for 1 hour.

Place a baking sheet in the middle of the oven and preheat to 400°F. (The pan will catch any pie filling that might bubble over the edge.)

In a mixing bowl, combine the drained blueberries with the remaining ½ cup (100 grams) of sugar, 1 tablespoon (14 grams) of lemon juice, ½ teaspoon (3 grams) of salt, and the lemon zest. Taste a bit of the filling and adjust the seasoning as needed. Sift the cornstarch over the berries and stir well to thoroughly incorporate.

CONTINUED

MAKES ONE 9-INCH PIE

5 cups fresh wild Maine blueberries or cultivated blueberries

1⅓ cups (300 grams) granulated sugar

3 tablespoons (43 grams) fresh lemon juice

1 teaspoon (6 grams) kosher salt

Pie Dough (recipe follows), doubled batch

Finely grated zest of 1 large lemon

¼ cup (30 grams) cornstarch

1 egg, beaten

Turbinado sugar for sprinkling

Note: We use a combination of butter and shortening in our pie dough to achieve a light, flaky, and rich (but not too rich) crust. Feel free to play around with the ratio of butter to shortening to find out what you like the best. We've found that macerating and draining the fruit before making the pie filling helped to make a more consistently set filling. Double this recipe for the blueberry lattice pie to make the lattice top.

BLUEBERRY LATTICE PIE

CONTINUED

Remove the pie plate with the dough from the refrigerator and pour in the filling, leaving a little bit of space between the top of the filling and the top of the plate (you may have some filling left over). Brush some of the beaten egg onto the edges of the dough hanging over the edge of the plate (to act as glue for the lattice strips), then lay half of the strips out evenly in one direction on top of your filling, leaving ½ inch between strips. Rotate the pie plate 90 degrees and weave the remaining strips through the first ones by lifting up the strips and laying them down, spacing them the same distance apart as the first.

Trim the overhanging bottom dough and lattice strips to a uniform length, leaving ½ inch beyond the edge for crimping the edges. Starting in one spot, use your fingers to crimp the bottom dough edge and lattice edges together. Work your way around the edge of the pie plate. Then go back around and, using a fork or your fingers, crimp or flute the edges to make the edge look even and uniform. Brush the remaining beaten egg over the top of the lattice and the crust and sprinkle with the turbinado sugar.

Place the pie plate on the preheated baking sheet and bake for about 30 minutes, until the edges of the crust are light golden brown. Tear a piece of aluminum foil slightly larger than the diameter of the plate and place it on a cooling rack. Remove the pie from the oven and place it in the center of the foil, then carefully roll the foil up and over the crust to help prevent it from getting too dark. Return the pie to the oven, lower the temperature to 350°F, and bake for another 45 to 60 minutes, until the filling is bubbly and thickened (or the center of the pie reads 200°F).

Remove the pie from the oven and let cool to room temperature completely before serving. Leftovers can be wrapped in plastic and kept at room temperature for up to 3 days or in the fridge for up to 5 days.

PIE DOUGH

MAKES 1 PIE SHELL

1½ cups (210 grams) all-purpose flour

⅔ teaspoon (4 grams) kosher salt

1 teaspoon (4 grams) sugar

1 tablespoon plus 2 teaspoons (13.3 grams) vegetable shortening

8½ tablespoons (1 stick plus ½ tablespoon/ 121 grams) cold unsalted butter, cubed

2 tablespoons (30 grams) ice water

In a large bowl, mix the flour, salt, and sugar. Add the shortening and rub it into the flour mixture between the palms of your hands until you have a crumbly, sandy texture, around 3 minutes. Add the butter, toss to coat in the flour mixture, and then use your fingers to break up the butter into pea-size or smaller pieces. Make a small well in the center of the bowl and add the water a little at a time, gently mixing and tossing until the dough just holds together when squeezed. You may end up not using all of the water.

Press the dough together into one piece, wrap it tightly in plastic wrap, then flatten it into a disk and chill for at least 1 hour. You can make this ahead and hold it in the fridge for up to 3 days, or freeze it for up to 1 month, thawing completely before using.

APPLE PIE WITH
OAT CRISP TOPPING

OAT CRISP TOPPING

¾ cup plus 1 tablespoon (110 grams) all-purpose flour

1 heaping tablespoon (13 grams) granulated sugar

¼ cup (51 grams) light brown sugar

⅓ teaspoon (1.5 grams) kosher salt

Pinch of ground cinnamon

3½ tablespoons (50 grams) cold unsalted butter, cubed, plus 1½ tablespoons (22 grams) unsalted butter, melted

½ cup (51 grams) old-fashioned rolled oats

PIE FILLING

8 large firm apples (like Granny Smith), peeled, cored, and either chopped or sliced

1½ cups granulated sugar

2 tablespoons fresh lemon juice

Kosher salt

½ teaspoon ground cinnamon

¼ teaspoon freshly grated nutmeg

¼ cup all-purpose flour, sifted

Pie Dough (page 224)

Blueberries in the summer, apples in the fall. While many more types of fruit grow in Maine, these are the two big crops. From early September to early November, the smell of apple pie and cider donuts hangs thick in the air once you get a couple of miles outside Portland. We love our apple pie with this oat crisp, but you can make a lattice or closed top as well. —*Andrew*

To make the oat crisp topping, in a large bowl, mix the flour, sugars, salt, and cinnamon. Add the cold butter and rub handfuls of the mix between the palms of your hands until you have a crumbly, sandy texture. Add the melted butter and oats and toss everything together by hand until combined. Cover and chill while you prepare the filling and pie shell.

To make the pie filling, in a large nonreactive bowl, toss together the apples, 1 cup of the sugar, the lemon juice, and a pinch of salt. Let sit for about 15 minutes, stirring occasionally, then pour into a colander and let drain for 10 to 15 minutes, until the apples are clumped in a mass and not swimming in liquid.

Spray cooking spray in a 9-inch deep-dish pie plate and generously flour a work surface.

Roll out the pie dough into a circle about 1 inch wider than the rim of the pie plate and lay it centered over the plate. Gently push down in the center first, then move out to the corners, and finally up the sides of the dish, pressing it firmly to the plate to avoid trapping any air bubbles underneath the crust. Carefully trim any dough overhanging the rim of the pie plate if it isn't generally a uniform length. Starting in one spot, roll the overhanging dough up under itself to the rim of the plate and press together, and work your way around. Then go back around and crimp or flute to the edges. Wrap it up well and chill in the refrigerator for 1 hour.

Place a baking sheet in the middle of the oven and preheat to 400°F. (The pan will catch any pie filling that might bubble over the edge.)

In a large bowl, mix the drained apples with the remaining ½ cup of sugar, 1 teaspoon salt, and the cinnamon and nutmeg. Taste an apple and adjust the seasoning, if necessary. Sprinkle the flour over the apples and mix until evenly distributed.

Take the shaped pie crust out of the fridge. Pour in the filling, mounding it slightly in the center but leaving a little bit of space between the top edge of the filling and the top of the plate (you may have some left over). Sprinkle the oat crisp topping over the filling until you cannot see any of the apples below.

Place the pie plate onto the preheated baking sheet and bake for about 30 minutes, until the edges of the crust are light golden brown. Tear a piece of aluminum foil slightly larger than the diameter of the plate and place it on a cooling rack. Remove the pie from the oven and place it in the center of the foil. Carefully roll the foil up and over the crust to help prevent it from getting too dark. Return the pie to the oven, lower the temperature to 350°F, and bake for another 45 to 60 minutes, until the filling is bubbly and thickened (or the center of the pie reads 200°F).

Remove the pie from the oven and let cool to room temperature completely before serving. You can make this ahead and hold it in the fridge for up to 3 days, or freeze it for up to 1 month, thawing completely before serving.

COCKTAILS

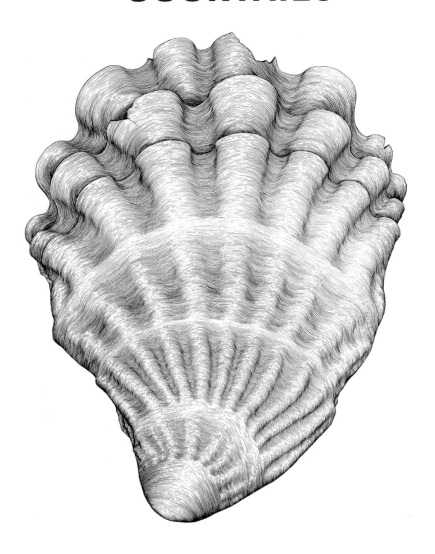

It will not surprise you to hear that the Eventide beverage program is just like everything else we do: casual but thoughtful, reliant on local and seasonal products, often experimental, and always meant to lift up the seafood shack experience without stepping on people's nostalgia. It was designed by Arlin in partnership with our opening bar manager and beverage director, John R. Myers. His skills behind the bar, instinct for hospitality, and prim mustache are the stuff of legend.

In designing the program, we were stylistically most interested in things that fit with our culture and our food. Crisp, light, flavorful, and funky were the organizing principles, because those profiles go best with seafood. The space constraints we had (and still have) demand that we keep everything as tight and well-curated as possible, which has always been a formidable challenge.

Beer is the most classic seafood shack beverage, so we'll start there. Our focus is always on local products and purveyors, which is easy in New England, where the craft beer culture is strong. In Maine particularly, we have the granddaddy, Allagash Brewing, which makes consistently great beers. Rob Tod and the Allagash team blazed the way for a bunch of other upstart breweries around Portland, including Oxbow Brewing Company, Bunker Brewing Company, and Maine Beer Company. You'll always find the locals represented on our six taps.

As much fun as it is to explore the next great trend in American beer, we have always maintained a healthy respect for classic imports, like Saison Dupont from Dupont Brasserie in Belgium; Reissdorf Kölsch from Heinrich Reissdorf brewery in Cologne, Germany; all the offerings from Samuel Smith's Brewery in Yorkshire, England; Old Speckled Hen from Morland/Greene King Brewery in Suffolk, England; and Murphy's Irish Stout from Lady's Well Brewery in Cork, Ireland. In general, there's something for everyone listed on our big specials board and our menu, from Ritterguts Gose for the beer nerd to the Anchor Porter from Anchor Brewing your girlfriend's dad swears by.

Our approach to wine is similarly focused on affordable types that go well with seafood, like crisp whites and lively sparkling wines. You will always find a bone-dry, laser-sharp Muscadet from the France's Muscadet Sèvre et Maine region being poured by the glass, alongside more esoteric offerings like the delicate and exquisitely floral Rosato di Cabernet Franc from Channing Daughters in Bridgehampton, New York. Our bottle list has a wealth of options to please even the most discriminating oyster eater. From crisp Chablis Grand Cru to funky grower Champagnes, we've left no shell unturned in our endeavor to deliver the perfect shellfish pairing. We would be remiss not to mention that we are huge fans of large-format bottles that are a little more adventurous, like the Steininger Grand Grü Grüner Veltliner from Austria. We thrill at the sight of a big table of boisterous eaters sharing a magnum of wine while taking down dozens of shells alongside round after round of crudos and lobster rolls. That is the way life should be.

The cocktail list is where we allow ourselves to get the most creative. We have taken really good care to make sure we use high-quality local spirits where possible, like New England Distilling Gunpowder Rye Whiskey and Hardshore Original Gin from Hardshore Distilling Company (both in Portland). We wanted cocktails that were pitch-perfect matches for the key parts of our menu and our ethos overall. The Celery Gimlet (page 239) goes great with oysters. The tiki-style drinks (Scorpion Bowl, page 235; Walking Dead, page 235) are all about familial good cheer. Coffee and Cigarettes (page 240) is perfect as a digestif after you've eaten yourself into near oblivion (or if you're the "I just got out of work" industry person). We denote specific types of alcohol that we love in the following recipes, but you can substitute according to preference and availability.

We hope you'll mix it up with these cocktail recipes!

ET&G

This is our version of a gin and tonic, which may be the greatest of all cocktail accompaniments for slurping shellfish. Good tonic is essential, so naturally we've experimented with many variations of tonic syrup over the years and the current recipe on page 245 is definitely our favorite. The cinchona bark supplies the quinine bitterness, while the lemongrass and coriander bring a depth of citrus flavor that goes beyond the lime and lemon zest. This syrup hold its own with any full-bodied, robustly flavored gin.

In a Collins glass, combine the gin and tonic syrup over ice. Top off with club soda. Stir. Garnish with lime.

MAKES 1 COCKTAIL

2 ounces Beefeater gin

¾ ounce House Tonic Syrup (page 245)

Club soda for topping

Lime slice for garnish

Walking Dead

SCORPION BOWL

As a bartender making the first Scorpion Bowl on any given evening, I always know that it won't be the last. The sight of an ornate, flaming bowl of rum being paraded through the dining room will inevitably cause heads to turn and copycat orders to start rolling in. Designed to be shared, our Scorpion Bowl has graced the table of countless bachelorette parties and transformed many an awkward first date. You know what they always say . . . go big or go home! —*Arlin*

In a cocktail mixing glass, stir together the Black Seal and Brugal Añejo rums, gin, sherry, orgeat, grenadine, and citrus juices and pour over ice in a large, Scorpion Bowl–style goblet. Make it pretty with novelty umbrellas, citrus twists, and any over-the-top garnish. Nestle the half-lime shell in the drink (bowl-side up), fill with the Overproof rum, and carefully light it on fire.

MAKES 1 LARGE COCKTAIL

3 ounces Gosling's Black Seal dark rum

2 ounces Brugal Añejo rum

1 ounce Beefeater gin

1.5 ounces amontillado sherry

1.5 ounces orgeat, store-bought or homemade (page 244)

1 ounce grenadine, store-bought or homemade (page 244)

2 ounces fresh lime juice, plus the shell of half a lime for garnish

3 ounces fresh orange juice

1 ounce overproof rum

WALKING DEAD

Our take on the tiki classic Zombie, which we call the Walking Dead, is as delicious as it is potent. The drink's success hinges on a blend of quality rums, fresh juices, and our house-made falernum. Falernum is a rum-based, syrupy liqueur that originated in the Caribbean. Flavored with ginger, lime, almonds, and spices, it lends a distinctive depth and intriguing warm spice notes to many of our favorite drinks.

In a cocktail shaker, combine the rums, fruit juices, falernum, grenadine, and bitters. Add ice, shake until well chilled, and strain into a tiki glass filled with crushed ice. Garnish with mint and a novelty drink umbrella spearing lime and orange slices and a cherry, and serve with a paper straw.

MAKES 1 COCKTAIL

1 ounce Gosling's Black Seal black rum

1 ounce Brugal Añejo rum

1 ounce Cruzan 151 rum

1 ounce fresh lime juice

1 ounce fresh orange juice

1 ounce fresh pineapple juice

½ ounce falernum, store-bought or homemade (page 245)

½ ounce grenadine, store-bought or homemade (page 244)

3 dashes Angostura bitters

Mint, lime slice, orange slice, and maraschino cherry for garnish

NEGRONI BIANCO

MAKES 1 COCKTAIL

1½ ounces Beefeater gin

1 ounce Cocchi Americano aromatized wine

1 ounce Dolin Blanc vermouth

Grapefruit peel for garnish

The Negroni Bianco was concocted as a lighter, refreshing take on its classic Italian namesake. We kept the base spirit—gin—the same, but swapped in Dolin Blanc for the typical red sweet vermouth and Cocchi Americano for the Campari. The Dolin Blanc is a colorless sweet vermouth from Chambéry, France, that is a little less spicy and a little more herb-forward than the traditional Italian style of rosso vermouth. Cocchi Americano is an aromatized wine with a lower proof and restrained bitterness compared to Campari. By dialing back both the bitterness and the alcohol, we ended up with a cocktail that was at home with both raw seafood and warm patios.

In a mixing glass, combine the gin, Cocchi Americano, and Dolin Blanc. Add ice and stir. Strain into a rocks glass filled with ice. Garnish with a twist of grapefruit peel.

KENTUCKY CYCLIST

MAKES 1 COCKTAIL

1½ ounces Old Grand-Dad Bonded bourbon

1 ounce Bonal Gentiane-Quina liqueur

½ ounce green chartreuse

½ ounce yellow chartreuse

2 dashes orange bitters

Orange peel for garnish

The Kentucky Cyclist is a Manhattan-esque stirred cocktail that showcases one of my personal favorite aperitif wines, Bonal Gentiane-Quina. Bonal is floral, bitter, and sweet all at the same time and derives its character from gentian root, cinchona, and herbs from the Chartreuse Mountains. Bonal was one of the early sponsors of the Tour de France; at the turn of the century, spectators would hand bottles of it to flagging cyclists to help fortify them against the long ride. Here, Bonal is balanced against the aggressive herbal bite of green chartreuse and the honeyed sweetness of yellow chartreuse, with a backbone of good old-fashioned American whiskey. As they say in France, *vive la bourbon*! —*John R. Myers*

In a mixing glass, combine the bourbon, Bonal, chartreuses, and bitters. Add ice and stir. Strain into a martini glass and garnish with a twist of orange peel.

Kentucky Cyclist

DIRTY DIRTY MARTINI

The drink so dirty we named it twice! The Dirty Dirty began as a convenient outlet for the copious amounts of oyster brine we were generating in the kitchen when we first opened, and it quickly became our most popular cocktail. Pairing that oyster brine with olive brine and a dash of hot sauce brings a roundness and pop of heat to a drink that tastes like what we imagine it would be like to drink a martini at the bottom of the ocean. It doesn't get much dirtier—in a good way—than that. —*Arlin*

In a cocktail shaker, combine the vodka, olive brine, oyster liquor, and Tabasco sauce. Add ice, shake until well chilled, and strain into a martini glass. Garnish with an olive.

MAKES 1 COCKTAIL

2½ ounces vodka or gin

½ ounce olive brine

½ ounce oyster liquor

Several drops of Tabasco sauce

Olive for garnish

CELERY GIMLET

If we were handing out cocktail superlatives, the celery gimlet would win for the best unexpected pairing with a bivalve. This cocktail resonates with an abundance of both acidity and minerality that perfectly harmonizes with an oyster's crisp, cold brine. The celery itself imparts vegetal, nearly salty flavors and, along with a hint of earthy green chartreuse, it lends the cocktail its alluring emerald coloring. —*Arlin*

In a cocktail shaker, combine the gin, celery juice, lime juice, chartreuse, vinegar, and bitters. Add ice, shake until well chilled, and strain into a coupe glass.

MAKES 1 COCKTAIL

2½ ounces Beefeater gin

1 ounce fresh celery juice (from 1 or 2 ribs)

½ ounce fresh lime juice

½ ounce green chartreuse

¼ ounce apple cider vinegar

3 dashes celery bitters

Note: If you do not have a juicer, you can puree celery in a blender and then wring it out in a cheesecloth or pass it through a fine-mesh strainer.

COFFEE AND CIGARETTES

MAKES 1 COCKTAIL

1½ ounces espresso vodka

1 ounce Johnnie Walker
Black Label scotch

1 ounce Fernet-Branca liqueur

¼ ounce simple syrup
(page 244)

Lemon peel for garnish

This may be the perfect after-dinner drink. It tastes a lot like it sounds, with smoky scotch going up against highly caffeinated espresso-infused vodka, all held together by a bitter Fernet-Branca top note. The scotch mellows you out while the vodka perks you up and the Fernet helps soothe your stomach after the somewhat questionable decision to have another fried oyster bun for dessert. —*Arlin*

In a cocktail shaker, combine the vodka, scotch, Fernet, and simple syrup. Add ice, shake until well chilled, and strain into a whiskey glass. Garnish with a twist of lemon peel.

TEA WITH A TWIST

Have you ever enjoyed one of the many iced tea–flavored malt beverages on a hot summer day? If so, you're familiar with one of my guiltiest pleasures. By combining tea-infused vodka with fresh lemon juice and real iced tea, our twist on classic iced tea infused with booze is one of the most crowd-pleasing cocktails on our list. We made a big breakthrough when we figured out that cold-infusing the tea into the vodka, rather than into water, would give this drink a more clarified flavor and not dilute it too much. —*Arlin*

In a very large bowl, combine the Sobieski vodka with the tea bags and infuse at room temperature for 3 hours. Discard the tea bags and pour in the mandarin vodka, iced tea, lemon juice, and simple syrup, stirring to combine. Serve in swing-top bottles, large jars, or other suitable containers. Any extra tea will keep in the refrigerator in airtight containers for up to 1 month.

MAKES ENOUGH FOR AN ENORMOUS PARTY

2 (1.75-liter) bottles Sobieski vodka

4 black tea bags

2½ (750-milliliter) bottles Hangar 1 Mandarin Blossom vodka

4 quarts unsweetened black iced tea (store-bought)

2 quarts fresh lemon juice (from 40 to 50 lemons)

2 quarts simple syrup (page 244)

COCKTAIL ESSENTIALS

Our bar program is no different than our kitchen program—if we can handmake it to our specifications, we will! Some of our key cocktail-building elements, like grenadine, are well known, while others are new and experimental, like falernum and orgeat. Pretty early on, we decided that if we couldn't find something local, we'd try to make it ourselves. An example of this is falernum, the weird, wonderful, almond-driven liqueur that is found in the Caribbean.

GRENADINE

MAKES 6 CUPS

1¾ cups pomegranate concentrate

1¾ cups water

4¼ cups sugar

Small pinch of citric acid

Small pinch of kosher salt

In a small pot, combine the pomegranate concentrate, water, sugar, citric acid, and salt and bring to a simmer over medium-low heat. Cook for about 15 minutes until reduced to a thick syrup the consistency of maple syrup. Let cool, then use or store in a covered jar in the refrigerator for several months.

SIMPLE SYRUP

MAKES 1½ CUPS

1 cup sugar

1 cup water

Combine the sugar and water in a small pot. Heat over medium-high heat, stirring often, until the sugar dissolves, which should take only 1 to 2 minutes. Let cool and store in a lidded container in the fridge for 2 weeks.

VARIATION:

To make rich simple syrup for the Eventide Falernum (opposite), combine 2 cups sugar with 1 cup water and prepare as in the main recipe.

Note: Using the 1:1 ratio for sugar and water, you can scale this recipe to the moon. If you're making a larger batch, the cooking time may increase. Just keep stirring until the sugar is fully dissolved.

ORGEAT

MAKES 5 CUPS

1 cup whole almonds

2 cups hot water

1 gram Ticaloid 210 S Powder (optional; see glossary)

1⅔ cups sugar

1 ounce Hangar 1 Mandarin Blossom vodka

In a skillet over medium-high heat, toast the almonds until they have darkened in color, 3 to 5 minutes. Combine the almonds and hot water in a blender and puree until it looks like thick almond milk. Allow to cool completely. Strain the mixture through a fine-mesh strainer lined with cheesecloth set over a large bowl, being sure to press out all of the liquid from the remaining pulp. Pour the almond liquid back into the blender and add Ticaloid powder, blending until incorporated. Add the sugar and vodka and blend again. Pour into a large jar, cover, and store in the refrigerator for 2 weeks.

EVENTIDE FALERNUM

MAKES ABOUT 6 CUPS

8 limes

40 whole cloves

2 star anise pods

1 tablespoon allspice berries

1½ cups whole almonds

1¼ cups Pusser's rum

½ cup overproof rum

1 cup peeled and minced fresh ginger

2 tablespoons fresh lemon juice

1¼ cups Rich Simple Syrup (see variation, page 244)

With a vegetable peeler, peel the limes and reserve the peels, then juice the limes (you should have ½ cup lime juice).

In a large skillet over medium heat, toast the cloves, star anise, and allspice for 30 to 60 seconds, until fragrant. Set aside.

In the same skillet, toast the almonds over medium-high heat, shaking them often, until they have darkened in color, 3 to 5 minutes. Combine the almonds and rums in a food processor and pulse to break down the almonds into small crumbs (stop short of creating a puree of almond flour).

Set an immersion circulator to 126°F. Combine the rum and almond mixture, toasted spices, ginger, and lime peels in a large vacuum-seal bag. Seal the bag, then cook in the immersion circulator for 2 hours, or put the ingredients into a high-quality zip-lock freezer bag, bring a large pot of water to a simmer, turn off the heat, lower the freezer bag into the hot water, and leave the bag in the water for 2 hours. Check during that time to make sure the water stays hot to the touch. Set up an ice bath.

Cool the bag in an ice bath and strain the contents through a fine-mesh strainer lined with cheesecloth into a very large jar or bowl. Add the ½ cup lime juice, the lemon juice, and the simple syrup and shake or stir thoroughly to combine. Use immediately or cover the jar and store in the refrigerator for up to 1 month.

HOUSE TONIC SYRUP

MAKES 6 CUPS

6 stalks lemongrass

1 tablespoon coriander seeds

2 limes

2 lemons

4 cups water

¼ cup cinchona bark (see Glossary)

2 cups sugar

¼ cup citric acid

¼ teaspoon kosher salt

Chop the lemongrass into chunks and bruise in a mortar and pestle or on a cutting board with the back of a knife, then reserve in a bowl. Pulverize the coriander seeds in the mortar and pestle or a spice grinder, then add to the bowl with the lemongrass.

With a vegetable peeler, peel the limes and lemons, and set the peels aside, reserving the fruit for another use.

In a pot, combine the water, lemongrass, cinchona bark, lime peels, lemon peels, and coriander. Bring to a boil, turn down to a simmer, and cook for 10 minutes. Remove the pot from heat, cover with foil, and let steep for 1 hour.

Strain the contents multiple times through a cheesecloth-lined fine-mesh strainer, replacing the cloth each time (the goal is to remove as much solid material and pulp as possible).

In a pot, combine the strained liquid, sugar, citric acid, and salt, stirring to dissolve everything. Allow to cool and use immediately or store in a sealed large bottle or jar in the refrigerator for 2 weeks.

GLOSSARY

Eventide is an intersection for so many things: tradition and modernity, local and global, low tech and high tech, casual and elevated. We are constantly exploring the space between all of those things to discover new ways to make people happy in the restaurant, and over the past few years, we've landed on some cool tools, techniques, and ingredients that make things a little easier and more interesting. Here are a few that help our kitchen hum and could help you take on some of the recipes in this book.

EQUIPMENT

Bamboo steamer basket: Ubiquitous in Asian cooking, the bamboo steamer basket is a cylindrical, perforated vessel that gets filled with food, covered, and placed over boiling water to steam whatever is inside. They're better and cheaper than microwaves; you should buy several. At Eventide, we use them for our family-style clambake, which is reproduced in the book as the Efficiency Apartment Clambake (page 102). We recommend buying 12-inch baskets.

Cold smoking at home: We are all big fans of smoked seafood and use it a lot at our restaurants. There are many creative ways to do smoke at home, too, but here's our method. You'll need cool weather, something like a Weber grill and an A-maze-n smoker, which you can buy online. It's a clever little unit made of perforated metal in the shape of a small maze. Fill the maze with wood chips or wood pellets, light one end, and put it under the grate on the opposite side of the grill from the food on top of the grate. The smoker will produce hours of consistent smoke with almost no heat. Check out our recipes for smoked seafood on pages 204 and 206.

Fine-mesh strainer: This kitchen tool allows for straining out impurities from stocks, broths, and sauces. Passing a puree or a sauce through a fine-mesh strainer results in a smoother, more refined

Bamboo steamer basket

preparation. You'll see it all over this book, because as Thomas Keller says, "when in doubt, strain."

Food dehydrator: A food dehydrator is an appliance that draws the moisture out of food and concentrates its flavor. We use it for a variety of garnishes and other ingredients, including the Daikon Bushi (page 181) and Kalamata Olive Crumb (page 62) preparations in this book. Excalibur is the high-end version that you can buy online, but you can also get a cheaper version from Nesco. An alternative to using a food dehydrator is as follows: turn your oven on to 350°F and let it run for a few minutes, then turn it off and leave the oven door slightly ajar for a couple of minutes. Place your ingredient in the oven on a baking sheet and close the door. Leave it for 8 hours or overnight and you should get a similar result.

Immersion circulator: This electrical appliance is attached to a tub of water to make sous vide (French for "under vacuum") cooking possible. It heats the water to a precise temperature and can hold it there over long periods of time while circulating the water, allowing you to cook an ingredient uniformly and to an exact temperature. It basically gives you complete control in a way that no other cooking implement can. It's used all over the restaurant world, from high-end restaurants to catering kitchens, and entrepreneurs have brought a lot of different home-use versions to market in recent years. We use an immersion circulator for a variety of things at Eventide, including very precise fish cookery, or for the eggs in our House Mayonnaise and its valuable spinoffs (page 172). There's really not an easy substitute for this cooking technique, although for fish or some proteins, lightly poaching in liquid can create somewhat similar outcomes.

Refractometer: We are proud of the unique flavored ices (page 32) we serve as accoutrements with our shellfish program, and the name of the game for pulling them off is sugar content. Sugar is essential to making the ice easy to work with and giving it the right texture in the end. A refractometer is a tool often used in the culinary world to measure the sugar content (also known as the Brix level) of liquids, and while it's not critical to have one in your home kitchen to pull of shaved ices, we make large enough amounts in the restaurant that it's worth being able to measure things precisely. The sweet spot, no pun intended, is a Brix level of 14°. We don't have a particular favorite brand, but there are quite a few available online.

Thermometers: There are quite a few recipes (particularly fried dishes) in this book that call for a digital instant read thermometer, which you can buy online, at some grocery stores, or at kitchen goods or hardware stores. We like the Thermapen brand, but any version will suffice.

INGREDIENTS

Barley koji: There is a deep, deep rabbit hole behind koji (*Aspergillus oryzae*), which is the fungus that, when inoculated on cooked grain, becomes the mother fermentation agent of soy sauce, bean pastes (including misos), sake, and *shochu*. Koji can be deployed in a variety of ways to enhance the sweetness, richness, or savoriness of a given dish. We use barley inoculated with koji to make a knock-out vinaigrette with calamansi lime (page 154). You can buy it online or in Asian grocery stores.

Bonito flakes: Made from dried skipjack tuna, bonito flakes are commonly used as a garnish on hot food. The heat rising from the dish causes the flakes to dance. You can buy it online or in Asian grocery stores.

Calamansi vinegar: Calamansi is a wonderfully fragrant citrus common to Southeast Asia that has mandarin orange and kumquat qualities and resembles a lime. We use Huilerie Beaujolaise brand *vinaigra de calamansi*.

Calcium chloride: An additive commercially known as Pickle Crisp, these granules help keep pickled products crisp in their pickling medium. We use it in our Bread and Butter Pickles (page 193), which are sliced before pickling and can turn mushy more quickly than whole vegetables. It can be found online or at most grocery stores.

Cinchona bark: Cinchona bark is harvested from the cinchona tree, an evergreen plant native to the Andes of South America. The bark contains a naturally occurring form of quinine and has long been used in the treatment and prevention of malaria. Quinine on its own is extremely bitter, and to make it more palatable, British colonials in India began mixing quinine water with citrus, sugar, and gin. Thus, the gin and tonic was born. Cinchona bark can be bought at natural foods or herbal supplement stores or websites, or from online craft cocktail suppliers.

Citric acid: This powder derived from citrus has a number of culinary uses, most notably in canning and preserving, where it is added to lower the pH of ingredients and make them shelf stable. It is useful in discouraging oxidization of baked goods and is helpful in seasoning when acidity is needed but moisture is not. We rely on the powder to give an acidic kick to our nori potato chips (page 187). It can be purchased online or in the baking aisle of many supermarkets.

Golden Mountain sauce: This stir-fry sauce, used extensively in Thai cooking, is a saltier, sweeter cousin to soy sauce. It adds savory depth to just about anything, like our Lobster Stew (page 126). You can buy it online or in Asian grocery stores.

Hijiki. *See* Seaweeds

Katsuobushi flakes: Another core ingredient in the Japanese pantry, katsuobushi flakes are made from smoked and dried bonito. They impart a deep, smoky essence to Dashi (page 177), which is a really important part of our repertoire at Eventide. You can buy it online or in Asian grocery stores.

Kombu. *See* Seaweeds

Masa harina: This corn flour goes through the ancient nixtamalization process to make it edible and digestible before being made into tortillas, tamales, pupusas, and other products. We fry it into crispy bits to garnish the black bass ceviche dish (page 66) at Eventide. You can but it online or at most grocery stores.

Micro sorrel and micro mustard greens: Specially grown because they are beautiful and pack a surprising amount of flavor, microgreens make great additions to a salad and they can be used as a dynamic garnish. You can find them at farmers' markets or specialty food stores, but they're often pricey. They're also extraordinarily easy to grow at home (check info and instructions at online seed sellers, such as johnnyseeds.com), and we grow our own at the restaurants. Micro sorrel has an

amazing tartness that works nicely in our Lightly Cured Char (page 47) and micro mustard greens are peppery and pair well with full-flavored fish, like in our Cured Salmon (page 64).

Mustard oil: Made by pressing mustard seeds into oil, this spicy, peppery ingredient adds a nice punch to dressings, as for our Coleslaw (page 197) and the Pickled Ramp Relish in our Chu-Toro (page 82). You can buy it online or at Asian grocery stores. We like the Rhee Bros brand.

Palm sugar: A sweetener derived from the sap of palm trees, palm sugar is used a lot in Southeast Asian cooking. It has a caramel or maple-like flavor (light brown sugar is a good substitute in equal quantity) and brings balance to sauces like our Nam Phrik (page 176). You can buy it online or in Asian grocery stores.

Pink salt: A curing salt for meats that staves off bad bacteria growth. It is also known as Insta Cure #1 or Prague powder. We use it for Salt Pork (page 202), a staple of New England cooking. You can buy it online at www.butcherandpacker.com.

Salt: We use kosher salt and finishing salt throughout this book and our favorite brands are Diamond Crystal kosher salt and Maldon finishing salt.

Salted black beans: Another secret weapon brought to us by koji (see Barley koji, page 249), these fermented, dried soybeans are like little umami jewels that lend deep savoriness to our Hoisin Sauce (page 269). You can buy it online or in Asian grocery stores, where it's usually sold in sealed bags or jars.

Seaweeds (kombu, hijiki, wakame): Abundant, sustainable, nutritious, and versatile, seaweeds of all kinds can be found on the Eventide menu. Kombu, a large, flat type of seaweed that is sold fresh and dried, shows up in our Dashi (page 177). Hijiki, a black sea vegetable harvested on the coasts of Japan, Korea, and China and sold dried, goes into our Pickled Sea Vegetables (page 85) with dried wakame, another commonly used type of seaweed. Wherever you use it, seaweed brings its briny, ocean-y essence. You can buy it online or in Asian grocery stores.

Shaoxing rice wine: The most common spirit in Chinese cooking, this amber-hued liquid adds an aromatic, nutty element to sauces (like our Korean BBQ Sauce on page 168), marinades, fillings, and other products.

Shiro miso: Also known as white miso, shiro miso is a mild, salty-sweet seasoning paste popular in Japanese cooking. We use it for the spicy miso glaze (page 132) and sesame sauce (page 80) recipes in the book. You can buy it online in sealed containers or find it refrigerated in Asian grocery stores.

Tapioca starch: A flourlike ingredient derived from cassava, it is used widely in gluten-free baking. We like using it for our puffed snacks because it is almost completely flavorless.

Tellicherry peppercorns: The Cadillac of black peppercorns has a deeper, more pungent flavor than your average little peppercorn, making it a great addition to our Black Pepper and Lemon Ice (page 35). You can buy it online or in most grocery stores.

Ticaloid 210 S Powder: A perfect mix of natural gums designed to stabilize and thicken foods. For years our orgeat required regular shaking to prevent separation and it wasn't until we read Dave Arnold's *Liquid Intelligence* that we learned about the dark magic that is Ticaloid 210 S Powder.

Umeboshi: The word usually refers to ultra-sour, salty pickled plums popular in Japan, but *umeboshi* also refers to a style of salting and preserving that can be applied to a lot of different ingredients. Check out the Tuna Tartare recipe on page 84 to see how we use umeboshi to make a punchy vinaigrette for dressing the dish. You can buy it online or in Asian grocery stores.

Wakame. *See* Seaweeds

Xanthan gum: A powder that is used for thickening sauces and keeping them from separating, like in our Mussels en Escabeche (page 67). You can buy it online or in most grocery stores. There are not great substitutes, frankly, but you can leave it out of a recipe.

Yuzu kosho: This fermented Japanese condiment is made with red or green chiles, salt, and the juice and zest of the yuzu fruit, which is tart like grapefruit and fragrant like mandarin orange. It is one of the greatest hot sauces on earth, and a very small bit goes a long way. We use both the red and green versions. The former is grassier and the latter has more of a chile-forward flavor, but both are delicious. Check out the Yuzu Kosho Ice (page 35) and the Cure Salmon (page 64) to see how we incorporate this powerful little number into Eventide dishes. You can buy it online or in Asian grocery stores.

ABOUT THE AUTHORS

ARLIN SMITH

Owner and general manager Arlin Smith hails from Buffalo, New York, and holds a degree from the Culinary Institute of America. Early in his career, his appreciation for all things hospitality drew him out of the kitchen. He has since led Big Tree's front of house teams and spearheaded the melding of function and design in establishing each of the Big Tree Hospitality restaurants. He has become something of an authority on hospitality and has spoken on the subject in podcasts, on panels, and to many print journalists. Arlin leads by example in his commitment to instilling a spirit of generosity in the company's staff by managing all of Big Tree Hospitality's philanthropic efforts.

ANDREW TAYLOR

Big Tree Hospitality chef-owner Andrew Taylor's appreciation for the history of New England's food grew out of an affinity for fishing and foraging. He is a James Beard Award–winning chef and father of four who has become adept at culinary improvisation, crafting innovative cuisine out of the most seasonal ingredients Maine provides. When he isn't stomping through the woods searching for matsutakes or reviewing the company's financials, Andrew can be found cooking alongside his team. He is constantly looking toward the future and leading the company in new and exciting directions.

MIKE WILEY

Big Tree Hospitality owner Mike Wiley is a James Beard Award–winning chef. His inquisitive nature carried him through a six-year stint in academia, and ultimately left him with a masters in rhetoric and a determination to get back in the kitchen. His tireless curiosity has since led him to become the company's resident culinary nerd and an authority on sustainable sourcing and fermentation. Mike's intellectual approach to culinary work keeps him close to menu development on a daily basis, as well as mentoring and training new chefs.

SAM HIERSTEINER

Sam Hiersteiner is a food writer whose work has appeared in the *Boston Globe*, *First We Feast, Eater, Lucky Peach, Huffington Post, Art of Eating*, and other publications. He lives in Boston with his wife, Jacqueline, and two children, Caroline and Rowan.

Arlin Smith

Andrew Taylor

Mike Wiley

ACKNOWLEDGMENTS

I would like to thank my Nana for making me roasted fat sandwiches with mayo, my Mom for all of the support and love, Steller for your laughter, Norm and Ry for being proud and loving siblings to the brother that drove you both crazy, Rob and Nancy for seeing something in me and putting me in my place, Brian Smith and Bill Guilfoyle for pushing and believing, Sam and Don for all of your insight, and Rich and Maya for getting my ass to Portland. Much Love.
–*Arlin*

To all who have conspired to put me where I am now, I thank you. Chefs, mentors, family, and friends: you have all pushed me to where I need to be. But most of all to Rachel, Lincoln, Oliver, Julian, and Georgia; who inspire and support me every day. I love you all.
–*Andrew*

Thanks to my mom for getting me going in the kitchen early and thanks for supporting ruinous professional decisions that happened to pan out. Thanks, Dad, for teaching me to appreciate the glories of a thing done well. Ben, thanks for being better at making scallion pancakes than me (and for reminding me who I am). Abby, thank you for your patience with my schedule and my wandering obsessions, I love you.

   Restaurant family, I'm still trying to keep up with the compound. Thank you.
–*Mike*

We'd like to also thank our customers as well as our incredible staff, especially Kira Butera, John Myers, and Kimberly Rodgers—this cookbook and these restaurants couldn't have happened without you! To Rob Evans and Nancy Pugh, thank you for believing in us. Don and Sam, thanks for your guidance over the years, and during this book project. Will Droste and Peter Considine: thanks for keeping the faith, fellas. Dick McGoldrick, we're so glad that you like oysters more than Scandinavian knick knacks! And many thanks to Emma Rudolph and everybody at Ten Speed: Lisa Regul, Kelly Snowden, Isabelle Gioffredi, Jane Chinn, Chloe Aryeh, Allison Renzulli, and Jana Branson.

   Sally Ekus and Sam Hiersteiner, you guys were right, thanks for the push. And Sam: Sam, Sam, Sam, you put up with a lot of hyperbole, snark, and waffling, and we *deeply* appreciate it!

INDEX